INTERNATIONAL ACCOUNTING: A USER PERSPECTIVE

Second Edition

Shahrokh M. Saudagaran, PhD, CPA
Oklahoma State University

THOMSON

SOUTH-WESTERN

Australia · Canada · Mexico · Singapore · Spain · United Kingdom · United States

THOMSON

SOUTH-WESTERN

International Accounting: A User Perspective, 2nd Edition
Shahrokh M. Saudagaran

Acquisitions Editor:
Melissa S. Acuña

Marketing Manager:
Keith Chasse

Developmental Editor:
Janice Hughes

Senior Production Editor:
Marci Combs

Manufacturing Coordinator:
Doug Wilke

Production House:
Navta Associates, Inc.

Cover Design:
Rik Moore

Cover Photo:
©PhotoDisc

Printer:
Globus Printing, Inc.

COPYRIGHT © 2004 by South-Western, a division of Thomson Learning. Thomson Learning™ is a trademark used herein under license.

Printed in the United States of America
1 2 3 4 5 05 04 03 02

For more information contact South-Western, 5191 Natorp Boulevard, Mason, Ohio 45040. Or you can visit our Internet site at: http://www.swcollege.com

ALL RIGHTS RESERVED. No part of this work covered by the copyright hereon may be reproduced or used in any form or by any means–graphic, electronic, or mechanical, including photocopying, recording, taping, Web distribution or information storage and retrieval systems–without the written permission of the publisher.

For permission to use material from this text or product, contact us by
Tel (800) 730-2214
Fax (800) 730-2215
http://www.thomsonrights.com

ISBN: 0-324-18620-7

Library of Congress Control Number: 2003100916

DEDICATION

To My Family

Always there
Always loving
Always giving
Never demanding

PREFACE

INTRODUCTION

As business and capital markets have continued to grow more globalized over recent years, the need for cross-border financial information has correspondingly increased. This has brought international accounting to the forefront. As products, services, and capital increasingly cross domestic borders, the likelihood that various parties to business transactions are based in different countries increases. These parties must contend with the reality that information on their business partners often exists in an accounting language other than their own. In order to make informed decisions in a global environment, one needs to be educated in international accounting. While the required level of detailed knowledge of international accounting issues varies between organizations, there will be very few businesses in the twenty-first century that are not impacted by globalization and hence by some aspect of international accounting.

TARGET AUDIENCES

The primary audiences for this book are upper-division undergraduate students, graduate students, and participants in corporate university courses. In undergraduate programs, most Advanced Accounting books focus on business combinations with little or no coverage of international accounting topics. The typical Advanced Accounting book has some coverage on foreign currency translation as its ode to international accounting. *International Accounting: A User Perspective* provides a much more comprehensive coverage of international accounting issues than is available in Advanced Accounting texts. Given the target audience, every effort has been made to present the material completely yet succinctly and in a writing style that is easy to read. In terms of its coverage of international accounting issues, this book is placed somewhere between Advanced Accounting texts that cover very little and traditional international accounting texts that are too long and expensive for most undergraduate, graduate and executive programs. Similar to the first edition, this edition has been kept to a reasonable length, ensuring that most of the chapters will be used in the programs and courses where it is adopted.

USER PERSPECTIVE

This book is designed to provide an understanding of international accounting issues to students in graduate and undergraduate business programs and for executives involved either directly or indirectly in international business. As indicated in its title, the book takes a user perspective (as opposed to a preparer perspective) to international financial reporting. This approach makes sense because most business executives are more likely to be users of transnational financial information than preparers of it. Very few businesspersons are ever called upon to prepare financial statements in their domestic environment, let alone in another country. However, many executives are regularly called upon to make decisions based on financial information that originates in another country. This might take the form of evaluating the performance of a subsidiary, affiliated organization or joint venture in another country, making credit decisions on customers located in other countries, or making investing and financing decisions based on opportunities in other countries. Being educated in international accounting is an important asset in the portfolio of skills required of managers in companies engaged in global business.

RESEARCH COMPONENT AND OTHER IMPORTANT FEATURES

An important feature of the book is that it facilitates the transfer of international accounting research to students who typically would not access the academic literature on their own. It does this by discussing research findings where appropriate and by extensively citing scholarly references related to the subject matter. Since much of the text is based directly or indirectly on research evidence it helps bring "state of the art" international accounting material into the classroom. The extensive coverage of **Financial Reporting in Emerging Capital Markets** is another distinguishing feature of this book. As these countries grow in importance so does the need to learn of the special accounting issues facing them. Other distinguishing features of the book are its coverage of accounting for changing prices (in Chapter 4), and information technology (in Chapter 7).

SUMMARY OF CONTENTS

Based on feedback received from reviewers and other colleagues that have used the book, the length and coverage has been kept similar to the first edition. However, revisions have been made as necessitated by recent developments in the business and research arenas. The book is organized as follows:

- *Chapter 1* examines the interaction between accounting and its environment, the diverse roles of accounting in countries, the effects of accounting diversity, and the major challenges facing accounting globally. This chapter was updated.
- *Chapter 2* is about the global harmonization of accounting and auditing standards. It looks at various aspects of harmonization including the reasons for and against harmonization, the measures of harmonization, the organizations engaged in harmonization, and the various harmonization models and scenarios. This chapter was revised to include coverage of the International Accounting Standards Board and other relevant developments.

- *Chapter 3* deals with accounting for currency exchange rate changes. This chapter was updated to reflect the formal adoption of the Euro in 2002.
- *Chapter 4* delves into selected financial reporting and disclosure issues in the global context including accounting for changing prices, accounting for goodwill and intangible assets, geographic segment reporting, and environmental and social disclosures. This chapter was revised to include several new illustrations.
- *Chapter 5* covers various issues related to using corporate financial reports across borders. It examines corporate responses to foreign users of financial statements, and how preparers and users cope with transnational financial reporting. It also covers a number of issues related to international financial statement analysis. This chapter contains several new illustrations as well as revisions in the discussion of cross-country analysis.
- *Chapter 6* looks at financial reporting in emerging capital markets. The coverage includes the role of financial reporting in emerging capital markets, and the characteristics and policy issues related to financial reporting in developing countries. This chapter has new sections on accounting in China and Mexico and several new illustrations.
- *Chapter 7* deals with a number of managerial issues in international accounting. These include budgeting and performance evaluation, global risk management, transfer pricing, and information technology.

END OF CHAPTER MATERIALS

Each chapter ends with a summary of the main points contained therein, discussion questions, exercises, and where appropriate, cases. The discussion questions are relatively straightforward applications of chapter materials. In keeping with the user perspective of the book most of the exercises involve hands-on application of domestic and foreign annual reports.

INSTRUCTORS' MANUAL

The book is accompanied by an instructor's manual that includes 1) an outline of each chapter, 2) solutions for selected exercises and cases at the end of the chapter, 3) a test bank consisting of true/false and multiple choice questions, and 4) transparency masters.

ACKNOWLEDGMENTS

I thank my mentor, Professor Gerhard Mueller, for his guidance, friendship and support over more than two decades. He was the reason I chose to go to the University of Washington to work on a PhD in international accounting—a decision that was a life-changing event for me. He provided many useful suggestions on the first edition of the book that I have tried to incorporate in this edition. Words cannot adequately express my gratitude to him.

I am grateful to the many colleagues all over the world who chose to use the first edition of this book despite (or because of) its innovative and novel approach.

The positive feedback received from many of these colleagues was instrumental in the decision to proceed with this edition. It has been heartening to see that the book has had global appeal and is used at universities in over 20 countries on four continents.

I would also like to acknowledge a number of individuals who have helped in a variety of ways in the production of this book. Febiana Rinasari and Susie Le provided able research assistance and administrative support. The students in my MBA and undergraduate international accounting elective courses provided valuable feedback on various aspects of the draft chapters. I am grateful to the professional and friendly team at South-Western/Thomson International Publishing for their assistance and support during the entire process. Special thanks to Melissa Acuña, Keith Chasse, Marci Combs, Janice Hughes, and Nikki Wise for providing their production, editorial, and marketing expertise.

The following individuals have provided editorial guidance by reviewing portions of my developing manuscript. I appreciate the feedback provided by the following:

Victor Beard, *University of North Dakota*
Robert Bloom, *John Carroll University*
Teresa Conover, *The University of North Texas*
Michael Cummings, *Salem Academy and College*
Orapin Duangploy, *University of Houston—Downtown*
Hans J. Dykxhoorn, *Western Michigan University*
Teresa Gordon, *University of Idaho*
Don Herrmann, *Oregon State University*
Steven Kachelmeier, *The University of Texas at Austin*
Il-Woon Kim, *University of Akron*
Robert Larson, *Penn State—Harrisburg*
Walter O'Conner, *Fordham University*
Joseph R. Razek, *University of New Orleans*
Juan Rivera, *University of Notre Dame*
Lynn Rees, *Texas A & M University*
Eamonn Walsh, *New York University*
Michele Wingate, *University of Colorado at Denver*
Jeanne H. Yamamura, *University of Nevada*

Finally, I would like to thank my wife, Unhi (Iris), and my daughters, Mina and Maryam, for their patience and support. The hours spent working on the book sometimes caused me to miss attending a *tae kwon do* class, piano and violin recitals, and dance performances because there was a deadline looming ahead. I thank them for their love and understanding through it all.

Despite the best efforts of all involved, users might identify some errors in the book. I accept responsibility for these errors and welcome constructive comments from professors and students who have occasion to use this book.

Shahrokh M. Saudagaran

TABLE OF CONTENTS

About
the Author

SHAHROKH M. SAUDAGARAN

Shahrokh Saudagaran PhD, CPA is the Arthur Andersen Alumni Centennial Professor and Head of the School of Accounting at Oklahoma State University. He is Secretary General of the Asian Academic Accounting Association and Past-President of the American Accounting Association's International Accounting Section.

Dr. Saudagaran has distinguished himself both in teaching and in research. In addition to receiving several teaching awards, he has also been recognized for his research. In 2002, the Japanese Association for International Accounting Studies awarded him a lifetime honorary membership in recognition of his contributions to international accounting. He is known for his research on the impact of international accounting diversity on global capital markets and on financial reporting in emerging capital markets, particularly those in the Asia-Pacific region. His work has been published in the top accounting, finance and international business journals. He consults and teaches executive seminars in international accounting and finance for corporations in Asia, Europe, and the United States. He is currently joint editor of *Research in Accounting in Emerging Economies*, associate editor of *Journal of International Accounting Research*, and also serves on the editorial boards of the *Journal of International Financial Management and Accounting, Issues in Accounting Education, Review of Accounting and Finance*, and *Accounting, Accountability & Performance*. He has previously served on the editorial boards of several other journals including the *Accounting Review* and *Accounting Horizons*.

Saudagaran obtained his Ph.D. from the University of Washington (Seattle), his MBA from the Iran Center for Management Studies, and his Bachelor of Commerce from the University of Bombay. He is also licensed as a CPA in Washington State. He is a member of the Academy of International Business, the American Accounting Association, the Asian Academic Accounting Association, the European Accounting Association, and the International Association for Accounting Education and Research. Before entering academia, he worked as a management consultant with Ernst & Young and as Financial Controller with Van Leeuwen Buizenhandel, a Dutch multinational.

CHAPTER 1

FINANCIAL REPORTING IN THE GLOBAL ARENA

LEARNING OBJECTIVES

- Identify the main environmental variables that shape accounting.

- Recognize the differing role of accounting throughout the world.

- Demonstrate the economic effects of accounting diversity.

- Appreciate the benefits of classifying countries into accounting clusters.

INTRODUCTION

The purpose of accounting is to provide information that is useful for making business and other economic decisions. For this reason, accounting is commonly referred to as the language of business. Over the past few decades, as business across borders has continued to grow, the need for global communication has correspondingly increased. This has cast a spotlight on the need for international accounting. As increasing amounts of goods, services, and capital flow across domestic borders, the probability increases for global parties to the transaction. From a decision-making perspective, these parties must obtain relevant information on those they conduct business with and increasingly this information is presented in an accounting language different from their own. To make informed decisions in a global environment, one needs to have an understanding of international accounting issues. Naturally, the level of detail required varies depending on the extent of global involvement. However, as businesses grow, few can escape the impact of globalization and international accounting.

To get a sense of the pace of globalization in recent years, let's look at capital markets. Between 1990 and 2000, transactions in U.S. shares between U.S. investors and non-U.S. investors grew from US$362 billion to more than US$6 trillion. Similarly, transactions in non-U.S. shares between U.S. investors and non-U.S. investors grew from US$255 billion to more than US$3 trillion. In 2002, 468 non-U.S. companies with a combined market capitalization of US$5 trillion (from a total of US$16 trillion) were listed on the New York Stock Exchange. These companies were from 51 countries.[1] These statistics illustrate the phenomenal pace of globalization in a relatively short time period. They also point to the need for capital market participants to understand accounting information from countries other than their own, so as to make well-informed financing and investing decisions across domestic borders.

This book is designed to provide an understanding of international financial reporting issues to students in graduate and undergraduate business programs, and for executives involved either directly or indirectly in international business. The book takes a user perspective (as opposed to a preparer perspective) to international financial reporting. Very few businesspersons are ever called upon to prepare financial statements in their domestic environment, let alone in another country. However, many executives are regularly called upon to make decisions based on financial information that originates in another country. This might take the form of evaluating the performance of a subsidiary, an affiliated organization, or a joint venture in another country; making credit decisions on customers located abroad; or making investing and financing decisions based on opportunities globally. An education in international financial reporting is an important asset in the portfolio of skills required of managers in companies engaged in global business.

The book is organized into seven chapters. This chapter discusses the interaction between accounting and the environment in which it develops. It explores the causes of accounting diversity globally, discusses the differing roles of accounting across countries, and considers the economic effects of accounting diversity. It concludes with a discussion of global challenges facing accounting. This leads into Chapter 2, which deals with the harmonization of financial reporting globally. Included therein are sections on the rationale and pressures for, and the obstacles to, harmonization; measuring accounting harmonization; the organizations engaged in the harmonization

---

[1] New York Stock Exchange Fact Book 2001 Data.

effort, and the level of harmonization achieved thus far. Chapter 3 covers the conceptual and practical issues related to accounting for changes in the foreign currency exchange rate. Chapter 4 deals with selected financial reporting and disclosure topics in international financial reporting. These include 1) accounting for the effects of changing prices; 2) accounting for goodwill and other intangible assets; 3) geographic segment reporting; and 4) environmental and social disclosures. Chapter 5 covers specific issues related to using corporate financial reports across borders. It examines the corporate response to foreign users of financial statements, the user response to financial reports of foreign companies, and some do's and don'ts in analyzing foreign financial statements. Chapter 6 addresses issues related to financial reporting in emerging capital markets. In the past, very little attention has been paid to financial reporting in those countries with emerging capital markets. Specifically, Chapter 6 considers the nature and importance of emerging capital markets, the role and the desired characteristics of financial reporting in these countries, and challenges facing regulators and investors in emerging markets. Chapter 7 covers managerial accounting issues for companies as they do business globally, including transfer pricing, budgeting, and performance evaluation.

INTERACTION BETWEEN ACCOUNTING AND ITS ENVIRONMENT

As a social science, accounting is the product of its environment. However, accounting also influences the social environment. Thus, there is an interdependence between accounting and the environment in which it exists. A country's accounting regulations and practices are the product of a complex interaction of social, economic, and institutional factors. It is unlikely that the mix is identical in any two countries, and therefore diversity is to be expected. The factors that impact accounting development at the national level also contribute to accounting diversity at the international level. In this section, we identify 10 environmental factors which are likely to shape accounting development in a country. They are: 1) the type of capital market, 2) the type of reporting regimes, 3) the type of business entity, 4) the type of legal system, 5) the level of enforcement, 6) the level of inflation, 7) political and economic ties with other countries, 8) status of the accounting profession, 9) existence of a conceptual framework, and 10) quality of accounting education. This is by no means an exhaustive list, and there might be additional factors that influence accounting development in countries. To the extent that these factors vary among countries, they contribute to diversity in accounting.

Nature of Capital Markets

Several aspects of a capital market affect the system of financial reporting that prevails in a country. These include whether the market is predominantly equity-oriented or debt-oriented, the level of sophistication of financial instruments, and the level of globalization of capital markets.

In countries such as the United States and Canada, when companies reach a certain size they turn to the stock market as their main source of capital. These capital markets are characterized as equity-oriented capital markets. In countries such as Germany, Japan, and Switzerland, on the other hand, companies depend on bank financing as their primary source of capital, and are characterized as debt-oriented. Whether a country's capital market is equity-oriented or debt-oriented has a significant impact on the financial reporting that develops in the country. The type of capital market affects financial reporting at both the cosmetic and the substantive levels.

At the cosmetic level, in equity-oriented countries, one observes companies investing considerable resources in their annual reports and other financial communications to investors. Since anybody with investing power is a potential provider of capital, companies treat the annual report as a marketing device to attract investors from among the general populace. As such, they strive to make their annual report a public relations document that will present a positive image of the company. Considerable resources are devoted to the preparation of annual reports in equity-oriented capital markets. Exhibits 1-1 and 1-2 contain samples of two annual reports. The first has super-model Cindy Crawford on the front cover, on the back cover, and throughout the annual report. The second example is designed to look like a children's book and even has a hard-bound cover. In debt-oriented countries, corporate annual reports tend to be more spartan and matter-of-fact. This makes sense since bank debt is the main source of financing for companies in those countries. The banker providing the loan does not typically do so on the basis of a glossy annual report, and hence there is little reason to spend large amounts on the annual report production.

More importantly, one also observes important differences at the substantive level between financial reporting in equity- and debt-oriented countries. In the former,

EXHIBIT 1-1 Extract from the PepsiCo, Inc. 1994 Annual Report

EXHIBIT 1-2 Extract from the Adaptec 1996 Annual Report

ABC&D

All About
Being Connected
to Data

ADAPTEC 1996 ANNUAL REPORT

companies try to make their accounting numbers as positive as possible (hopefully, within what the accounting rules permit). There is generally an optimistic bias to reporting earnings in equity-oriented countries since stockholders are the primary providers of capital. Even when the performance of the company has not been good, the company tries to put the best face on the accounting numbers since capital markets can and do punish companies that report disappointing performance. However, in debt-oriented countries there is a tendency to underreport earnings. For example, there is much anecdotal evidence which shows that German firms' earnings computed in German accounting principles are consistently lower than their earnings prepared in U.S. accounting principles.[2] As discussed below, other factors might also explain this difference in reporting philosophies among countries.

The level of sophistication of capital markets impacts financial reporting because accounting constantly has to keep up with finance in terms of drafting accounting rules for new financial instruments. Thus, in countries such as the United States, where Wall Street constantly brings out highly complex and innovative financial instruments, the financial reporting must be constantly changing to account for the economic substance of the new financial instruments. On the other hand, in countries with relatively simple capital markets and financing instruments, there is less need for accounting to constantly change to keep up with financial innovations.

---

[2]An article by Richard Morais in *Forbes* [December 15, 1986] indicated that Volkswagen's 1985 earnings were understated by $344 million in German accounting principles (relative to what they would be under U.S. accounting principles). Similarly, the German chemical giant Bayer understated earnings by $374 million, while BASF, another German chemical giant, understated its earnings by 60%. More recently, Cairns reported that Volkswagen lopped off DM1.85 billion from its 1997 reported earnings by taking advantage of German tax laws [*Accountancy International*, April 1999, p. 81].

The level of globalization of a country's capital market also impacts the financial reporting that occurs in a country. The exact nature of the influence will vary with the type of non-domestic firms that enter a country's capital market. If the entering firms are from a country with high financial reporting and disclosure requirements, this will tend to raise the general level of financial reporting in that country (e.g., U.S. firms listing on the London Stock Exchange). On the other hand, if the entering firms are from a country with lower reporting requirements, then it might not have much impact on the financial reporting practices in the host country (e.g., Indonesian firms listing on the Australian Stock Exchange).

Type of Reporting Regime

It is possible to dichotomize countries into groups based on whether they have a dual or a single set of rules for financial reporting and tax reporting. Countries such as the United Kingdom and the United States have mostly independent sets of rules for financial reporting and tax reporting. In contrast, countries such as Austria and Germany set detailed rules that have to be followed for both tax reporting and external financial reporting. As one would expect, the presence or absence of this tax linkage dramatically affects the nature of financial reporting. In countries with dual reporting regimes, it is perfectly legal for companies to engage in a form of financial reporting schizophrenia—to look rich in their financial reports to investors and poor in their tax reports to the tax collector (both within the scope of each law). This enables companies to take an optimistic view to reporting earnings in their financial reports since the latter do not typically determine their tax liability. However, in countries with a single reporting system, inflating earnings in financial reports comes at a high price in the form of a higher tax liability. Therefore, it should come as no surprise that in countries with single reporting regimes, firms have traditionally tended to understate earnings. (Examples of this were cited earlier in footnote number 2.)

Type of Business Entities

The level of economic development of a country is likely to influence the type of business entities that exist in a country. Developed countries are characterized by large and complex conglomerates that often sell hundreds of products, employ thousands of people, and do business in many countries. In some instances, the value-added generated by these companies exceeds the economic output (i.e., gross domestic product) of some countries. According to the United Nations Conference on Trade and Development (UNCTAD), 29 of the world's largest 100 economic entities are multinational companies. ExxonMobil is larger than all but 44 national economies.[3] By contrast, countries with emerging economies are characterized by small, simple business entities that are often family owned. Financial reporting rules in each country will therefore reflect the needs of its business entities. In developed economies, the rules will be detailed and complex to capture the economic substance of the business entities they are accounting for. Simpler financial reporting rules will suffice for the smaller and less complex business entities typical of developing countries.

---

[3]ExxonMobil, with an estimated value-added of US$63 billion, was about the same size as the economy of Pakistan. Ford, DaimlerChrylser, General Electric and Toyota were all comparable in size to the economy of Nigeria, while Philip Morris was comparable in size to Tunisia, Slovakia, and Guatemala.

Type of Legal System

The legal system in most countries can be classified as either code law (legalistic) or common law (non-legalistic). Code law has its origin in Continental Europe (i.e., Roman, German, French Napoleonic), while common law originated in England and was exported to other countries during their colonization by Britain. The code law system is sometimes characterized as mandating acceptable behavior, while the common law system focuses on deterring undesirable behavior. In code law countries such as France and Germany, accounting is regulated mainly through an accounting code that tends to be highly detailed, prescriptive, and procedural, and is generally set by the legislature. The emphasis is on protecting the creditors of the company. By contrast, in common law countries, such as the United States and Australia, accounting regulations are set on a piecemeal basis, typically by a private sector standard-setting body. The emphasis in financial reporting in common law countries is to present a true and fair picture to shareholders. Research evidence suggests that financial reporting in common law countries tends to be more transparent and timely than in code law countries.[4] The common law environment is generally regarded as being more adaptive and innovative in terms of financial reporting.

Level of Enforcement of Regulations

When studying the financial reporting regimes of various countries, it is important to differentiate between accounting regulations and the actual accounting practices that prevail in the country. The proximity or distance between accounting regulations and accounting practice often depends on the level of enforcement. In countries with high levels of enforcement, one is likely to observe that accounting practices are largely in compliance with the requirements. However, in countries with low levels of enforcement, accounting practices of business entities are likely to exhibit very little compliance with regulations. The level of enforcement in countries can, in turn, be attributed to a number of factors that affect the willingness or the ability to enforce the rules on the books. One factor is the type of political system and leadership in the country. The recent Asian financial crisis has been blamed in part on cronyism in countries where political patronage and ties to the ruling group enabled business entities to circumvent existing financial reporting requirements. Investors who assumed that companies were complying with reporting requirements suffered significant financial losses when the true financial position of these companies was disclosed. This, in a sense, represents a lack of willingness to enforce the rules. However, countries that adopt accounting standards of other countries might not have the resources to implement and enforce these standards. While it is relatively inexpensive to adopt sophisticated accounting standards that were designed by other countries, it takes a lot more resources to actually implement and enforce these standards. Business entities need trained personnel to apply these standards, while regulatory agencies need adequate budgets to monitor compliance. When countries lack the necessary resources, there is a significant divergence between accounting regulations and accounting practice. Even in an economically developed country like the United States, scarcity of resources can impact the level of enforcement, as evidenced by recent financial reporting scandals.

---

[4]See, for example, Ball, Kothari, and Robin [2000] and Jaggi and Low [1999].

Level of Inflation

The historical-cost model is the dominant basis of accounting in most countries. Under this model, economic transactions are mostly recorded at values that prevailed on the date of the transaction. Thus, under the historical-cost model, a piece of property purchased many years ago would still appear in the financial statements at its original purchase price. While there are questions about the decision relevance of this model even in a low-inflation environment, it certainly loses relevance in a highly inflationary environment. Countries that have generally held inflation in check, such as the United Kingdom and United States, typically use the historical-cost model for financial reporting purposes, based on the premise that inflation does not seriously impact them. However, countries that have suffered high levels of inflation, such as Bolivia and Mexico, do not have the luxury of persisting with the historical-cost model of financial reporting. They use inflation-adjusted models of financial reporting to provide more decision-relevant information in the context of their economies. Inflationary accounting models are covered in Chapter 4.

Political and Economic Ties

Another important factor shaping accounting development in countries is their political and economic ties with other countries. Accounting systems, like legal systems and educational systems, are often imported and exported among countries. In the past, countries have adopted the accounting regime of other countries, both voluntarily and involuntarily. Where a country was colonized for an extended period of time, it typically adopted the accounting system of the colonial power. Prime examples are the countries in the British Commonwealth. All these countries were colonies of Britain at some point in their history and, as a result, ended up with accounting systems either similar or identical to that of Britain. Similarly, we observe that accounting in the Philippines is based on accounting in the United States, an obvious legacy of its colonial history. Until Indonesia gained independence from the Netherlands, accounting in Indonesia was essentially identical to Dutch accounting. In the case of colonization, the colony typically had little choice in the matter. However, post-independence, former colonies have taken two distinct paths. In some situations, countries have made a deliberate choice to continue their close association in accounting (and other) matters with the former colonial power. Examples of this are Singapore and Malaysia, which chose to stay with the British system, and the Philippines, which chose to stay with the U.S. system even after gaining independence. In other situations, the former colony has replaced the system imposed upon it by the colonial power with a different system. An example of this is Indonesia, which discarded the Dutch system of accounting after gaining its independence and chose to move towards the U.S. model of accounting.

Economic ties between countries also have the potential to influence accounting development. Thus, one sees that accounting in Canada is greatly influenced by accounting in the United States, partly due to geographic proximity but also because the United States represents the largest export market for Canada. A large number of Canadian firms are also listed on U.S. stock exchanges, and this too affects their accounting. In recent times, it has become increasingly popular for countries to enter into regional economic alliances. Examples include the European Union (EU), the North American Free Trade Agreement (NAFTA), and the Association of South East Asian Nations (ASEAN). If member countries receive a boost in economic activity, they try to harmonize many of their business regulations, including those for financial reporting, to reduce the transactions cost of doing business with each other. It is important to emphasize that proximity in regulations between countries will work only because it provides economic gains. Thus, we observe a greater effort towards harmonization of accounting regulations in the EU than in ASEAN, consistent with the fact that EU countries trade considerably more with each other relative to ASEAN countries which trade more with countries outside ASEAN.[5]

Status of the Accounting Profession

Another factor that affects accounting development in countries is the status of the accounting profession. In common law countries such as the United States and Canada, despite the recent financial reporting and auditing problems at some very visible corporations, the accounting profession has generally been held in high esteem. In such countries, the accounting profession is largely self-regulating and plays a major role in setting accounting and auditing standards, as well as establishing educational and licensing requirements for entering and staying in the profession. In code law countries such as France and Germany, the accounting profession has considerably less stature and power, and the government takes the lead role in regulating the profession. In yet other countries like Russia, accounting has historically been equated with bookkeeping, a clerical task implying a lower status.

The stature of the accounting profession has an important influence on the quality of financial statements produced. Where there is a strong accounting profession, audit reports are more likely to be respected as independent and reliable. In countries with weak accounting professions, there are questions as to the quality of financial statements and whether auditors have the stature and independence to stand up to the companies that they audit. Finally, the stature of the accounting profession is also likely to influence the size of the accounting profession. Exhibit 1-3 on the following page provides evidence on the size (scaled by population) of the accounting profession in selected countries. Even among developed countries, there is a considerable range, with New Zealand topping the list at 550 auditors per 100,000 population and Japan at the bottom with 10 auditors per 100,000 population.

Existence of a Conceptual Framework

A conceptual framework of accounting has been defined as "a coherent system of interrelated objectives and fundamentals that can lead to consistent standards and that prescribes the nature, function, and limits of financial accounting and financial statements" [FASB, 1976, p. 2]. Conceptual frameworks appear to be associated uniquely with countries that embrace a micro-user oriented accounting system.[6] Countries such as Australia, Canada, New Zealand, the United Kingdom, and the United States, in particular, are at the forefront of developing and adopting their own particular versions of conceptual frameworks. More similarities than differences characterize existing conceptual frameworks in countries with micro-user oriented accounting systems. Most conceptual frameworks contain:

- a statement of aims or objectives of financial accounting,
- targeted users of financial statements,

---

[5]See Saudagaran and Diga [1997a].

[6]Micro- and macro-user oriented systems are defined and compared in the next section of this chapter.

EXHIBIT 1-3 Accountants and Auditors in Emerging and Developed Markets

Emerging Markets	No. of Auditors Per 100,000 Population	Developed Markets	No. of Auditors Per 100,000 Population
Chile	87	New Zealand	550
Argentina	71	Australia	539
Malaysia	48	U. K.	352
South Africa	35	Canada	350
Philippines	31	Singapore	273
Taiwan	17	Ireland	262
Mexico	15	U. S.	168
Poland	14	Hong Kong	110
Greece	12	Italy	110
Zimbabwe	11	Denmark	106
India	9	Switzerland	53
Sri Lanka	9	Netherlands	52
Nigeria	8	France	45
South Korea	7	Sweden	41
Thailand	5	Belgium	38
Columbia	2	Germany	26
Indonesia	2	Spain	18
Pakistan	2	Finland	10
Brazil	1	Japan	10

Source: Saudagaran and Diga (1997c)

- financial accounting statements that ought to be issued,
- qualities and characteristics of good financial accounting,
- limitations of financial statements,
- scope of applicability of conceptual framework,
- definition of reporting entity,
- definition and basis of recognizing financial statement elements,
- measurement of financial statement elements and concept of capital maintenance.

Thus, accounting in countries that have developed or adopted a conceptual framework is likely to be more similar to each other than to countries that lack a conceptual framework. While a conceptual framework does not have mandatory status in every country, it provides a reference point for developing and adopting accounting standards. One also observes similarities in the accounting of developing countries that adopt conceptual frameworks from developed countries (e.g., the Philippines and the United States, since the former patterned its conceptual framework—Statement of Financial Accounting Standard No. 1, "Basic Concepts and Accounting Principles Underlying Financial Statements of Business Enterprises"—on U.S. APB Statement No. 4).

While it has been suggested that conceptual frameworks provide a logical and consistent guide to formulating accounting standards, it is not yet apparent how they contribute to accounting standard setting. What is clear, however, is that professional accounting bodies in a number of developing countries (e.g., Indonesia, Malaysia, Singapore) have followed the lead of their counterparts elsewhere, particularly accounting bodies in industrialized countries with micro-user oriented accounting systems (e.g., Australia, Canada, New Zealand, United Kingdom, United States), and have introduced their own versions of conceptual frameworks. Overall, the existence of these conceptual frameworks in countries characterize their accounting systems as:

- emphasizing decision-usefulness as an important function of accounting,
- institutionalizing the flexibility in measurement and disclosure that is characteristic of financial reporting in these countries, and
- signaling the important role played by professional accounting bodies in shaping accounting development in these countries.

Quality of Accounting Education

Finally, the quality of accounting education in countries has a significant impact on the type of accounting that develops. Naturally, the quality of education is impacted by a number of factors discussed above such as the level of economic development, the political and economic ties with other countries, and the stature of the accounting profession. Certain countries have a long history of including accounting in their tertiary institutions of higher education. In these countries, students are able to choose accounting as a major field of study in undergraduate (i.e., bachelor's), graduate (i.e., master's) and even doctoral (i.e., Ph.D.) programs in universities. Students are able to receive a rigorous education in accounting and emerge as well-trained individuals ready to enter the accounting profession. Upon graduation, these individuals are recruited by public accounting firms as well as corporations. This helps enhance the attractiveness of accounting as a field of higher education. However, in many other countries, the quality of accounting education is relatively weak, because accounting is often equated to bookkeeping and is regarded as a vocation rather than a profession. It is limited to secondary education and is unavailable in universities. The result is that it is very low on the totem pole in terms of its prestige and attractiveness as a career choice.[7] The accounting profession in these countries suffers as a result of its inability to attract the best and brightest students into accounting careers.

DIVERSE ROLES OF ACCOUNTING IN COUNTRIES

It is important for users of accounting information to recognize that the primary role of accounting in another country might differ from that in their home country. This is likely to affect the orientation and information content of financial statements produced in those countries, which, in turn, might influence how the accounting reports should be interpreted and used.

Domestic capital markets can have a subtle, yet pervasive and enduring, impact on the development of accounting systems in countries. Accounting, however, appears to be both a cause and an effect of change in domestic capital markets. On one hand, demands arising from capital markets provide a rationale for adopting particular forms of accounting. Reciprocally, accounting is perceived as a prerequisite for the growth of domestic capital markets.

Financial accounting is central to the process of allocating financial resources in capital markets. In the non-securities sector, financial accounts provide an important

---

[7]A recent study [Enthoven et al. 1998] reports that in Russia, "the prestige of accounting was extremely low." Secondary school graduates in Russia rated accounting as 91st out of 92 career choices available to them.

basis for lending decisions of financial institutions in most countries. As a matter of policy, financial institutions require borrowers to furnish detailed financial information as part of the loan extension process to evaluate the relative credit risk of prospective and existing borrowers.

Conversely, financial reporting requirements are essential for the adequate oversight and supervision of banks and other financial institutions in countries. Financial institutions are usually required to submit their financial statements to government agencies (and, in some countries, publish in major newspapers) as part of discharging their accountability requirements. Regulatory requirements for banks and other financial institutions are often based on accounting information furnished by these enterprises. As will be discussed in greater detail in Chapter 6, this issue has been dramatically spotlighted by financial crises in a number of emerging capital markets (e.g., Argentina, Brazil, Indonesia, Malaysia, Russia). Inquiries into the cause of these crises have concluded that lack of financial reporting transparency and inconsistent application of auditing standards were among the factors that exacerbated the magnitude of the problems experienced by these countries.[8]

Extensive evidence, both empirical and anecdotal, suggests that accounting reports are relevant to investors' buy and sell decisions on corporate securities. The importance of accounting reports for stock market investors has been demonstrated through multi-country capital market studies and in surveys of financial statement users. Anecdotally, it is also evident every time the stock price of a company drops precipitously when questions arise about the reliability of its financial reporting.[9] The link between accounting information and well-developed securities markets is a particularly crucial policy matter for less-developed countries (LDCs) aiming to attract increased capital flows to develop their economies. As indicated by Walter [1993, p. 15], "The nature and extent of information production and disclosure is central to equity market development and the ability to attract cross-border flows. . . . The stronger and more independent the information infrastructure, the more attractive an emerging market will be to foreign equity investors."

The emerging consensus that financial accounting is important for the efficient operation of capital markets has permeated policy making at the national and international levels. The regulation of corporate financial reporting is a pervasive phenomenon worldwide. At an international level, organizations such as the International Accounting Standards Board (IASB) and the International Organization of Securities Commissions (IOSCO) are concerned with ensuring an adequate supply of reliable and relevant financial information necessary for cross-border financial transactions. Moreover, multilateral lending institutions such as the International Monetary Fund (IMF), the World Bank, and the Asian Development Bank (ADB), among others, are at the forefront of recommending to LDCs the need to ensure a robust accounting system to enhance the development of their financial systems.

Notwithstanding the emerging consensus regarding the importance of having an adequate domestic accounting system, the debate over which form of financial reporting system is most appropriate for a country is far from settled. The extent and persistence of diverse financial reporting regulations and practices worldwide attests to

---

[8]See "Big Five criticised over global audit standards," by Jim Kelly [*Financial Times*, October 19, 1998, p. 1].

[9]See, for example, "Fraud probe announcement sends Xerox shares falling," [*Financial Times*, September 25, 2002, p. 18] and "Sodexho falls after account anomalies," [*Financial Times*, September 20, 2002, p. 16].

EXHIBIT 1-4 Hierarchy of Accounting Policies

Element of Accounting	Accounting Policy Issues
Broad aims of financial accounting	• What should be the *aim* of financial accounting in terms of the user orientation of the accounts? • What should be the role of financial accounting in regard to capital markets, fiscal (tax) policy, and macroeconomic planning policy?
Institutional setting for accounting regulation	• Which approach(es) to *formulating* accounting regulation should be adopted? • Which approach(es) to *enforcing* accounting regulation should be used?
Specific accounting rules and requirements	• Which specific *disclosure* and *measurement* rules should be adopted and to whom should these rules apply?
Corporate accounting practices	• Which specific *disclosure* and *measurement* methods will be used in presenting the company's accounts?

Source: Saudagaran and Diga (1997b)

different views on what constitutes proper accounting. A significant stream of research in comparative international accounting has sought to address such issues from a contingency perspective, aiming to explain current features of accounting systems in terms of various contingent economic, political, and socio-cultural variables.[10] Results of these studies, however, are far from conclusive and suggest the need for an in-depth understanding of the impact of specific factors, such as domestic capital markets, on accounting policy development.

Policy Choices in Accounting

Accounting policy here refers to making choices with respect to the broad aims established for accounting, the institutional framework for setting and implementing accounting regulations, detailed accounting rules, and corporate accounting practices. The aim of analyzing financial accounting systems from a policy perspective is to determine the nature, rationale, and process giving rise to different accounting systems in different countries. The pertinent policy issues in regard to specific accounting elements are summarized in Exhibit 1-4.[11]

The relative scope and importance of policy decisions increases as one climbs the accounting policy hierarchy. Decisions regarding the broad aims of financial accounting have a profound and long-term impact on the institutional basis, specific accounting rules, and corporate accounting practices in a country. At the same time, the available alternatives increase significantly as one descends the hierarchy. There are significantly more options, for example, in regard to specific accounting practices as

[10]See Saudagaran and Diga [1999] for a review of the contingency-based literature in international accounting. Doupnik and Salter [1995] state that the aim of contingency-based research in comparative international accounting is to arrive at a "general model" that could explain and predict patterns of accounting systems worldwide on the basis of specific environmental factors.

[11]The notion of "accounting policy" in this chapter is a broad one that encompasses choices with respect to different elements of an accounting system. In contrast, the term "accounting policy" is used in some studies in the context of accounting measurement and disclosure rules and/or practices adopted by reporting enterprises. See, for example, May and Sundem [1976], Foster [1980], Beaver [1981], Lev [1988].

compared to types of institutional arrangements for regulating accounting.[12] In regard to the broad aims of accounting, empirical evidence from comparative international accounting research suggests that two general preferences have been demonstrated thus far. One is to emphasize the usefulness of the accounting system for private-sector users (i.e., individual and institutional participants in capital markets) and the other is for public-sector users (i.e., government ministries and agencies responsible for tax collection or economic planning). In this section, we specifically examine the broad accounting aims with respect to domestic capital markets.

Countries can be compared based on the relative importance attached to particular roles of accounting in society. On this basis, prior research strongly supports a dichotomization between a macro-user oriented and a micro-user oriented accounting system. Exhibit 1-5 outlines the differences between these two systems in relation to the main roles of accounting in society. As indicated in Exhibit 1.5, the overall difference relates to the intended users of accounting information. In macro-user oriented systems, government agencies, particularly tax and economic planning agencies, are the principal users of accounting reports. By comparison, a diverse set of capital providers is perceived to be the most important user group of accounting reports in micro-user oriented systems.

Differences between the two systems are also quite pronounced with respect to the role of accounting in capital markets. In countries, such as Canada and the United States, that have adopted micro-user oriented accounting systems, the goal of accounting has traditionally been to provide "true and fair" or "fairly presented" financial statements. The notions of "true and fair" and "fairly presented" are generally associated with the need to provide adequate and reliable financial disclosures, and the use of accounting methods that reflect the economic substance, rather than the legal form of transactions.

EXHIBIT 1-5 Accounting in a Macro-User and Micro-User Oriented Environment

Functional Core	Role in Macro-User Oriented	Role in Micro-User Oriented
Capital markets	Accounting helps ensure financial stewardship, i.e., non-dissipation of assets and protection of creditors.	Accounting provides relevant and reliable information about an enterprise's "true" state of economic well-being.
Taxation	Accounting plays a primary role; no difference between tax accounting and financial accounting methods.	Accounting plays an indirect and supportive role; tax accounting and financial accounting methods differentiated clearly.
National economic planning	Accounting: • ensures the effect of government economic policies are reflected in enterprise accounts • provides inputs for industry or national accounting reports.	Accounting plays an incidental role. Government relies indirectly, if at all, on enterprise accounts in preparing national or industry economic plans.

Source: Saudagaran and Diga (1997b)

---

[12]Studies that compare the alternative approaches to accounting regulation in industrialized countries include Puxty et al. [1987], Bloom and Naciri [1989], and Gorelik [1994].

In comparison, the goal of providing fairly presented accounts has not been acknowledged explicitly in countries with macro-user oriented accounting systems.[13] The traditional aim of accounting, particularly in regard to providers of long-term capital, has been to guard against the surreptitious loss of assets. This goal was supposedly attained through the use of conservative accounting measurement methods that understated reported assets and profits of the enterprise.

The contrasting goals of accounting in the context of domestic capital markets indicates fundamentally different assumptions between macro-user and micro-user oriented accounting systems in regard to the role of accounting in effective corporate governance.[14] In micro-user oriented environments, the role of accounting is viewed in terms of providing a reliable benchmark for evaluating management performance. A major determinant of management's performance is maintaining an adequate track record of earnings performance and cash or dividend flows. In view of the incentives for management to bias reported results, there is a perceived need for neutral and unbiased accounting methods that could mitigate potential conflicts of interests between enterprise managers and owners. Conversely, debates regarding the economic consequences of accounting have raised the possibility that accounting methods could be adopted in order to promote specific desired effects, e.g., boosting spending on research and development to increase enterprise competitiveness. The dominant view in the micro-user oriented environments, however, is that accounting should remain for the most part insulated from wrangling over potential beneficial or adverse economic consequences. Otherwise, the neutrality and, hence, credibility of accounting reports would suffer.[15]

In contrast, in most macro-user oriented accounting systems in Continental Europe, such as in France, Germany, and Sweden, the role of accounting is viewed in terms of contributing to enterprise stability and continuity.[16] This view arises from conditions typically prevalent in these countries. First, institutional creditors often play a significant role in corporate governance through representation in the enterprise's board of directors and executive management, or through a system of cross-ownership between borrowing and lending enterprises. Conservative accounting methods prevent management from distributing dividends perceived to be detrimental to creditors, and provide rock-bottom asset values that do not overstate the security potential of assets in case of liquidation. Moreover, the entitlements of a wider set of corporate stakeholders appear to be well recognized in Continental Europe and Japan. The requirements of government agencies (primarily tax and economic planning agencies) and employees (including management) are ranked of the same, if not

---

[13]The European Community's (EC) Fourth Directive on Company Law (Art. 2) states that "the annual accounts shall give a true and fair view of the company's assets, liabilities, financial position and profit or loss." Apparently, the United Kingdom insisted that the phrase be inserted in the directive primarily to protect the traditional framework of U.K. accounting. Despite the presence of the "true and fair" requirement in the company laws of all EC member countries, evidence suggests that Continental European countries have largely maintained intact their macro-user oriented accounting systems.

[14]See, for example, Benston [1982], Macdonald and Beattie [1993], and Tricker [1994].

[15]As emphasized by FASB [1978, par. 107]: "Neutrality in accounting is an important criterion by which to judge accounting policies, for information that is not neutral loses credibility." The same view is expressed by Solomons [1991, p. 294]: "If accounting is to retain any credibility—and without credibility it is worthless—its guiding light must be neutrality in financial reporting."

[16]See Alexander and Archer [2001] for a detailed description of the financial reporting regime in 25 European countries.

greater, importance as capital providers.[17] The enterprise is viewed as helping to guarantee long-term, if not lifetime, employment and contributing towards national economic goals.[18] In this environment, neutrality in accounting procedures is subordinated to the goal of deliberately influencing the behavior of enterprise agents towards certain pre-defined goals, an arrangement deemed unacceptable in micro-user oriented accounting systems (because it leads to biased accounts).

Until the collapse of the Soviet Union, one could observe a very specific role of accounting in planned economies with a communist system of government. In these countries, since private property and investment were frowned upon, the government was typically the only direct stakeholder in economic entities. Since there were no external stakeholders and few competitive markets for goods and services, there was no real concern with traditional measures of performance such as profitability or cost containment. The main role of accounting in these countries was to facilitate the economic plans under which the government would set priorities and targets at the national level, which would translate to production goals and quotas at the individual factory level. Accounting was used almost entirely to collect data to prepare national statistics and to determine whether the government's economic targets had been achieved.

There is little evidence that these differing views of the role of financial accounting can be reconciled in the short term. One school of thought believes that deliberate efforts towards accounting harmonization can reduce the gap regarding the broad aims of countries. Even in the European Union (EU), where the greatest visible effort towards attaining regional accounting harmony has been made, there remain substantial differences in terms of the broad aims of accounting and, consequently, of the methods and practices among countries. Evidence suggests that accounting differences are, to a significant extent, perpetuated by underlying differences in these countries' capital markets. Whereas the United Kingdom and United States have had a long tradition of active securities markets, Germany and France (two of the largest economies in the EU) have, until now, relied on bank finance as a source of industrial capital. An intriguing, albeit unexplored, dimension in comparative accounting research is the extent to which these differences in customary sources of capital, i.e., securities markets versus banks, are themselves a reflection of more enduring ideological and cultural characteristics in a country.[19]

---

[17]It is common practice in Continental Europe, for example, to have representatives from labor unions or workers' councils to sit as members of the company's board of directors. France has specifically required enterprises to publish an annual *bilan social* ("social balance sheet") to report on matters relevant to employees.

[18]The most notable example of this practice is the system of accounting for untaxed reserves in Finland, Germany, and Sweden, where companies are allowed to make appropriations of their pre-tax profits in order to stabilize future earnings. The government sanctions this practice to allow companies to smooth their reported earnings according to their respective business cycles.

[19]Hofstede [1987], for example, identified at least four models of economic organization. The Anglo-U.S. model is portrayed as a village market where the ultimate and optimal mode of control was believed to be through market forces. In comparison, the French model was described as a pyramid with a strict hierarchy and set of rules while the German model was that of a well-oiled machine organized around rules but where hierarchical positions mattered less. Developing countries, such as Indonesia and Thailand, were depicted as following the family model of organization of having an undisputed leader but few formal rules. These different perspectives of economic organizations suggest varied roles for accounting in these societies.

EFFECTS OF DIVERSITY ON CAPITAL MARKETS

In this section, we examine the economic effects of global accounting diversity. As will be discussed in detail in Chapter 2, there is much ongoing activity that is aimed at reducing global diversity in accounting. This activity, which generally falls under the rubric of "harmonization initiatives," is a fairly expensive exercise. One can only assume that the economic rationale for the harmonization efforts is that there are significant costs from accounting diversity that harmonization will help reduce. If accounting diversity presents a barrier to the free flow of capital across borders, then reducing or removing this barrier should help direct capital to the most efficient users (and uses) globally. A related rationale for reducing accounting diversity is that it will improve comparability of financial statements, making them easier to use across countries.

The recent move towards a single currency (i.e., the euro) in 11 European Union member countries is a relevant analogy that helps explain the effects of diversity. By signing the Treaty of Maastricht in 1991, the authorities in the European Union agreed to move towards unifying their currencies. The economic rationale for moving towards a single currency presumably was that the diverse currencies imposed significant costs to doing business within Europe, and thus limited intra-EU trade. It is clear that in the short run, Europe faces significant costs in its efforts to achieve monetary union. Phasing out the individual national currencies and introducing the euro is estimated to have cost European businesses US$65 billion in the period immediately preceding July 2002. Critics contend this cost is too high. However, proponents point out that the long-term benefits of melding an 11-nation, US$6.5 trillion, 290 million-person region into one economic and financial bloc will outweigh the costs. Yet others estimate that the removal of transactions costs involved with diverse currencies will result in economic gains estimated at 0.5 percent of the EU members' gross domestic product.[20] Again, the euro analogy is a good example of the perceived economic effects of diversity between countries and the rationale for removing the diversity.

There is considerable evidence on the diversity in financial reporting practices and its effect on firms. Some of the issues examined include the effects of differences in disclosure levels on listing decisions,[21] the effects of regulatory differences on user groups,[22] and the effects of differences in goodwill treatments on mergers and acquisitions.[23]

Research has examined how accounting and regulatory factors that result in differing levels of financial disclosure affect where companies list their stocks. There has been a fairly heated debate as to the level of disclosure that should be required by regulators and stock exchanges from foreign firms listing within their jurisdiction.[24] From the regulators' perspective, the goal of protecting domestic investors from potentially misleading financial disclosures by foreign firms must be weighed against demands for

---

[20]See "We have liftoff!" [*Business Week*, January 18, 1999, pp. 34–37]

[21]See, for example, Biddle and Saudagaran [1991], Saudagaran and Biddle [1992, 1995].

[22]See, for example, Choi and Levich [1991], and Bhushan and Lessard [1992].

[23]See, for example, Choi and Lee [1991], Lee and Choi [1992], Dunne and Rollins [1992], and Dunne and Ndubizu [1995].

[24]See, for example, Torres [1990, 1991], LaBaton [1991], Freund [1993], Breeden [1994], and Cochrane [1994].

increased access to investment opportunities in foreign firms. The competitiveness of domestic stock exchanges and securities industries often hangs in the balance. In the United States, the Securities and Exchange Commission (SEC) and the New York Stock Exchange (NYSE) have been on opposite sides of the issue. The SEC insists that foreign firms' financial statements must be reconciled to U.S. GAAP for the protection of U.S. investors. The NYSE and others have argued that the reconciliation requirement imposes an unnecessary burden on foreign issuers that is keeping them from listing their securities on the NYSE and other U.S. stock exchanges, and is adversely affecting the U.S. economy. The requirement deprives U.S. investors of the opportunity to invest in many global blue chip companies. It reduces the competitiveness of domestic stock exchanges and securities industries relative to countries where the net regulatory burden is less than in the United States.

Biddle and Saudagaran [1991] address three main issues related to the interaction between accounting diversity and the increasing globalization of the world's capital markets. They discuss 1) the benefits and costs of listing on a foreign stock exchange, 2) the effects of accounting disclosure levels on foreign listing decisions, and 3) accounting policy issues posed by foreign stock exchange listings and how authorities have responded. From the accounting and financial reporting perspective, a key question is whether choices regarding alternative foreign stock exchange listings are influenced by financial disclosure levels. Research provides evidence that exchange choices are influenced by financial disclosure levels. Three of these studies [Biddle and Saudagaran, 1989; Saudagaran and Biddle, 1992 & 1995] looked at large samples of companies from the largest capital markets. Another study [Mittoo, 1992] surveyed Canadian companies listing in the United States and the United Kingdom. The majority of Canadian firms that participated in the survey indicated that they regarded the financial reporting and compliance requirements of the U.S. Securities and Exchange Commission to be the greatest cost of listing their shares on U.S. stock exchanges. This is particularly significant because Canada is very similar to the United States in terms of its business environment. Exhibit 1-6 contains a ranking of the level of financial reporting disclosure in the eight countries with the most internationalized capital markets. If firms from Canada, which is ranked just below the United States, consider the differences in financial reporting between Canada and the United States to be the most important barrier to tapping U.S. capital markets, then accounting diversity must surely impose an even higher cost on companies from countries such as Germany and Switzerland whose financial disclosure levels are ranked lowest.

In related research, other surveys gauge the behavioral effects of accounting diversity on major categories of capital market participants. They found that accounting differences are important and affect capital market decisions (i.e., the geographic spread of investments, the types of securities selected, assessment of security returns or valuation, and information processing costs) of a significant number of the surveyed capital market participants regardless of nationality, size, experience, scope of international activity, and organizational structure.[25] There is also evidence that while investors might prefer foreign companies to reconcile their financial statements in the investors' domestic accounting regulation, they do not consider it essential because they still regard the company's primary financial statements and local valuation as being most important.[26]

---

[25]See Choi and Levich [1991].

[26]See Bhushan and Lessard [1992].

EXHIBIT 1-6 Survey of Financial Reporting Disclosure Levels in Eight Major Capital Markets

	Mean Ranks				
	Statutory Reporting Requirements	Exchange Reporting Requirements	Capital Market Expectations	Overall Disclosure Levels	Disclosure Level Rank (DLR)
United States	7.27	7.29	7.17	7.28	8
Canada	6.48	6.38	5.91	6.41	7
United Kingdom	5.84	5.87	6.09	6.02	6
Netherlands	4.68	4.80	4.50	4.75	5
France	4.11	4.50	4.13	4.17	4
Japan	3.82	4.04	4.22	3.83	3
Germany	3.96	3.90	4.04	3.81	2
Switzerland	2.70	2.78	3.17	2.60	1

Spearman Rank Correlation
between Overall Disclosure Levels and

Statutory Reporting Requirements	.976
Exchange Reporting Requirements	1.000
Capital Market Expectations	.952

*Ranks are in descending order with '8' ('1') indicating highest (lowest) disclosure level.

Source: Saudagaran and Biddle (1992)

Another stream of research studies the effects of differing rules of goodwill on merger activity. It examines whether national differences in the accounting treatment of purchased goodwill are associated with differences in merger premiums offered by non-U.S. acquirers when bidding for U.S. target companies. It finds that merger premiums offered by foreign acquirers based in countries with more favorable accounting and tax treatments for goodwill than the United States to be higher than those offered by U.S. acquirers. The evidence shows that goodwill accounting treatment does explain merger premiums, and that the premiums paid by British firms are substantially more than those paid by German and Japanese firms.[27] Also, because Japan allowed the amortization of goodwill to be deducted for tax purposes, Japanese firms had a cash flow and, therefore, a competitive advantage over firms from the United States and United Kingdom. U.K. acquirers experienced the highest reported income and rates of return because they were able to write off goodwill immediately against stockholders' equity. U.S. acquirers enjoyed neither a cash flow nor a reported earnings advantage relative to firms from Japan and the United Kingdom.[28] Yet another study found that non-U.S. companies that write off goodwill against a reserve account transfer more wealth to the target shareholders than those that amortize goodwill

---

[27]See Choi and Lee [1991], and Lee and Choi [1992].
[28]See Dunne and Rollins [1992].

against income. Foreign acquirers that deduct goodwill for tax purposes transfer more wealth to the target stockholders at the acquisition announcement than other acquirers. The conclusion was that this put U.S. bidders at a disadvantage in their competition with foreign bidders to acquire U.S. firms.[29] Overall, these findings indicate that diversity in accounting and/or tax treatments affects international merger activity.

The evidence presented in this section demonstrates that international accounting diversity affects various capital market participants and the terms of international transactions. As such, diversity imposes costs on the resource allocation system worldwide. Harmonization of this diversity may provide one solution and is discussed in the next chapter.

CLASSIFICATION OF FINANCIAL ACCOUNTING AND REPORTING SYSTEMS

The object of classification (or clustering) in international financial reporting is to group countries according to the common elements and distinctive characteristics of their financial accounting systems. Classifications should reveal fundamental structures that countries have in common and that distinguish them from countries in other groups. By identifying similarities and differences, descriptions and analyses of accounting are sharpened and our overall understanding is thereby improved. There are also some practical benefits. First, the countries comprising a particular group are likely to react to new circumstances in similar ways. Countries may anticipate accounting problems and solutions by looking at the experiences of other countries in the same group. Second, developing countries that lack the resources to develop their own accounting standards may identify a particular cluster that can serve as a model for the types of standards that are most appropriate for them. Third, patterns can help organizations such as the International Accounting Standards Board in their global harmonization efforts. In order to succeed, global standard-setting organizations need to understand the differences that are likely to be encountered and whether the patterns are changing, merging, etc. By revealing patterns, clustering studies can provide useful insights to global standard-setting groups as they try to craft accounting standards that are likely to be acceptable to the important parties. Fourth, financial statement communication problems are more severe when reporting across groups rather than within. Multinationals that are interested in attracting foreign investors may want to provide additional disclosures when users of their financial statements are from countries outside their own cluster.

Review of Selected Classification Studies

Considerable research has been conducted in international financial reporting to classify countries into groups based on the similarity of their financial reporting regimes. Some studies have resulted in judgmental classifications while others have generated classifications by empirically analyzing the accounting standards or practices prevailing in countries.[30] Next, we discuss selected classification studies in order to gain an appreciation of how the research on accounting classifications has evolved over the past 30 years.

---

[29]See Dunne and Ndubizu [1995].

[30]See Meek and Saudagaran [1990] for a review of the early classification studies in international accounting.

EXHIBIT 1-7 Nobes' Classification of Accounting Systems

A Hypothetical Classification of Financial Reporting Measurement Practices in Developed Western Countries in 1980

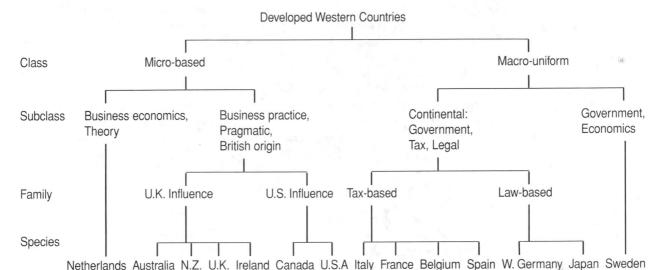

Source: Nobes (1983)

Mueller [1967] is generally considered to be the pioneering classification study. Using a judgmental approach, Mueller identified the following four patterns to accounting development in Western market-oriented economies: 1) macroeconomic pattern, 2) microeconomic pattern, 3) independent discipline approach, and 4) uniform approach. Several points about Mueller's classification deserve mention. The first is that the macroeconomic and uniform approaches overlap. (For example, Germany has features of both.) Second, the Netherlands seems to be the only country where accounting developed along microeconomic lines. Third, the categories are not specifically concerned with accounting and reporting practices, though it would seem reasonable that practices follow from approaches. Nevertheless, in practice, accounting in the Netherlands is quite similar to that in the United States and United Kingdom.[31]

In 1983, Nobes proposed a classification, laid out in Exhibit 1-7, that added a hierarchy of comparative distances between the groups. For example, it accommodated separate U.S. and U.K. groups, yet also demonstrated that the two groups are more like each other than they are to the countries of Continental Europe. Nobes' classification is consistent with certain environmental variables discussed earlier in this chapter. For example, micro-based and macro-uniform roughly correspond to nonlegalistic and legalistic systems of jurisprudence. Also, the influence of the United Kingdom on its former colonies, Australia, New Zealand, and Ireland, can be discerned. The classification is consistent with Mueller [1967] in that the four subclasses are the same. It is important to recognize that these accounting classifications are dynamic and change over time. Thus, groupings of countries based on research conducted previously may no longer be valid.

In 1993, Doupnik and Salter produced a classification applying statistical analysis to accounting measurement and disclosure practices in fifty countries. They grouped

---

[31]In a subsequent study, Mueller [1968] provided an alternative classification based on the following four characteristics of the business and social environment of countries: 1) stage of economic development, 2) business complexity, 3) political system, and 4) legal system.

countries into narrow clusters to assess whether their classification was consistent with that of Nobes. Despite using more recent data (1990 versus 1980) and more countries (50 versus 14), their results supported Nobes' classification. As indicated in Exhibit 1-8, their results contained a two-group and a nine-group classification. The two-group classification is consistent with Nobes' macro/micro split. Further, the micro-based group subdivides into U.K.- and U.S.-based groups consistent with previous classifications by Nobes and others. In the nine-group classification, there are both similarities and dissimilarities to Nobes' classification. Germany and Japan split into separate single-country groups, while the Netherlands is part of the U.K.-based group. Spain, France, and Italy remain part of a European group which surprisingly includes Colombia, while Belgium joins an Arab group which also includes Thailand and Panama. Another counterintuitive result is the inclusion of the Philippines with the U.K. group rather than the U.S. group. Doupnik and Salter also investigated the relationship between measurement and disclosure practices and found that countries with more conservative accounting practices generally have lower levels of disclosure, and vice versa.

One purpose of classification is revealing fundamental characteristics that members of a group have in common, and which also distinguish various groups from one another. Despite different research methods and databases, the studies cited in this section are consistent with one another. Evidence suggests that no single classification system can include all accounting systems. Differences between disclosure and meas-

EXHIBIT 1-8 Groups of Accounting Systems Derived by Doupnik and Salter

Micro groups		Macro groups	
Group 1		**Group 3**	**Group 7**
Australia	UK	Costa Rica	Finland
Botswana	Zambia		Sweden
Hong Kong	Zimbabwe	**Group 4**	
Ireland		Argentina	**Group 8**
Jamaica		Brazil	Germany
Luxembourg		Chile	
Malaysia		Mexico	**Group 9**
Namibia			Japan
Netherlands		**Group 5**	
Netherlands Antilles		Colombia	
New Zealand		Denmark	
Nigeria		France	
Philippines		Italy	
Papua New Guinea		Norway	
South Africa		Portugal	
Singapore		Spain	
Sri Lanka			
Taiwan		**Group 6**	
Trinidad and Tobago		Belgium	
		Egypt	
Group 2		Liberia	
Bermuda		Panama	
Canada		Saudi Arabia	
Israel		Thailand	
USA		UAE	

Source: Doupnik and Salter (1993)

urement systems might affect classifications, as might the types of companies studied (i.e., multinational or domestic). The classification studies examined measurement practices; however, it is disclosure practices that are more likely to have changed over time. Similarly, while the studies have examined domestic accounting practices, multinational companies are more likely to use transnational accounting practices, which blur differences between countries. These factors may raise questions about the conclusions of the earlier classification studies.

MAJOR CHALLENGES FACING ACCOUNTING GLOBALLY

This section provides an overview of immediate challenges that face accounting in the global arena.

Global Harmonization

As businesses increasingly operate in multiple countries, they encounter the costs of dealing with diversity in financial reporting requirements. Various constituents have been lobbying for harmonization of accounting regulations to reduce the costs resulting from accounting diversity. As we will discuss in Chapter 2, a number of organizations have a stake in the harmonization regime that ultimately emerges. While these efforts have been in process for more than 25 years, the restructuring of the IASC into the IASB may provide new momentum for progress in attaining global convergence in accounting standards.[32] Worldwide capital market participants are immensely interested in this issue since its resolution will have a significant impact on their investing, financing, and business decisions. (Global harmonization is covered in detail in Chapter 2 of this book.)

Quality of Financial Reporting in Developed and Emerging Economies

The recent accounting scandals in the United States and elsewhere has brought the issue of the quality of corporate financial reporting to the forefront.[33] This is in addition to the existing concerns about the quality of financial reporting in countries with emerging economies. Moreover, the wave of economic and financial crises in a number of countries has also highlighted the need for reliable and transparent financial reporting from business entities based in these countries. While multilateral lending and developing agencies such as the International Monetary Fund, the World Bank, and the United Nations have raised questions about the quality of the financial reporting and auditing standards and practices in developing countries, domestic regulators such as the Securities and Exchange Commission are grappling with financial reporting problems in the developed economies. Organizations such as the United States Agency for International Development (USAID) are devoting considerable resources to establish accounting and capital market regulations in developing countries. A

---

[32]See, for example, the following articles, all appearing in *Accountancy International:* "IASB quizzed over long-term plans" [March 2002]; "EU agrees to adoption of IAS by 2005," "Enron paranoia is green light for IAS," "Fast-track convergence on the cards," "European business leaders embrace IAS" [all in July 2002]; "IAS is coming – ready or not!" [August 2002].

[33]See "Global scandals and the high street practice" by Bob Reynolds [*Accountancy*, August 2002], "WorldCom: Could it happen here?" by Beth Holmes [*Accountancy*, August 2002], and "Audit committees: The cure for corporate ills?" by John House [*Accountancy*, August 2002].

sound financial reporting system is perceived as a vital part of the infrastructure necessary for economic development and fair and efficient capital markets in all countries. (Chapter 6 examines issues related to financial reporting in emerging capital markets.)

Social and Environmental Reporting

One consequence of the globalization of business enterprises is that companies now have stakeholders not just in their home country but also in all the countries where they operate. Until now, companies that were based in countries with little or no regulations on social and environmental reporting did not feel the need to disclose this information as part of their financial reporting package. However, as they venture into countries with these requirements, there is increasing pressure to provide social and environmental disclosure. Even in the absence of disclosure requirements, the emergence of socially conscious investors is another source of pressure on companies to report on the environmental and social impact of their business decisions. In certain countries, companies publish environmental reports in addition to their annual reports. Finally, companies with foreign competitors who provide social and environmental disclosure (either voluntarily or by requirement) feel the pressure to provide similar disclosure for competitive and public relations reasons. With the growth in environmental consciousness and the increase in related legislation, social and environmental reporting will grow in importance as an international accounting issue. (We provide a detailed coverage of this topic in Chapter 4.)

Financial Reporting in the High Technology Era

The phenomenal growth in internet, software, and telecommunication technology will have a significant impact on financial reporting practices globally. When one considers that investors expect information in a more timely manner, and software technology already exists that makes possible the preparation of daily consolidated financial statements, it is anyone's guess as to how much longer the traditional mode and frequency of financial reporting will be relevant. Technology has the effect of minimizing the significance of geographic distances, and investors will begin to demand timely electronic financial reporting regardless of the nationality or the geographical distance of the entities in which they invest. The traditional hard-copy annual reports may soon become obsolete. It will be fascinating to watch how these developments will impact the numerous constituents of international financial reporting in the coming years.[34]

SUMMARY

1. Accounting is a product of the complex interaction of social, economic, and institutional factors in a country. Ten environmental factors are likely to shape accounting development in a country: 1) the type of capital market, 2) the type of reporting regimes, 3) the type of business entity, 4) the type of legal system, 5) the level of enforcement, 6) the level of inflation, 7) political and economic ties with other countries, 8) status of the accounting profession, 9) existence of a conceptual framework, and 10) quality of accounting education.

---

[34]See "Identity Crisis for Online Annual Reports" by R. A. Kaplan [*Financial Executive*, July/August 1999], "On line and on Time" by L. Bury [*Accountancy International*, August 1999], and "Fast and furious" by B. Holmes [*Accountancy*, July 2002].

2. Countries can be compared based on the relative importance attached to particular roles of accounting in society. One basis of dichotomization is between a macro-user oriented and a micro-user oriented accounting system. In macro-user oriented systems, government agencies, particularly tax and economic planning agencies, are the principal users of accounting reports; in micro-user oriented systems, a diverse set of capital providers is perceived to be the most important user group of accounting reports.

3. Accounting diversity appears to affect capital markets. The chapter presents research evidence that accounting diversity affects global capital flows by influencing which foreign stock exchanges firms choose to list on, as well as differential accounting and tax treatments of goodwill resulting from mergers and acquisitions.

4. Classification studies group countries according to common elements in their financial reporting systems. They provide several practical benefits to national and international standard-setters, as well as to preparers and users of financial statements.

5. Some of the major global challenges facing accounting include 1) global harmonization, 2) quality of financial reporting in developed and emerging economies, 3) social and environmental reporting, and 4) financial reporting in the high technology era.

QUESTIONS

1. Select a company (perhaps where you work) and identify three of its international financial reporting issues. How important are these issues to the success of the company? Who is responsible for managing these issues?

2. Discuss the factors that are likely to shape accounting development. Select one country each from Africa, Asia, Europe, and Latin America and identify the major factors that have, in your view, shaped their financial reporting regime.

3. There is an interdependence between accounting and the social environment in which it exists. Provide evidence to support this statement in the context of any country that you are familiar with.

4. Discuss the different economic roles of accounting in countries across the world. What are some of the factors that determine the primary role of accounting in a country?

5. Describe the role of accounting in macro-user oriented and micro-user oriented economies. What are the main differences?

6. Consider the case of two countries in Southeast Asia—Indonesia and Singapore. Discuss the level of enforcement of rules in each country. What does this suggest about the quality of financial reporting practices that exist in each country?

7. In the United States, why are the New York Stock Exchange and the Securities and Exchange Commission at odds over the appropriate level of financial disclosure for foreign companies seeking to list on U.S. stock exchanges? What evidence exists of the effect of differences in disclosure requirements on the decision to list on foreign stock exchanges? Do you think foreign companies should be allowed to enter your country's capital market on the basis of their home country financial statements? Explain.

8. Select a global challenge facing international financial reporting and explain how preparers and users of financial statements and capital market regulators have a stake in the outcome.

9. Using specific examples, explain how accounting classifications are useful in global business.

10. In your view, how will technology affect international financial reporting in the next 20 years?

11. What are some other likely developments, either domestic or foreign, that could significantly affect international financial reporting in the next 20 years?

EXERCISES

1. Whether a country's capital market is equity-oriented or debt-oriented has a significant impact on the financial reporting that develops in the country, both at the cosmetic and substantive level. Choose an equity-oriented country and a debt-oriented country, and obtain two corporate annual reports from each. Comment on the similarities and differences of the reports.

2. The level of globalization within a country's capital market is an important factor in influencing the financial reporting practices. Choose three capital markets anywhere in the world and determine the number of non-domestic firms relative to domestic firms that are listed in each country's capital market. Are the foreign firms generally from countries with higher or lower financial reporting and disclosure requirements? In your opinion, has the penetration of non-domestic firms listed on these capital markets impacted the financial reporting practices of the host country?

3. The legal system in most countries can be classified into two categories: the code law system, characterized as mandating acceptable behavior; and the common law system, focusing on deterring undesirable behavior. In code law countries, accounting is regulated mainly through a highly detailed, prescriptive and procedural accounting code with an emphasis on protecting creditors. Conversely, common law countries set accounting regulations on a piecemeal basis with the emphasis on providing shareholders with decision-useful information. Choose a code law country and a common law country, and obtain two corporate annual reports from each. Comment on the similarities and differences of the reports. In your opinion, what is the influence of the legal system on financial reporting in each country? Explain.

4. Regional economic alliances [e.g., the European Union (EU), the North American Free Trade Agreement (NAFTA), and the Association of South East Asian Nations (ASEAN)] have the potential of influencing financial reporting regulations and practices between member countries. Choose a regional economic bloc of interest to you and discuss the impact of the alliance on financial reporting in the member countries.

5. The proximity or distance between accounting regulations and accounting practice often depends on the level of enforcement. Select two countries and discuss the level of enforcement of financial reporting regulations in each country. Identify the agencies and organizations in place that are responsible for enforcing the financial reporting requirements. How do they compare to one another?

6. Financial reporting has diverse roles in the economic and social landscape of different countries. This usually influences the orientation and informational content of financial statements produced in those countries. Choose a macro-user oriented and a micro-user oriented country, and obtain two corporate annual reports from each. Describe features of the annual reports that reflect the financial reporting perspective of that country.

7. The role of accounting in macro-user oriented accounting systems can be viewed as contributing intentionally towards enterprise stability and continuity to achieve certain pre-defined national economic goals. Identify a country that has a macro-user oriented approach to accounting and explain how this system has contributed to the country's national economic goals.

8. The chapter lists four practical benefits of classifying countries by their financial reporting environment. Select a country, from one of the multi-country groups presented in Exhibit 1.8, and discuss how it can benefit from a financial reporting perspective from other countries within the group.

CASES

Case

Hodge-Podge

Blake Green is a senior manager at a prestigious accounting firm, and was recently transferred to the international division of acquisitions and mergers. His first assignment is to make a recommendation to a client regarding the acquisition of a Swiss company. However, Blake has no knowledge or experience with Swiss companies or Swiss accounting. After spending hours analyzing the Swiss company's annual report, Blake concludes that Swiss accounting is a whole lot different than the U.S. accounting principles he is more familiar with.

During his analysis, Blake is astounded with the level of "unnecessary" detail that is included in the annual reports (e.g., social, environmental, and employee disclosures) and thinks that there is not enough information on the more important items (e.g., segmental disclosures). He also notices that the Swiss company understates net income by undervaluing assets and overvaluing liabilities. He doesn't understand why.

1. Are the disclosures included in the Swiss annual report really "unnecessary"? Explain. What social, economic, and institutional factors in Switzerland might be causing the inclusion of these disclosures?
2. Explain why Swiss companies take a conservative approach to financial reporting, resulting in the understatement of net income.

Case

Blue-zee

Bruce Carlson, having recently obtained his MBA, has been hired by a large investment banking firm. As part of his responsibilities, he is required to make recommendations on investing in securities of foreign companies.

During his lunch hour, Bruce runs into a colleague and complains about the difficulties he encounters with the lack of comparability in the financial statements of firms from different countries. He is puzzled by the inability of national accounting standard-setting bodies to agree on a uniform accounting regime globally since, in his view, this would represent a win-win situation for all concerned.

1. Pretend you are the individual that Bruce is talking to. Explain why only one uniform accounting and reporting standard may not necessarily represent a win-win situation for all concerned.
2. Discuss the advantages and disadvantages of having diverse accounting standards that are the product of each country's national environment.
3. In your opinion, should harmonization be pursued?

REFERENCES

Alexander, D., and Archer, S. 2001. *Miller European Accounting Guide*. New York: Aspen Law & Business.

Ball, R., Kothari, S. P., and Robin, A. 1999. The effect of international institutional factors on properties of accounting earnings. *Journal of Accounting and Economics* 29 (1): 1–51.

Beaver, W. H. 1981. *Financial Reporting: An Accounting Revolution*. Englewood Cliffs, NJ: Prentice-Hall.

Benston, G. 1982. An analysis of the role of standards in enhancing corporate governance and social responsibility. *Journal of Accounting and Public Policy*, 1 (1): 5–17.

Bhushan, R., and Lessard, D. R. 1992. Coping with international accounting diversity: Fund managers' views on disclosure, reconciliation, and harmonization. *Journal of International Financial Management and Accounting*, 4 (2): 149–165.

Biddle, G. C., and Saudagaran, S. M. 1989. The effects of financial disclosure levels on firms' choices among alternative foreign stock exchanges. *Journal of International Financial Management and Accounting*, 1 (1): 55–87.

Biddle, G. C., and Saudagaran, S. M. 1991. Foreign stock listings: Benefits, costs, and the accounting policy dilemma. *Accounting Horizons*, 5 (3): 69–80.

Bloom, R., and Naciri, M. A. 1989. Accounting standard setting and culture: A comparative analysis of the United States, Canada, England, West Germany, Australia, New Zealand, Sweden, Japan, and Switzerland. *International Journal of Accounting*, 24 (1): 70–97.

Breeden, R. C. 1994. Foreign companies and U.S. securities markets in a time of economic transformation. *Fordham International Law Journal*, 17: S77–S96.

Choi, F. D. S., and Lee, C. 1991. Merger premia and national accounting differences in accounting for good-will. *Journal of International Financial Management and Accounting*, 3 (3): 219–240.

Choi, F. D. S., and Levich, R. M. 1991. Behavioral effects of international accounting diversity. *Accounting Horizons*, 5 (2): 1–13.

Cochrane, J. L. 1994. Are U.S. regulatory requirements for foreign firms appropriate? *Fordham International Law Journal*, 17: S58–S67.

Doupnik, T. S., and Salter, S. B. 1993. An empirical test of a judgmental international classification of financial reporting practices. *Journal of International Business Studies*, 24 (1): 41–60.

Doupnik, T. S., and Salter, S. B. 1995. External environment, culture, and accounting practice: A preliminary test of a general model of international accounting development. *International Journal of Accounting*, 30 (3): 189–207.

Dunne, K. M., and Ndubizu, G. 1995. International acquisition accounting method and corporate multinationalism: Evidence from foreign acquisitions. *Journal of International Business Studies*, 26 (2): 361–378.

Dunne, K. M., and Rollins, T. P. 1992. Accounting for good-will: A case analysis of U.S., U.K., and Japan. *Journal of International Accounting Auditing and Taxation*, 1(2): 191–207.

Enthoven, A. J. H., Sokolov, Y. V., Bychkova, S. M., Kovalev, V. V., and Semenova, M. V. 1998. *Accounting, Auditing, and Taxation in the Russian Federation*. Institute of Management Accountants (Montvale: New Jersey) and University of Texas at Dallas (Richardson: Texas).

Financial Accounting Standards Board (FASB) 1976. *Scope and Implications of the Conceptual Framework Project*. Stamford, CT: FASB.

Financial Accounting Standards Board (FASB) 1978. *Statement of Financial Accounting Concepts No. 1: Objectives of Financial Reporting by Business Enterprises*. Stamford, CT: FASB.

Foster, G. 1980. Accounting policy decisions and capital market research. *Journal of Accounting and Economics*, 2 (1): 29–62.

Freund, W. C. 1993. That trade obstacle, the SEC. *Wall Street Journal*, August 27: A12.

Gorelik, G. 1994. The setting of accounting standards: Canada, the United Kingdom, and the United States. *International Journal of Accounting*, 29 (2): 95–122.

Hofstede, G. 1987. The Cultural Context of Accounting. *Accounting and Culture—Plenary Session Papers and Discussants' Comments from the 1986 Annual Meeting of the AAA* (B. E. Cushing, ed.): 1–11.

Jaggi, B., and Low, P. K. 1999. Impact of culture, market forces, and legal system on financial disclosures. *International Journal of Accounting*, forthcoming.

LaBaton, S. 1991. U.S. may erase rules affecting foreign stocks. *New York Times*, June 5: 17.

Lee, C., and Choi, F. D. S. 1992. Effects of alternative goodwill treatments on merger premia: Further empirical evidence. *Journal of International Financial Management and Accounting*, 4 (3): 220–236.

Lev, B. 1988. Towards a theory of equitable and efficient accounting policy. *Accounting Review*, 63 (1): 1–23.

Macdonald, N., and Beattie, A. 1993. The corporate governance jigsaw. *Accounting and Business Research*, 23 (91A): 304–310.

May, R., and Sundem, G. L. 1976. Research for accounting policy: An overview. *Accounting Review*, 51 (4): 743–763.

Meek, G. K., and Saudagaran, S. M. 1990. A survey of research on financial reporting in a transnational context. *Journal of Accounting Literature*, 9: 145–182.

Mittoo, U. 1992. Managerial perceptions of the net benefits of foreign listing: Canadian evidence. *Journal of International Financial Management and Accounting*, 4 (1): 40–62.

Mueller, G. G. 1967. *International Accounting*. New York: Macmillan.

Mueller, G. G. 1968. Accounting principles generally accepted in the United States versus those generally accepted elsewhere. *International Journal of Accounting*, 3 (1): 91–103.

Nobes, C. W. 1983. A judgmental international classification of financial reporting practices. *Journal of Business Finance & Accounting*, Spring: 1–19.

Puxty, A. G., Willmott, H. C., Cooper, D. J., and Lowe, A. 1987. Modes of regulation in advanced capitalism: Locating accountancy in four countries. *Accounting, Organizations, and Society*, 12 (3): 273–291.

Saudagaran, S. M., and Biddle, G. C. 1992. Financial disclosure levels and foreign stock exchange listing decisions. *Journal of International Financial Management and Accounting*, 4 (2): 106–148.

Saudagaran, S. M. and Biddle, G. C. 1995. Foreign listing location: A study of MNCs and stock exchanges in eight countries. *Journal of International Business Studies*, 26 (2): 319–342.

Saudagaran, S. M., and Diga, J. G. 1997a. Accounting regulation in ASEAN: A choice between the global and regional paradigms of harmonization. *Journal of International Financial Management and Accounting*, 8 (1): 1–32.

Saudagaran, S. M., and Diga, J. G. 1997b. The impact of capital market developments on accounting regulatory policy in emerging markets: A study of ASEAN. *Research in Accounting Regulation*, (Supplement 1): 3–48.

Saudagaran, S. M., and Diga, J. G. 1997c. Financial reporting in emerging capital markets; Characteristics and policy issues. *Accounting Horizons*, 11 (2): 41–64.

Saudagaran, S. M. and Diga, J. G. 1999. Evaluation of the contingency-based approach in comparative international accounting: A case for alternative research paradigms. *Journal of Accounting Literature*, 18: 57–95.

Solomons, D. 1991. Accounting and social change: A neutralist view. *Accounting, Organizations, and Society*, 16 (3): 287–295.

Torres, C. 1990. NYSE's new chief seeks to make Big Board more international. *Wall Street Journal*, December 21: C1.

Torres, C. 1991. Big Board facing serious erosion as market for stocks, chief warns. *Wall Street Journal*, March 13: C1.

Tricker, R. I. 1994. *International Corporate Governance: Text, Readings, and Cases*. New York: Prentice-Hall.

Walter, I. 1993. Emerging Equity Markets: Tapping into Global Investment Flows. *ASEAN Economic Bulletin*, (1): 1–19.

CHAPTER 2

HARMONIZING FINANCIAL REPORTING STANDARDS GLOBALLY

LEARNING OBJECTIVES

- Recognize the arguments for and against harmonization.
- Identify the pressures for and the obstacles to harmonization.
- Become familiar with the main organizations involved in harmonization.
- Examine some previous harmonization efforts.
- Compare harmonization approaches in EU and ASEAN.

With the dramatic growth in global trade and the accelerated internationalization of capital markets, financial statements produced in one country are used in other countries more frequently. This has brought accounting harmonization to the forefront as an international business issue. While accounting academics and others have offered several definitions of harmonization, very simply stated, it is the process by which differences in financial reporting practices among countries are reduced with a goal of making financial statements more comparable and decision-useful across countries. This chapter addresses a number of issues in the area of accounting harmonization, including: 1) the rationale for harmonization, 2) factors promoting and impeding harmonization, 3) appropriate measures of harmonization, 4) the organizations engaged in harmonization, and 5) some previous harmonization efforts. We also discuss the level of harmonization that has been achieved to date, and compare harmonization efforts in two regional economic blocs.

RATIONALE FOR HARMONIZATION

The debate over the need for and desirability of accounting harmonization began in the 1960s and has continued unabated since. The primary economic rationale in favor of harmonization is that major differences in accounting practices act as a barrier to capital flow. Ideally, investors would like to direct their capital to the most efficient and productive companies globally, provided they are able to understand their accounting numbers. However, if the accounting practices between countries are different to the point of imposing unreasonable burdens on capital providers, then investors may direct their capital to less efficient companies simply because they understand their financial statements and thus regard them as less risky. A rationale for harmonization is that it will enhance comparability of financial statements, thus making them easier to use across countries. Two former members of the U.S. Financial Accounting Standards Board (FASB), Arthur Wyatt and Dennis Beresford, have both reiterated the need for harmonization in view of the rapid growth in international capital markets and increased cross-border financing.[1] They have asserted that harmonization is necessary to produce comparable and credible data for use across borders. Beresford has disputed suggestions that the FASB has been uninterested and uncooperative regarding the international harmonization of accounting standards, and has reiterated the positive aspects of internationalization and the FASB's commitment to improving international standards.

Among those who oppose harmonization, some consider it to be unnecessary and others view it as being harmful.[2] Opponents argue that full harmonization of international accounting standards is probably neither practical nor truly valuable. They predict that global GAAP will not likely be achieved given the institutional impediments in the standard-setting process. Also, a well-developed global capital market already exists, so there is no real need to increase reporting requirements in the already robust international capital markets. Investors and issuers can make investment decisions without the presence of international accounting standards. Another argument against the need for harmonization is that investors are rational enough to spend the necessary time and money to correctly analyze investment opportunities and focus on real economic results.

---

[1] See Wyatt [1997] and Beresford [1997].
[2] See Fantl [1971], Samuels and Oliga [1982], Goeltz [1991], and Hoarau [1995].

Opponents also cite differences in the economic, political, legal, and cultural environment in countries as a justification for financial reporting differences. They typically express concerns that the accounting regimes in developed Western countries are likely to dominate global harmonization efforts. Imposing Western accounting practices on developing non-Western countries, they argue, is likely to do more harm than good. Critics have even questioned accounting harmonization among developed Western countries. In a recent article,[3] a French academician, C. Hoarau, raised questions about the international accounting harmonization movement based on France's experience with implementing international standards. Hoarau contends that, in France, the influence of international harmonization is limited to consolidated financial statements and that because harmonization disregards the economic, social, and cultural context of French accounting, it has broken down the homogeneity of the French accounting model, ruptured its unity, and reduced the social functions of accounting in France. Hoarau considers the current harmonization process to be aimed at conformance to the Anglo-Saxon (and particularly the American) accounting model and its focus on the stockholder as the primary stakeholder. According to Hoarau, questions remain about the nature and means of achieving harmonization, about its consequences at a national level, and about the obstacles and political difficulties to be overcome.

As more companies switch to IAS or U.S. GAAP in order to gain entry to global capital markets, there are more questions of whether non-domestic GAAP adequately reflects the financial performance and position of companies. The case of Deutsche Bank is illustrative of some of the challenges of using non-domestic GAAP. In 2002, Deutsche Bank voluntarily switched to U.S. GAAP in preparing its financial statements as part of its stock listing on the New York Stock Exchange (NYSE). Analysts argued that the switch to U.S. GAAP was detrimental in that it confused investors, reduced transparency, and increased earnings volatility. They blamed the switch to U.S. GAAP for making Deutsche Bank's financial statements more opaque and its earnings more difficult to forecast. Specifically, U.S. GAAP was deemed inappropriate for Deutsche Bank because a tax rule forced it to take a synthetic tax charge when it sold industrial shareholdings, even though there was no actual payment. The charge produced net profit distortions ranging from minus 88 percent in 2001 to plus 220 percent in 2002. The U.S. rules resulted in canceling out capital gains of $1.89 billion and earnings per share of $3.00. Critics contend that U.S. GAAP is not suitable for German banks, which, unlike their U.S. counterparts, have large portfolios of industrial shareholdings.

While most developed countries such as France and Germany have the political will and clout to act in their perceived national interest, including in the arena of accounting harmonization, a number of industrializing and economically developing countries lack the resources to develop their own standards. The concern is that these developing countries might adopt international accounting standards (IAS) in an effort to gain global respectability for their financial reporting without considering whether these standards are suitable for their economies. In the context of developing countries, critics have portrayed harmonization as a form of accounting colonialism with the accounting standards of the developed countries becoming the de facto international standards, regardless of whether they are suitable for developing countries. Developing countries should endeavor to make their voices heard in the deliberations

---

[3]See Hoarau [1995].

of the International Accounting Standards Board (IASB) so that their concerns and requirements are considered in any international standards that emerge.[4]

PRESSURES FOR HARMONIZATION

While the initial efforts at harmonization were championed mainly by political bodies and professional accounting organizations, current pressures to harmonize are driven by investor groups who use financial statements, multinational companies that prepare financial statements, regulators who monitor capital markets, the securities industry (including stock exchanges) which views itself as being significantly impacted by the global diversity in financial reporting requirements, and developing countries that often lack the resources to develop indigenous accounting standards.

INVESTORS. The dramatic acceleration in the globalization of capital markets that started in the 1980s has shifted sentiment among financial statement users towards an organized effort aimed at harmonizing accounting principles. The surge in cross-border securities listings has increased the number of investors who use financial reports of foreign companies. However, since accounting standards are still determined on a country-by-country basis, investors and financial analysts are concerned with the reliability and comparability of financial statements prepared in countries other than their own. They favor harmonization because they perceive that it will help lower the cost of investing abroad and enhance their ability to make effective investment decisions across borders.

MULTINATIONAL COMPANIES. As capital, product, and labor markets become increasingly globalized, most large companies find themselves having to diversify geographically (both in terms of their input and their output) in order to compete effectively with the major players in their industry. The increasing pace of cross-border investments and sales by multinational companies means that they are accounting for a larger percentage of global trade. Much of the new foreign investment by multinationals occurs in developing countries, which may have very different accounting regimes from developed countries. This results in multinationals having to devote greater resources to preparing their consolidated financial statements due to the differences between financial reporting in their domiciles and those in the foreign countries in which much of their new investment is taking place. Differences in reporting requirements also adversely affect multinational companies' efforts to tap foreign investors, leading preparers of financial statements to support the harmonization effort. Multinational companies can also reap additional benefits from harmonization such as the reduced cost of preparing consolidated financial statements, ease in monitoring subsidiaries abroad, more meaningful managerial accounting reports, and more relevant performance evaluation methods.

REGULATORS. With the increase in cross-border listings by companies, regulators in many countries face higher costs since they now have to monitor compliance not just by domestic firms but also by foreign firms that are listed in their jurisdiction. One way of coping with this might be to simply require foreign firms to provide

---

[4]See Saudagaran and Diga [2003].

financial statements that conform to the host country's requirements, but there is considerable debate as to the wisdom of this approach. Critics argue that the high costs of financial reporting and other regulatory compliance thereby imposed on foreign firms cause them to stay away. Empirical evidence supporting this claim has been provided by Biddle & Saudagaran [1989], and Saudagaran & Biddle [1992, 1995]. This practice can hurt the very investors that the regulator is mandated to protect by depriving them of attractive investment opportunities. Regulators might then benefit from harmonization because it would reduce their monitoring costs yet allow domestic individual investors the option of investing in foreign companies without incurring unduly high transaction costs. Through their multilateral association—the International Organization of Securities Commissions (IOSCO)—regulators have been engaged in an initiative aimed at streamlining and harmonizing financial reporting requirements for cross-border listings. This initiative will be discussed in more detail later in this chapter.

THE SECURITIES INDUSTRY AND STOCK EXCHANGES. Another effect of the dramatic increase in cross-border listings has been that many stock exchanges now look to foreign companies for growth in listings and the volume of securities transactions within their market. For example, the number of non-U.S. firms listed on the NYSE has increased from 59 in 1986 to 468 in 2002, while on NASDAQ it has grown from 244 in 1986 to 419 in 2002. The growing importance of non-U.S. firms to the U.S. stock exchanges and securities industry are also evident in the trading volume and market capitalization of the U.S. stock exchanges. The value of total transactions in non-U.S. equities by U.S. investors has grown from US$362 billion in 1990 to over US$6 trillion in 2000. The market capitalization of non-U.S. companies listed on the NYSE in 2001 was $4.8 trillion out of a total of $16 trillion for the NYSE as a whole. The London stock exchange had 409 foreign firms listed on it in 2001. Similarly, foreign firms represented significant portions of the total listings on the German (31 percent), Swiss (57 percent), and New Zealand (35 percent) stock exchanges.[5] There is therefore a significant constituency in such countries that supports facilitating the listing process in order to make their stock exchanges more attractive to foreign companies. Since there is evidence to suggest that accounting differences impose costs on companies seeking to list abroad, it is not surprising that stock exchanges and other securities industry participants have been strong supporters of reducing differences in financial reporting requirements globally.

DEVELOPING COUNTRIES. In recent years, with the fall of the communist system in Eastern Europe and the former Soviet Union, a number of countries are attempting to switch to market-oriented economic policies. In order to attract foreign capital, they are often called upon to implement accounting standards that inspire confidence in foreign investors. Few of these countries have the time or the economic resources to devise accounting standards from scratch; international accounting standards provide a low-cost option. Because time is of the essence to these countries as they seek to develop their economies, drawing upon international accounting standards can help. Moreover, adopting a harmonized set of international accounting standards also saves developing countries from having to provide expensive reconciliations to the GAAP of foreign providers of capital.

---

[5]From various issues of the annual fact books of the New York Stock Exchange and NASDAQ, and the annual statistical reports of the International Federation of Stock Exchanges.

The real and perceived economic consequences to the various groups discussed above have resulted in their exerting significant pressure on standard-setters and securities commissions around the world to accelerate the process of developing harmonized accounting and disclosure requirements.

OBSTACLES TO HARMONIZATION

A number of obstacles to global accounting harmonization remain that have thus far prevented it from becoming a reality. Some of these are economic, while others are political. Harmonization is often opposed due to its economic impact on countries or segments of society within countries. Grinyer & Russell [1992] discuss the lobbying effort in the United Kingdom in the case of accounting for goodwill and provide evidence that managers and auditors lobbied against the IASC proposal to further their own vested interests. Guenther & Hussein [1995] find that support for LIFO during IASC discussions originated exclusively from countries where use of LIFO provided clear tax benefits to companies. Kenny & Larson [1993] also provide evidence that large professional organizations lobby strongly in the development of IASs based on their self-interest. Thus, because economic consequences of accounting practices vary by country and to the extent that they are considered in the standard-setting process, this acts as an important stumbling block to harmonization.

Nationalism represents a political obstacle to harmonization. As in many other arenas, countries are wary of ceding control of their accounting regulation to outsiders, particularly if it is perceived as replacing their own accounting regulations with those of other countries. It helps if the external standards originate in a supranational organization such as the IASC since it is politically more palatable for countries to adopt "international standards" rather than the standards of another country. Wallace [1990] discusses the emergence of the IASC as a legitimate organization due to its acceptance by its constituents. According to Wallace, a global accounting standard-setter is viable because of 1) the increasing internationalization of business and finance which make global harmonization of accounting and disclosure practices desirable, 2) the composite nature of its standards and its preoccupation with topics of a general nature, 3) its evolutionary strategy, and 4) the absence of a rival organization with keen and prolonged interest in the development and marketing of global accounting standards.

Another political obstacle is the absence of strong professional accounting bodies in a number of countries.[6] This means that an organization such as the IASB, which seeks to operate through national accounting bodies, will not be effective in a number of countries. This obstacle may be overcome, at least as it relates to listed companies, if the International Organization of Securities Commissions (IOSCO) endorses international accounting standards and encourages enforcement by its member organizations in their respective countries. As discussed later in this chapter, there are indications that progress is being made in this arena.

In the view of Arthur Wyatt, former FASB board member and IASC chairman, other obstacles to harmonization include the divergence between the needs of large multinationals and smaller business entities in developing countries, difficulties in coordinating change among the large number of IASC members, and emotional resistance to change.[7] The fact that there are significant differences between large

---

[6]See Nobes and Parker [1991].
[7]See Wyatt [1997].

multinationals, who primarily report to investors and creditors, and smaller entities in developing countries whose primary audience tends to be governments and other stakeholders has been an obstacle to international harmonization. There is a view that accounting standards that are primarily designed for behemoth multinationals are neither relevant nor cost effective for use by smaller companies. The IASB's lack of enforcement power results in difficulties in coordinating change. The degree of harmonization attainable is thus contingent on the ability and willingness of national standard setters and capital market regulators to see that IASB standards are adopted within their own country.

Finally, Wyatt cites the emotionalism that proposed changes evoke as another obstacle to harmonization. He refers to Germany's opposition to accounting for inflation on the grounds that it institutionalizes inflation—a phenomenon that Germans are very sensitive about based on their experience with hyperinflation in the first half of the twentieth century. In the United States, the business community has previously responded emotionally when accounting changes were proposed (such as foreign currency gains and losses or mark-to-market for investments) which were perceived as likely to increase earnings' volatility. This resistance, often evoking emotional responses, can thwart the harmonization effort. A current example of such an issue is the IASB's stated position on expensing the cost of employee stock options, which is strongly opposed by many corporations and politicians in the United States.[8]

MEASURING HARMONIZATION

Harmonization, in the accounting context, may be defined as the process aimed at enhancing the comparability of financial statements produced in different countries' accounting regulations. Accounting scholars [Meek & Saudagaran 1990, and Tay & Parker 1990] draw a distinction between harmonization of accounting practices (*de facto* harmonization) and harmonization of accounting regulations (*de jure* harmonization). In addition, they distinguish between measurement and disclosure issues. They suggest that the harmonization of both accounting practices and accounting regulations can focus either on measurement issues such as methods of recognition, valuation, and estimation, or on disclosure issues such as the level of transparency provided by entities via their financial reporting. Harmonization measurement studies purport to explore the similarity, or lack thereof, of accounting practices and requirements.

In a research paper that critiques and attempts to streamline harmonization terminology as used in the international accounting literature, Tay & Parker [1990] analyze six harmonization studies to demonstrate problems involved in measuring the concepts of harmonization and standardization in international accounting. They discuss methodological issues and problems related to the definition and operationalizing of terms, data sources, and statistical methods. They draw distinctions between the terms *harmonization* (which is a movement away from total diversity) and *standardization* (which is a movement towards uniformity), regulation and practice (i.e., *de jure* versus *de facto*), and strict and less strict regulation (applying to all companies versus applying to some companies; the law versus a professional accounting standard; defined precisely versus defined loosely to allow discretion). Finally, they also distinguish between *harmony* and *uniformity*, which are states, and *harmonization* and *standardization*, which

---

[8]See "To expense or not to expense" in *Business Week*, July 29, 2002, pp. 44–45.

are processes. They point out that there are numerous differences between how the six studies in their analysis approach their stated task of measuring harmonization, and consequently it is not surprising that the six studies come up with different conclusions. In their view, the focus ought to be on the harmonization of accounting practice (de facto) rather than on accounting regulation (de jure). They recommend that data be obtained from annual reports or surveys of annual reports, rather than surveys of accounting standards and securities regulation.

SUPRA-NATIONAL ORGANIZATIONS ENGAGED IN ACCOUNTING HARMONIZATION

This section provides a brief overview of the main organizations that are involved in various aspects of global accounting harmonization. More detailed and current information on these organizations can be obtained from their respective web sites.

INTERNATIONAL ACCOUNTING STANDARDS COMMITTEE. The International Accounting Standards Committee (IASC), the predecessor of the current International Accounting Standards Board (IASB), was established in 1973 by professional accounting organizations from ten countries—Australia, Canada, France, Germany, Ireland, Japan, Mexico, the Netherlands, the United Kingdom, and the United States. Over the past 25 years, the IASC evolved into the most visible international accounting standard-setting organization.

The IASC's early standards were criticized for being too broad and allowing too many alternative accounting treatments. Critics charged that, as a result, comparability was lacking in financial statements that claimed to be in compliance with IASC standards. This was a serious weakness since comparability is at the heart of any harmonization effort. In 1987, the IASC responded to this criticism by initiating the Comparability Project, which was aimed at enhancing comparability of financial statements by reducing the alternative treatments available under IASC standards.[9] The Comparability Project achieved some reduction in the number of options permitted under IASC standards. There was broad support among user groups and in the International Organization of Securities Commission (IOSCO) for the Comparability Project. IOSCO consists of securities regulators from more than 100 regulatory agencies around the world. Since the IASC lacked the authority to enforce its standards globally, it sought the backing of the IOSCO for its standards in countries that are IOSCO members.

In an effort to gain acceptance of its standards by securities regulators around the world, the IASC adopted a work plan to produce a comprehensive core set of high-quality accounting standards, commonly referred to as the "core standards" program. In July 1995, the IOSCO declared its agreement to support the IASC's core standards program. This was considered significant at the time because, conditional to the IASC's successfully completion of the program, financial statements prepared in accordance with IASs were to be acceptable in cross-border security listings as an alternative to national accounting standards.

In 1997, the IASC formed a Strategy Working Party (SWP) to consider what the IASC's strategy and structure should be upon completion of the core standards program. Concurrent with the deliberations of the SWP, the accounting G4 consisting of standard setters in Australia, Canada, the United Kingdom and the United States

---

[9]See Purvis et al. [1991].

started demanding a restructuring of the IASC. The confluence of these two developments led to a total revamping of the IASC into a new standard setter in the image of the U.S. FASB.

INTERNATIONAL ACCOUNTING STANDARDS BOARD In March 2001, the IASC Foundation was formed as a not-for-profit entity incorporated in the State of Delaware, USA. The IASC Foundation is the parent entity of the IASB, an independent accounting standard setter based in London. Effective April 2001, the IASB assumed accounting standard-setting responsibilities from the IASC. This was the culmination of a restructuring based on the recommendations contained in the report, *Recommendations on Shaping IASC for the Future.*

The IASB structure contains the IASC Foundation as an independent organization with two main bodies, the Trustees and the IASB, as well as the Standards Advisory Council and the International Financial Reporting Interpretations Committee. The IASC Foundation Trustees appoint the IASB members, exercise oversight, and raise the funds needed, whereas the IASB has the sole responsibility for setting standards.

The objectives of the IASB, as stated in its constitution, are:

a) to develop in the public interest, a single set of high quality, understandable and enforceable global accounting standards that require high quality, transparent, and comparable information in financial statements and other financial reporting to help participants in the world's capital markets and other users make economic decisions.

b) to promote the use and rigorous application of those standards; and

c) to bring about the convergence of national accounting standards and International Accounting Standards to high quality solutions.

EXHIBIT 2-1 Countries With Member Organizations in the IASC

Argentina	Denmark	Ireland, Republic Of	New Zealand	Sudan
Australia	Dominican Republic	Israel	Nicaragua	Swaziland
Austria	Ecuador	Italy	Nicaragua	Sweden
Bahamas	Egypt	Ivory Coast	Nigeria	Switzerland
Bahrain	El Salvador	Jamaica	Norway	Syria
Bangladesh	Fiji	Japan	Pakistan	Taiwan
Barbados	Finland	Jordon	Panama	Tanzania
Belgium	France	Kenya	Paraguay	Thailand
Bolivia	Germany	Korea	Peru	Trinidad & Tobago
Botswana	Ghana	Kuwait	Philippines	Tunisia
Brazil	Greece	Lebanon	Poland	Turkey
Bulgaria	Guatemala	Lesotho	Portugal	Uganda
Cameroon	Haiti	Liberia	Romania	United Kingdom
Canada	Honduras	Libya	Saudia Arabia	Uruguay
Chile	Hong Kong	Luxembourg	Serbia	USA
China	Hungary	Malawi	SierraLeone	Venezuela
Colombia	Iceland	Malaysia	Singapore	Vietnam
Costa Rica	India	Malta	Slovenia	Zambia
Croatia	Indonesia	Mexico	South Africa	Zimbabwe
Cyprus	Iran	Namibia	Spain	
Czech Republic	Iraq	Netherlands	Sri Lanka	

Source: IASC web site (www.iasc.org.uk)

In 1998, for the first time, the number of countries represented in the IASC exceeded 100. Exhibit 2-1 contains a list of these countries. Since several countries have multiple professional accounting bodies that are members of the IASC, the number of accounting organizations that are IASC members exceeds 140. As of December 2001, the IASC had issued 41 International Accounting Standards (IAS). A list of the IASC standards is provided in Exhibit 2-2.

INTERNATIONAL FEDERATION OF ACCOUNTANTS. The International Federation of Accountants (IFAC) is comprised of national professional accounting organizations that represent accountants employed in public practice, business and industry, the public sector, and education, as well as some specialized groups that interface frequently with the profession. Formed in 1977, its goals are to develop the profession and harmonize its standards worldwide, to enable public accountants to provide services of consistently high quality in the public interest. Currently, IFAC has 156 member organizations in 114 countries, representing almost 2 million accountants.

The IFAC issues International Standards on Auditing (ISAs) that are aimed at harmonizing auditing practices globally. It also issues International Auditing Practice Statements (IAPSs) to provide practical assistance in implementing the ISAs and to promote good practice. IAPSs are not intended to have the authority of standards.

EXHIBIT 2-2 List of IASC Standards

IAS 1	Presentation of Financial Statements	IAS 22	Business Combinations
IAS 2	Inventories	IAS 23	Borrowing Costs
IAS 3	No longer effective. Replaced by IAS 27.	IAS 24	Related Party Disclosures
IAS 4	Depreciation	IAS 25	Accounting for Investments
IAS 5	Information to be Disclosed in Financial Statements	IAS 26	Accounting and Reporting by Retirement Benefit Plans
IAS 6	No longer effective. Replaced by IAS 15.	IAS 27	Consolidated Financial Statements and Accounting for Investments in Subsidiaries
IAS 7	Cash Flow Statements		
IAS 8	Profit or Loss for the Period, Fundamental Errors and Changes in Accounting Policies	IAS 28	Accounting for Investments in Associates
		IAS 29	Financial Reporting in Hyperinflationary Economies
IAS 9	Research and Development Costs		
IAS 10	Contingencies and Events Occurring after the Balance Sheet Date	IAS 30	Disclosures in the Financial Statements of Banks and Similar Financial Institutions
IAS 11	Construction Contracts	IAS 31	Financial Reporting of Interests in Joint Ventures
IAS 12	Income Taxes		
IAS 13	Presentation of Current Assets and Current Liabilities	IAS 32	Financial Instruments: Disclosures and Presentation
IAS 14	Segment Reporting	IAS 33	Earnings Per Share
IAS 15	Information Reflecting the Effects of Changing Prices	IAS 34	Interim Financial Reporting
		IAS 35	Discontinuing Operations
IAS 16	Property, Plant, and Equipment	IAS 36	Impairment of Assets
IAS 17	Accounting for Leases	IAS 37	Provisions, Contingent Liabilities and Contingent Assets
IAS 18	Revenue		
IAS 19	Employee Benefits	IAS 38	Intangible Assets
IAS 20	Accounting for Government Grants and Disclosure of Government Assistance	IAS 39	Financial Instruments: Recognition and Measurement
IAS 21	The Effects of Changes in Foreign Exchange Rates	IAS 40	Investment Property
		IAS 41	Agriculture

Source: IASB web site (www.iasb.org.uk)

The IFAC also works towards reducing differences in the requirements to qualify as a professional accountant in its member countries. It has also published the Code of Ethics for Professional Accountants to provide guidelines on a variety of issues faced by auditors such as independence, integrity, and objectivity. Similar to the IASC, the IFAC also sought the backing for its standards from the IOSCO. It received a significant boost in 1992 when the IOSCO voted to accept ISAs for cross-border filings with securities regulators.

Another current IFAC initiative is the establishment of international public sector standards applicable to all levels of government. These standards are intended to provide governments around the world with tools to improve their financial management and reporting practices. Another project relates to maintaining auditor independence in today's complex and competitive business environment. A number of recent reports by the SEC, World Bank, and the United Nations have expressed concerns related to auditor independence. The IFAC is also examining how accountants can play a role in reducing corruption. A recent study issued by the IFAC addresses the key issues related to the management and measurement of intellectual capital and the accountant's role in this process. Finally, the IFAC organized a Forum on the Development of the Accountancy Profession, bringing together various development banks and agencies to determine how best to marshal the combined resources of the accounting profession, local and national governments, and development agencies to meet the basic needs for an accounting framework in developing countries.[10]

INTERNATIONAL ORGANIZATION OF SECURITIES COMMISSIONS. The International Organization of Securities Commissions (IOSCO) was formed in 1983 and is comprised of securities regulators from more than 115 securities regulatory agencies from around the world, representing coverage of 85 percent of the world's capital markets. Its General Secretariat is based in Madrid. The IOSCO objectives include:

- to cooperate to promote high standards of regulation in order to maintain just, efficient, and sound markets;
- to exchange information on their respective experiences to promote the development of domestic markets;
- to establish standards and an effective surveillance of international securities transactions;
- to promote the integrity of the markets by a rigorous application and enforcement of the standards.

As discussed above, there was a movement to have the IOSCO endorse IASC standards to streamline cross-border listing globally and to provide enforcement of IASs. In 1993, the IOSCO and the IASC Board agreed to a list of core standards for use in financial statements of companies involved in cross-border listings. At that time, the IOSCO endorsed IAS 7, Cash Flow Statements, and indicated that 14 of the existing standards were acceptable without additional improvements. In 1995, the IOSCO's technical committee announced that successful completion of the IASC Board's Work Plan would mean that IASs comprised a comprehensive core set of standards which, in turn, would lead to the IOSCO's endorsement of IASC standards for cross-border listing in all global capital markets. In 2000, the IOSCO recommended that its

---

[10]More detailed information on IFAC and its programs is available on **www.ifac.org**

members allow incoming foreign issuers to use IASs to prepare their financial statements for cross-border listings with the supplementary information necessary to meet national or regional requirements.

Today, the IOSCO looks to the IASB to provide acceptable international accounting and financial reporting standards for use in cross-border listings and securities offerings. A number of stock exchanges require or permit foreign issuers to submit IAS-based financial statements. Consequently, in recent years, hundreds of companies prepared their financial statements using international accounting standards.[11]

UNITED NATIONS. The United Nations' (UN) involvement in international accounting harmonization has two distinct phases. In the 1970s, its Group of Experts on International Standards of Accounting and Reporting produced a list of financial and non-financial disclosures to be provided by multinational corporations. This effort was motivated by a desire to better monitor the activities of multinational companies doing business in developing countries. The UN list was fairly detailed, including requirements for disclosure of transfer pricing policies, segment information, research and development expenditures, and employment information. Since many of these items are regarded as proprietary information that is not required to be disclosed in many countries, and because the UN has no enforcement authority, its recommendations were rejected by most industrialized countries. The effort was perceived as primarily serving the needs of governments in developing countries where multinational companies did business.

More recently, the UN has played a less controversial role in the international accounting arena. It has worked to promote the harmonization of accounting standards by discussing and supporting best practices, including those stipulated by the IASC. It has also focused on issues such as environmental disclosures. The UN has provided funding and technical assistance to promote the speedy development of internationally accepted accounting standards in a number of former communist bloc countries that need a sound financial reporting regime if they are to successfully attract foreign investment. The UN's recent efforts have been received much more favorably by the international community. The Intergovernmental Working Group of Experts on International Standards of Accounting and Reporting (ISAR) was created in 1982. It is the only intergovernmental working group devoted to corporate accounting and auditing issues.[12]

ORGANIZATION FOR ECONOMIC COOPERATION AND DEVELOPMENT. The Organization for Economic Cooperation and Development (OECD) comprises 30 member countries that produce two-thirds of the world's goods and services. It is often called the "rich man's club." However, the OECD maintains that it is not an exclusive organization and that it welcomes all countries with a commitment to a market economy and a pluralistic democracy. The OECD considers itself to be an organization that provides governments with a setting in which to discuss, develop, and perfect economic and social policy. Exchanges between OECD governments flow from information and analysis provided by a Secretariat in Paris. In the area of accounting, the OECD's efforts include formation of an Ad Hoc Working Group on Accounting

---

[11]More detailed information on IOSCO and its programs is available on **www.iosco.org**

[12]Additional information on the UN's activities in global accounting harmonization can be obtained at **www.unctad.org**

Standards which 1) supports current efforts by international, regional, and national bodies to promote accounting harmonization, and 2) functions as a forum for the exchange of views on UN efforts on accounting and reporting standards.

The latter point hints at the OECD's role as a counterweight to organizations such as the UN and the International Confederation of Free Trade Unions (ICFTU) which it regards as acting contrary to the interests of its own members. Along the same lines, its views have resonance among industrialized countries because the OECD has taken a moderate stance on multinational companies, stressing voluntary restraint on issues such as transfer pricing in lieu of national regulation. In 1976, the OECD issued a code of conduct for multinational companies that includes recommendations for annual report disclosures. It has also tried to foster good governance in corporations and in the public sector.[13]

OTHER HARMONIZATION EFFORTS

BILATERAL OR MUTUAL AGREEMENTS. This approach consists of two or more countries negotiating agreements that involve mutual recognition of each other's standards with certain additional disclosures or reconciliations as part of the arrangement. We examine a highly visible effort at such an agreement between Canada and the United States to determine the viability of this approach to harmonization.

The Multijurisdictional Disclosure System (MDS) is a bilateral agreement negotiated between the SEC and Canadian regulatory authorities. The MDS was created to reduce multiple registration, listing, and reporting requirements for Canadian firms that dual-list in Canada and the United States, primarily to make access to the U.S. market less costly for Canadian firms. Under the MDS, eligible Canadian firms may satisfy most SEC requirements by filing documents prepared for Canadian regulators. Further, securities regulators review documents of firms filing only once, in the firm's home country, instead of in both markets. This was expected to significantly reduce the monetary costs as well as the time to market for companies listing outside their home market. Finally, the immediate elimination of the requirement to reconcile Canadian GAAP financial statements to U.S. GAAP for investment grade debt and preferred stock (but not common stock) for eligible Canadian firms was supposed to be another cost savings to firms. In addition to benefiting Canadian firms that met the MDS criteria, other Canadian firms were also expected to enjoy reduced financial reporting and disclosure costs as a result of the MDS since they were able to report to the SEC under the simplified Integrated Disclosure System (IDS) that had been available to other non-U.S. companies since 1982.[14]

The MDS became effective July 1, 1991, after six years of often difficult negotiations between U.S. and Canadian regulators. The SEC had originally selected Canada as the first country to enter into a bilateral agreement with because of the similarities between U.S. and Canadian accounting, auditing, and regulatory environments, as well as the significant market presence of Canadian firms in the United States. In 1985, when the negotiations for the agreement began, Canadian firms comprised more than half of the 463 foreign firms registered with the SEC. Their significance in the U.S. market was further illustrated by the magnitude of offerings by Canadian

---

[13]More detailed information on OECD and its programs is available on **www.oecd.org**
[14]See Saudagaran [1991].

firms in that period. During 1989 and 1990, the two years immediately prior to the MDS agreement, Canadian firms made 54 public offerings in the United States, totaling almost US$12 billion [SEC 1991, p. 13].

While the MDS was presented as a policy that would harmonize reporting requirements and reduce costs for Canadian firms entering the U.S. capital market, the actual evidence since its passage indicates that it falls short of being perceived as facilitating entry or reducing costs for Canadian companies. A recent study provided little evidence of significant benefit accruing to Canadian firms subsequent to the passage of the MDS.[15] Since very few Canadian firms list securities other than common stock in U.S. markets, most Canadian firms are still subject to the requirement to provide a reconciliation to U.S. GAAP. Ninety percent of respondents, from a sample of Canadian firms listed in the United States, responded that preparation of U.S. GAAP financial information continued to be extremely costly even after the passage of the MDS. Similarly, Canadian firms that were not listed in the United States responded that the MDS had not materially reduced the financial reporting requirements sufficiently to make a U.S. listing attractive.

This suggests that the MDS has not provided the benefits originally envisioned and leads to serious questions as to whether it is an appropriate model for harmonization efforts between countries. This approach is very time consuming, and the few benefits that result accrue primarily to the securities regulators. The MDS experience shows that users must continue to contend with alternative sets of accounting standards. This experience is particularly relevant since the two countries attempting the bilateral negotiation approach were Canada and the United States—countries that are not just geographic neighbors but also very similar in their business environments. If six years of negotiations between these two countries produced such modest results, one might ask what chance there is for bilateral agreements between countries that are very different from each other. Critics of this approach [e.g., Cochrane et al. 1996] point to the MDS process undertaken by the United States and Canada as an example of "how tortuous and relatively fruitless" this approach to accounting harmonization can be.

WORLD-CLASS ISSUER. This harmonization approach was primarily advocated by the New York Stock Exchange (NYSE). It involved establishing specific quantitative criteria to define a special category of companies as "world-class issuers." Qualifying criteria could include, for example, revenues of $5 billion and market capitalization of $2 billion along with average weekly trading volume outside the United States of at least $1 million or half a million shares. Non-U.S. companies that qualified as world-class issuers would be permitted to register securities with the SEC using their home country financial statements without the need for a quantitative reconciliation to U.S. GAAP. They would provide the SEC with a written explanation of any material differences from U.S. GAAP. This approach attempted to distinguish between the global blue chip companies and other non-U.S. companies. It advocated ease of entry into the U.S. capital market for world-class issuers on the basis that they presented less risk to U.S. investors.

There were a number of problems with this approach that made its adoption unlikely. The SEC was not impressed by this proposal and, in fact, was openly critical of it. It considered the world-class issuer approach as a dilution of the quality and

---

[15]See Houston and Jones [1999].

extent of disclosure requirements in the United States. There were also potential legal problems that could arise as a result of discriminating between companies on the basis of size. Other practical problems with this approach were obtaining agreement on the quantitative criteria for world-class issuers, and dealing with companies that were admitted upon meeting the criteria but that subsequently fell below the quantitative thresholds for world-class issuer. U.S. companies opposed it because they regarded it as likely to create an uneven playing field. They contended that this approach would discriminate against U.S. firms by allowing non-U.S. firms to tap U.S. capital markets with a relatively lower regulatory burden than that imposed on U.S. firms. Given that the SEC and U.S. companies were not in favor of this approach, it appears unlikely that the world-class issuer scenario will become a reality in the foreseeable future.

THE IASC/IOSCO INITIATIVE. As previously discussed in this chapter, until recently, the most promising scenario for the global harmonization of accounting principles appeared to be that of the standards issued by the IASC and endorsed by the IOSCO. As indicated earlier, a series of events led to the restructuring of the old IASC into the new IASB. On May 15, 2002, the IASB published its first major exposure draft, *Improvements to International Accounting Standards*, which includes proposals to revise 12 of the 34 active international accounting standards. The IASB appears to be the main hope for global accounting harmonization in the foreseeable future. Its efforts have been given added momentum by the European Union's requirement for publicly listed companies in its jurisdiction to use international accounting standards by 2005.

CURRENT EVIDENCE ON HARMONIZATION

This section considers the evidence on the level of accounting harmonization achieved to date. The evidence is examined at both the global level and the regional level, since both paradigms of harmonization have been attempted to varying degrees. The discussion on global harmonization focuses on the IASC initiative since that scenario has the greatest likelihood of success at this time. The discussion on regional harmonization examines the developments and evidence in the European Union (EU) and compares it to that of another regional economic group, the Association of South East Asian Nations (ASEAN).

Global

There has been very little empirical research to measure the success of harmonization at the global level. Meek and Saudagaran [1990] noted that the research on the extent of harmonization with the IASC's standards, prior to the start of its Comparability Project in 1989, showed that the IASC had had little impact on reporting practices even among multinational companies. They expressed the view that it was necessary to undertake a systematic analysis of the reasons for the apparent reluctance to adopt IASC standards before setting up enforcement mechanisms for these standards. The need for such research still remains. The less-than-enthusiastic initial response may be due to the fact that the original series of accounting standards promulgated by IASC were very broad and did little to enhance the comparability of financial statements. That particular concern ought to be alleviated to a considerable extent with the tightening of IASC standards through its Comparability Project started in 1989. This project was initiated to enhance comparability in part to gain the approval and, thereby, enforcement of its standards by the IOSCO. Research into whether the level of global harmony has increased as a result of the tightening of standards would be meaningful after the passage of a reasonable period of time since the establishment of the new IASB.

There is some anecdotal evidence which suggests that there has been a surge in de jure harmonization globally in the past decade. One measure of this is the number of stock exchanges that accept financial statements prepared using international accounting standards in lieu of the stock exchange's domestic standards. The 51 countries whose stock exchanges accept international accounting standards based financial statements either as is or with some adjustments in 2002 are listed in Exhibit 2-3. As discussed earlier in this chapter, Tay and Parker [1990] suggest that it is more appropriate to examine accounting practices (de facto) rather than accounting regulations (de jure) to get a true measure of the level of harmonization. In order to measure the extent of de facto harmonization with international accounting standards, one would have to identify the number and nationality of firms that prepare their financial state-

EXHIBIT 2-3 Stock Exchanges that Accept IAS Financial Statements

Argentina*	Buenos Aires Stock Exchange	Malta	Malta Stock Exchange
Australia	Australian Stock Exchange	Netherlands	Amsterdam Stock Exchange
Austria	Wiener Börse (Vienna Stock Exchange)	New Zealand	New Zealand Stock Exchange
		Norway	Oslo Stock Exchange
Bangladesh	Chittagong Stock Exchange	Pakistan	Karachi Stock Exchange
Belgium	Brussels Stock Exchange		Lahore Stock Exchange
Canada*	Montreal Stock Exchange	Peru*	Lima Stock Exchange
Cayman Islands	Cayman Islands Stock Exchange	Poland	Warsaw Stock Exchange
China (PRC)*	Shanghai Stock Exchange	Singapore	Singapore Exchange
	Shenzen Stock Exchange	Slovakia	Bratislava Stock Exchange
Croatia	Zagreb Stock Exchange	Slovenia	Ljubljana Stock Exchange
Cyprus	Cyprus Stock Exchange	South Africa	Johannesburg Stock Exchange
Czech Republic	Prague Stock Exchange	Spain*	Madrid Stock Exchange
Denmark	Copenhagen Stock Exchange		Barcelona Stock Exchange
Egypt	Cairo Stock Exchange		Bilbao Stock Exchange
Estonia	Tallinn Stock Exchange		Valencia Stock Exchange
Europe	EASDAQ Exchange	Sri Lanka*	Colombo Stock Exchange
Finland*	Helsinki Exchanges	Sweden	Stockholm Stock Exchange
France	Paris Stock Exchange	Switzerland	Swiss Stock Exchange
Germany	Deutsche Börse	Tanzania	Dar-es-Salaam Stock Exchange
	Frankfurt Stock Exchange	Thailand	The Stock Exchange of Thailand
	Bavarian Stock Exchange	Turkey	Istanbul Stock Exchange
	Stuttgart Stock Exchange	Ukraine	Ukraine Stock Exchange
Hong Kong*	Stock Exchange of Hong Kong	United Kingdom	London Stock Exchange
Hungary	Budapest Stock Exchange	United States*	New York Stock Exchange
Italy	Rome Stock Exchange		NASDAQ
Japan	Tokyo Stock Exchange		American Stock Exchange
Jordan	Amman Stock Exchange		Arizona Stock Exchange
Korea	Korea Stock Exchange		Boston Stock Exchange
Latvia	Riga Stock Exchange		Chicago Stock Exchange
Lithuania	National Stock Exchange of Lithuania		Chicago Board Options Exchange
Luxembourg	Luxembourg Stock Exchange		Pacific Stock Exchange
Macedonia	Macedonian Stock Exchange		Philadelphia Stock Exchange
Malaysia	Kuala Lumpur Stock Exchange	Zimbabwe*	Zimbabwe Stock Exchange

*Subject to certain conditions

ments in accordance with international accounting standards. Exhibit 2-4 provides summary statistics based on the list on the IASB web site of companies that report compliance with international accounting standards. As indicated therein, in October 2002, the list contains 224 companies from 38 countries that cite their use of international accounting standards. Interestingly, this list was considerably longer in September 2000 when almost 1,000 companies claimed to be preparing their financial statements in compliance with international accounting standards. The decrease is probably a result of Revised IAS 1, Presentation of Financial Statements, which states:

> An enterprise whose financial statements comply with International Accounting Standards should disclose that fact. Financial statements should not be described as complying with International Accounting Standards unless they comply with all the requirements of each applicable Standard and each applicable Interpretation of the Standing Interpretations Committee.

This is consistent with evidence provided by Street, Gray, and Bryant [1999] and Cairns [1999] indicating that, until 1998, among firms that claimed to prepare their financial statements in accordance with international accounting standards, the actual level of compliance was rather sketchy. It appeared that auditors asserted that financial statements were in compliance with international accounting standards even though the accounting policies footnotes and other notes indicated otherwise.

Regional

EUROPEAN UNION. The European Union (EU) has its origins in three pan-European treaties from the 1950s: 1) the European Coal and Steel Community (Treaty of Paris in 1950), 2) the European Atomic Energy Community (Euratom Treaty in 1957), and the European Economic Community (Treaty of Rome in 1957).

EXHIBIT 2-4   Companies Reporting under International Financial Reporting Standards

Countries	No. of Companies	Countries	No. of Companies
Austria	12	Italy	1
Bahrain	6	Japan	1
Belgium	2	Kuwait	1
Bermuda	1	Latvia	1
Botswana	3	Malta	4
Bulgaria	1	Netherlands	4
Canada	2	New Zealand	1
China	4	Norway	2
Croatia	2	Peru	1
Cyprus	2	Russia	3
Czech Republic	2	Slovakia	1
Denmark	11	Slovenia	4
Estonia	1	South Africa	3
Finland	5	Spain	1
France	2	Sweden	2
Germany	66	Switzerland	54
Greece	1	Turkey	2
SAR Hong Kong	5	United Arab Emirates	4
Hungary	3	Zimbabwe	1

Source: IASB web site (www.iasb.org.uk)

The Treaty of Rome, regarded as the most important of these agreements, was signed by 6 countries—Belgium, France, Germany, Italy, Luxembourg, and the Netherlands. Over the years, other countries have been admitted to the group—Denmark, Republic of Ireland, and the United Kingdom (1972), Greece (1981), Spain and Portugal (1986), Sweden, Finland, and Austria (1995)—raising its membership to 15 nations. Currently, several Central and Eastern European countries await the acceptance of their applications for full membership to the EU. The basic objective of the EU is to bring about a common market that allows for free mobility of capital, goods, and people between member countries.

The EU company law directives are the basis of the EU accounting harmonization effort. Under the 1957 Treaty of Rome, EU member countries agreed to harmonize their company laws in order to coordinate safeguards to protect the interests of member states and others, to make these safeguards equivalent across the EU. The laws of member states must be sufficiently similar to permit the proper functioning of the common market. To the extent that these laws differ, the accounting and reporting requirements across member countries is also likely to contain differences. EU directives consist of articles, each focusing on specific issues. The result to be achieved by a directive is binding on member countries. Once an EU directive becomes national law, it is binding for all companies in the jurisdiction affected. However, each country is free to choose the form and method of implementation and also to add or delete options, given that there are three types of articles found in directives:

- uniform rules to be implemented exactly in all member states,
- minimum rules that may be strengthened by individual governments, and
- alternative rules which give member states choices.

The EU has adopted a number of directives dealing with accounting matters. Of these, the Fourth Directive and the Seventh Directive are generally regarded as the most significant. The EU Fourth Directive addresses all aspects of the financial statements of individual companies. It aims to harmonize accounting principles, and thereby enhance comparability, by laying down minimum standards of presentation, publication, and audit to be applied in member countries. The Fourth Directive was adopted in 1978 after almost 15 years of negotiation, revision, and debate. The Fourth Directive was an important breakthrough in that it represented a compromise between the legalistic approach to accounting in most of continental Europe and the "true and fair" approach that characterizes accounting in the United Kingdom. Member countries have freedom in implementing and incorporating the directive in their national accounting regulation. They may require more than what the directive requires, and may also require different reporting rules based on company-specific variables such as size or line of business. Despite this flexibility, it took 13 years for all member states to be in compliance with the Fourth Directive, even though the targeted implementation date was within two years of its passage.

The Seventh Directive, passed in 1983, addresses the issue of consolidated financial statements. This was a very controversial issue within the EU because of the diversity of European consolidation practices and significant tax ramifications. Until the passage of the Seventh Directive, many EU countries did not have any requirements for consolidated financial reporting. For example, Germany only required consolidation of domestic subsidiaries, while France had no consolidation requirements. The Seventh Directive generally followed the British-American emphasis on legal control. However, disagreements on this issue are reflected in the more than 50 options available in the Seventh Directive. While the Directive has increased the number of European companies that must produce consolidated financial statements, it has not added appreciably to the degree of harmonization in consolidated financial reporting. The Eighth Directive, passed in 1984, does not deal directly with financial reporting issues but rather with minimum entry requirements for qualification as a statutory auditor. It provides considerable latitude to member countries on the educational level and required work experience, as well as on matters related to auditor independence. It does not deal with mutual recognition of auditors between EU countries. Consequently, regulations on key issues such as fraud reporting, requirements for entry into the profession, and auditor independence might still vary across EU countries after the Eighth Directive.

The EU effort at accounting harmonization has been a slow and challenging process. The EU Directives have highlighted European accounting diversity, which is rooted in different legal systems (code versus common law), different capital market structures (debt versus equity orientation), and different roles of accounting (macro- versus micro-user). The adoption of the directives in member countries has given rise to new differences, as political compromise has required the EU to sanction alternatives that hinder the goals of consistency and comparability. International accounting expert and former FASB board member, Gerhard Mueller, summarized the state of EU accounting harmonization as follows [Mueller 1997, pp. 11.26–27]:

1. The scope of the Directives is technically incomplete. Certain topics like accounting for foreign exchange transactions, leasing, pension accruals, tax effect allocations, and so on, are not directly covered.
2. The Directives were unevenly adopted into individual national legislation. Differential loopholes have cropped up between countries. The Fourth Directive was issued in 1978 with a two-year time frame for adoption into national legislation of member states. Italy did not implement this Directive until 1992.
3. All accounting-related EU Directives stand today as they were initially issued. Thus, they are static instruments missing updating and quality improvement mechanisms.
4. EU harmonization strategists selected mutual recognition as their policy concept for worldwide acceptance. The U.S. SEC has rejected mutual recognition as far as EU accounting is concerned. At the same time, European capital markets institutions readily accept financial reports prepared on the basis of U.S. GAAP.
5. Most EU member states (except Austria, Germany, and Luxembourg) have established national financial accounting standard-setting commissions or boards. Some of these boards have issued pronouncements which effectively "watered down" the EU Directives.
6. Large European corporations had hoped that compliance with EU accounting rules would be sufficient to reach international capital markets. This has not happened. German automaker Daimler-Benz is a case in point.

Mueller's assessment of the overall lack of success of the European accounting harmonization effort is borne out by research evidence. Since the EU is the only multi-country organization engaged in harmonization that is theoretically able to enforce its accounting directives, a number of studies have attempted to measure the level of harmonization attained within the EU. Some of these studies address accounting practice by examining corporate annual reports from selected EU member countries, while others look at the state of regulation on specific accounting items in selected countries. Hermann and Thomas [1995] looked at the level of harmonization in accounting measurement practices among eight member countries in the European Union.

They found that accounting for foreign currency translation of assets and liabilities, treatment of translation differences, and inventory valuation are harmonized, while accounting for fixed asset valuation, depreciation, goodwill, research and development costs, inventory costing, and foreign currency translation of revenues and expenses remain diverse. They also found some evidence that there is greater harmonization among fairness-oriented countries than among legalistic countries. Van der Tas [1992] tested for harmonization of accounting for deferred taxes in the EU, finding mixed evidence for the years 1978–88. Emenyonu and Gray [1992] found little evidence of harmonization across France, Germany, and the United Kingdom. Using groups of British and French accountants in a laboratory study, Walton [1992] found that not only is there a lack of harmonization in the application of the EU Fourth Directive between the two jurisdictions, but also a general absence of consensus even within each country group. Garrod and Sieringhaus [1995] compared the regulations for accounting for leased assets in Germany and the United Kingdom, concluding that the regulations are ambiguous and result in dissimilar accounting treatment in the two countries. Adhikari and Tondkar [1995] studied the success achieved by the EU in harmonizing stock exchange disclosure requirements for 11 EU stock exchanges. They found that EU requirements do not eliminate the differences in the disclosure requirements between stock exchanges. Rather, they establish a lower boundary below which the disclosure requirements may not fall. These studies indicate that the EU has achieved minimal harmony in its accounting practices and regulations.

In what was a clear break from its erstwhile emphasis on the regional model of harmonization, the EU announced in November 1995 that it would look to the IASC to proceed with the task of accounting harmonization. The EU indicated its support for the IASC/IOSCO initiative and announced its intent to make EU requirements consistent with IASs. The shift in strategy might be viewed as an acknowledgment by the EU of the lack of success of its efforts. In June 2000, the EU announced that all listed EU companies would be required to prepare their financial statements in accordance with International Accounting Standards. At least seven member countries (Austria, Belgium, Finland, France, Germany, Italy and Luxembourg) have since adopted measures specifically allowing listed companies to opt for preparing their financial statements in accordance with IAS or U.S. GAAP, rather than in their domestic national standards.

A TALE OF TWO REGIONS—COMPARING ASEAN TO EU. It is instructive to compare why the countries belonging to another regional organization, the Association of South East Asian Nations (ASEAN), adopted the global paradigm rather than the EU's regional paradigm of harmonization. Formed in 1967, one of ASEAN's principal objectives was to create a robust economic alliance in the region. The charter members of ASEAN were Indonesia, Malaysia, the Philippines, Singapore, and Thailand. Countries subsequently admitted were Brunei (1984), Vietnam (1995), Laos and Myanmar (1997). The ASEAN countries, with a total population of 450 million and a combined gross domestic product of almost a trillion dollars, represent a significant economic group.

Evidence indicates that ASEAN countries have followed the global paradigm of harmonization in that they have, for the most part, chosen to unilaterally adopt the accounting standards issued by the IASC rather than follow the regional approach attempted by the EU.[16] This raises the question as to why the ASEAN members have

---

[16]See Saudagaran and Diga [1997] for a detailed discussion of harmonization in ASEAN.

not pursued regional harmonization as a priority goal. It is useful here to draw parallels between the experience of ASEAN and that of the EU. Regional accounting harmonization has not been pursued in ASEAN because the requisite conditions that would make it an important policy objective are not present. These conditions include 1) an articulated rationale and a set of values that facilitate regional accounting harmony, 2) a high level of economic integration, 3) a political infrastructure to pursue harmonization within a broad policy framework, and 4) the economic and political clout to develop a regional vision without the fear of being marginalized in the global arena.

First, unlike the EU, ASEAN has not been able to articulate a clear rationale for why regional harmonization is a preferred course of action for the member countries. The rationale, while expressed in collective terms, must make the benefits of regional accounting harmonization explicit for each member state. Accounting systems in ASEAN countries, far from being homogeneous, are characterized by long-standing traditions engendered by each country's colonial history and regulatory preferences. The absence of tangible benefits for member countries would make policy-makers, particularly in government and the business community, reluctant to discard traditional approaches to accounting regulation. The EU was able to overcome resistance to change by presenting a clear case for regional accounting harmonization within the broader framework of common economic policy goals.[17] As stipulated in the EU's Common Industrial Policy [1970], the European Commission wanted a level playing field that would allow EU-based companies to remain competitive anywhere in the region. The presentation of corporate information was an essential component to maintaining regional competitiveness, therefore it appeared sensible to harmonize accounting regulation throughout the EU.

Second, the current level of economic integration in ASEAN is at a much earlier stage compared to the EU at the time when policies for regional accounting harmonization were being developed. The notion of an "ASEAN Inc.," a regional body with a coherent and coordinated set of economic policies, has yet to take shape. A comparison of the worldwide exports of EU and ASEAN member countries in 1993 reveals dramatic differences in the levels of economic importance attached to intra-regional markets by the two groups. While EU countries depend on other EU countries for over 60 percent of their worldwide exports, ASEAN countries' exports within the region only account for 20 percent of their worldwide exports. In all likelihood, this number has fallen further as a result of the Asian economic crisis in 1997. ASEAN countries are much more dependent economically on global partners outside ASEAN than are the EU countries. In the context of accounting harmonization, it appears more compelling from a policy standpoint for ASEAN countries to harmonize their accounting regulations globally to further encourage interest from existing and potential economic partners.

The third prerequisite for progress towards regional accounting harmonization is an organizational structure that would support harmonization goals. Related to this is the need for formal recognition that grants status and substantive legitimacy to the regional harmonization body by member countries through the national adoption of accounting standards developed at the regional level. During the period when the EU was making steady progress toward regional harmonization, support emanated from both the government and the accounting profession. Both were well represented in

---

[17]See Nobes [1992] and Van Hulle [1992] for a discussion on harmonization in Europe.

deliberations concerning European accounting harmonization. The EU, in particular, had a well-developed infrastructure for regional decision-making that included a separate civil service, parliament, various consultative committees, and councils of ministers. ASEAN, on the other hand, has never had a comparable structure. Also, the professional accounting bodies in Europe have had a relatively long history of intra-regional cooperation through the Union Européenne des Experts Comptables in 1951, the Groupe d'Etudes in 1966, and the Federation des Experts Comptables Européens (FEE) that took over the roles of the two earlier bodies in 1987. These regional accounting groups have influenced the nature and outcome of the Directives concerning company law in Europe. The ASEAN Federation of Accountants (AFA), by contrast, has yet to establish sufficient political clout to influence the agenda regarding the harmonization of corporate accounting regulations in ASEAN.

Finally, the differences in the experiences of EU and ASEAN may also be a function of different starting points in terms of economic and political clout on the global scene. The EU is a regional bloc consisting mainly of developed countries with significant political clout and generally well-established accounting traditions. Therefore, the EU was more confident of developing a regional vision without the fear of being marginalized. On the other hand, the ASEAN countries are mainly developing countries with young accounting traditions, and, therefore, may be less confident in developing a regional vision separate from the rest of the world. This was particularly true in the 1960s and 1970s, when these countries were considerably less developed than they are today. However, the EU's failed effort at regional harmonization and the consequence of the recent economic crisis in Asia are likely to reinforce the view of ASEAN countries that they are better off with the global paradigm of accounting harmonization. In the long run, it might also deter developing countries in other regions such as Africa and Latin America from attempting regional accounting harmonization.

SUMMARY

1. The primary economic rationale in favor of harmonization is that major differences in accounting practices act as a barrier to capital flowing to the most efficient users. Proponents of accounting harmonization argue that it is necessary to produce comparable and credible data for use across borders.

2. Opponents of harmonization argue that differences in the economic, political, and legal environments of countries justify financial reporting differences between countries. They express concerns that the Western accounting practices that tend to dominate harmonization efforts are not appropriate for developing countries.

3. Current pressures to harmonize are driven by investor groups who use financial statements, multinational companies that prepare financial statements, regulators who monitor capital markets, the securities industry (including stock exchanges) which views itself as being significantly impacted by the global diversity in financial reporting requirements, and developing countries that often lack the resources to develop indigenous accounting standards.

4. Some of the main obstacles to harmonization are nationalism, the perceived negative impact on countries or segments of society within countries, the absence of strong professional accounting bodies in certain countries, divergence between the needs of large multinationals and smaller business entities in developing countries, difficulties in coordinating change among the large number of IASC members, and emotionalism in the face of proposed changes.

5. There is a distinction between accounting harmonization (movement away from total diversity) and standardization (movement towards uniformity). It is also important to distinguish between the harmonization of accounting regulations (de jure) and accounting practices (de facto).

6. The harmonization effort over the past 25 years has been led by the International Accounting Standards Committee (IASC). Other organizations involved are the International Federation of Accountants (IFAC), the International Organization of Securities Commissions (IOSCO), and to a lesser degree the United Nations (UN) and the Organization for Economic Cooperation and Development (OECD). The IASC has recently been restructured and standard setting is now the responsibility of the newly formed International Accounting Standards Board (IASB).

7. The current evidence on harmonization is mixed. There appears to be more de jure harmonization with a number of countries adopting international accounting standards. However, the level of de facto harmonization is very modest with evidence of considerable differences in the financial statements of companies claiming to use international accounting standards.

QUESTIONS

1. Discuss the rationale for the global harmonization of financial reporting and disclosure requirements.
2. In recent years, there has been pressure from a variety of groups for pursuing global accounting harmonization. Who are these groups, and how do they stand to benefit from accounting harmonization?
3. What are the main obstacles to global accounting harmonization? In your opinion, are they likely to be overcome in the near future?
4. Define and distinguish the following terms as they apply to the international accounting literature:
   a) de jure harmonization versus de facto harmonization
   b) harmonization versus standardization
   c) strict regulations versus less strict regulations
   d) harmony versus harmonization
   e) uniformity versus standardization
5. Discuss the role of the following supra-national organizations in global accounting harmonization:
   a) International Accounting Standards Board (IASB)
   b) International Federation of Accountants (IFAC)
   c) International Organization of Securities Commissions (IOSCO)
   d) United Nations (UN)
   e) Organization for Economic Cooperation and Development (OECD)
6. Discuss the Multijurisdictional Disclosure System (MDS). Is this a viable approach to achieving global harmony in accounting?
7. Which organization is the main advocate of the "world-class issuer" approach to international accounting harmonization? What are the main obstacles to this approach?
8. In your view, will the IASB be more successful than the IASC in achieving global accounting harmonization? Explain.
9. Discuss the European Union's (EU) effort at achieving accounting harmonization within its member countries. Has the EU's attempt at regional accounting harmonization been successful? Explain.

10. How have the ASEAN countries differed from the EU countries in their approach to accounting harmonization? What were the main factors that might have caused the ASEAN countries to take a different approach?

11. Using the IASB web site (**www.iasb.org.uk**), identify five companies from each of five different countries that prepare their financial statements using international accounting standards. In your opinion, why has each of these firms opted for international accounting standards?

12. Select an OECD country and discuss whether it would benefit from the adoption of international accounting standards as its domestic GAAP. Explain.

13. Select a non-OECD country and discuss whether it would benefit from the adoption of international accounting standards as its domestic GAAP.

EXERCISES

1. Critics of harmonization say that the accounting regimes in developed Western countries are likely to dominate global harmonization efforts, and that the imposition of these Western accounting practices on developing non-Western countries, regardless of whether they are suitable, may do more harm than good. Go to the IASB home page and list the number of developing countries that have adopted international accounting standards as their accounting standard. Discuss some of the reasons why these countries might have chosen to adopt international accounting standards while other developing countries have not.

2. Obtain the annual reports of three companies (from the same industry) that prepare their financial statements using international accounting standards. Compare the disclosures, accounting policies and practices, and informational content between the three companies. In your opinion, are they truly comparable? Based on this comparison, are international accounting standards an effective global standard?

3. Select a country that allows companies to prepare their financial statements using either domestic GAAP or international accounting standards. Obtain two corporate annual reports within the same industry, one prepared in accordance with domestic GAAP and the other in accordance with international accounting standards. What are some of the similarities and differences between reporting under the two regimes? In your opinion, are the reports prepared using international accounting standards more or less informative than the annual reports under the domestic GAAP?

4. Exhibit 2.2 lists 41 international accounting standards. Choose four international standards and compare them to four corresponding standards in your home country. (To find summaries of each international accounting standard, go to the IASB web site at **www.iasb. org.uk**). What are the major similarities and differences between the standards? Explain.

5. In the January 1999 issue of *Accountancy International* (p. 9), then FASB member Jim Leisenring voiced his support for the IASC's mission to converge national standards around the world but asserted that IASs did not make the grade as "global standards." Leisenring also implied that the IASC was "sacrificing quality for the sake of convergence." Comment on Leisenring's statement. Do you agree or disagree? Explain.

6. Log on to the web site of an accounting organization of your choice and describe some of the steps this organization has taken to promote international harmonization, including any cooperative activities with other organizations and countries. Share your findings with the class.

CASES

Case

Harmonica

With the rapid growth of international capital markets and increased cross-border financing, the debate over harmonization has intensified. Supporters of harmonization reason that harmonization of accounting standards is necessary to produce comparability across financial statements worldwide. Opponents of harmonization argue that differences in financial reporting are justified due to the differing economic, political, legal, and cultural environments across countries, making the adoption of a global standard not truly valuable to users of financial statements.

1. You are on the International Accounting Standards Board (IASB) and must make a presentation to a national capital market regulator (e.g., the U.S. Securities and Exchange Commission (SEC), or the Japanese Ministry of Finance) and a national accounting standard-setter (e.g., the Canadian Accounting Standards Board, or the Nigerian Financial Accounting Standards Board) stating why harmonization of accounting standards is desirable. You have one week to prepare for these presentations, and you are drafting your speech. Make your case, pointing out at least three arguments in favor of harmonization.

2. You are a financial analyst and consultant to Merrill Lynch based in the United Kingdom. Your job is to recommend which stocks the company should include in its portfolio. Over the last 15 years, you have analyzed hundreds of corporate annual reports and have gained a great wealth of knowledge about Japanese and German accounting standards, along with their economic, political, legal, and cultural environments. Your boss is convinced that international accounting standards will soon emerge as the global standard and, consequently, has asked you to use only IAS-based financial statements in your analysis. Make a case on why using only IAS-based statements may not be an appropriate measure of the operating performance of a company.

3. Based upon your responses to both scenarios, should harmonization be pursued? If yes, to what extent? Explain.

Case

Penny Saver

Aaron Duley, the CEO of Nickel Corporation, was discussing with his CFO, Michael Cucciare, whether the company should adopt international accounting standards for financial reporting purposes. Nickel Corporation is based in a country that permits the use of either international accounting standards or domestic GAAP.

"Michael, reporting under our domestic GAAP is much more costly to the company than reporting under international accounting standards. I understand that fewer disclosures are required under international accounting standards. Moreover, international accounting standards provide more choices when it comes to applying accounting methods to our financial statements to produce the most favorable results. And, to be honest with you, the company is going to have to report its first operating loss in over 15 years if we continue to report under our current domestic GAAP. I certainly don't want that to happen while I'm CEO."

"I hear you, Aaron, but converting to international accounting standards might look bad to investors. What if the public finds out that we were trying to hide the operating loss or switched to international accounting standards to manipulate the bottom line? That could prove even more costly in the long run, while saving the company pennies now."

1. Referring to the conversation above, should Nickel Corporation prepare this year's financial statements in accordance with its domestic GAAP, or use international accounting standards? Justify your recommendation and address any concerns.

2. Assume you are the CFO of Nickel Corporation. How would you reply to the CEO's suggestion? Summarize your response including why you opted for or against the adoption of international accounting standards.

3. In your opinion, is there anything ethically wrong with the CEO's rationale for the adoption of international accounting standards? Explain.

4. As Nickel Corporation's auditor, would you agree to the switch to international accounting standards?

REFERENCES

Adhikari, A., and Tondkar, R. H. 1995. An examination of the success of the EC directives to harmonize stock exchange disclosure requirements. *Journal of International Accounting Auditing & Taxation*, 4 (2): 127–146.

Beresford, D. R. 1997. How to succeed as a standard-setter by trying really hard. *Accounting Horizons*, 11 (3): 79–90.

Biddle, G. C., and Saudagaran, S. M. 1989. The effects of financial disclosure levels on firms' choices among alternative foreign stock exchange listings. *Journal of International Financial Management and Accounting*, 1 (1): 55–87.

Canibano, L. and Mora, A. 2000. Evaluating the statistical significance of de facto accounting harmonization: A study of European global players. *European Accounting Review*, 9 (3): 349–369.

Chen, S., Sun, Z., and Wang, Y. 2002. Evidence from China on whether harmonized accounting standards harmonize accounting practices. *Accounting Horizons*, 16 (3): 183–197.

Cochrane, J. L., Shapiro, J. E., and Tobin, J. E. 1996. Foreign equities and U.S. investors: Breaking down the barriers separating supply and demand. *Stanford Journal of Law, Business & Finance*, 2 (2): 241–263.

Collett, P. H., Godfrey, J. M., and Hrasky, S. L. 2001. International harmonization: Cautions from the Australian experience. *Accounting Horizons*, 15 (2): 171–182.

Dye, R. A., and Sunder, S. 2001. Why not allow FASB and IASB standards to compete in the U.S.? *Accounting Horizons*, 15 (3): 257–271.

Emenyonu, E. N., and Gray, S. J. 1992. European Community accounting harmonisation: An empirical study of measurement practices in France, Germany, and the United Kingdom. *Accounting and Business Research*, Winter: 49–58.

Fantl, I. L. 1971. The case against international uniformity. *Management Accounting*, May: 13–16.

Financial Accounting Standards Board. 1999. *International Accounting Standard-Setting: A Vision for the Future*. Norwalk, CT: FASB.

Garrod, N., and Sieringhaus, I. 1995. European Union accounting harmonization: The case of leased assets in the United Kingdom and Germany. *European Accounting Review*, 4 (1): 155–164.

Goeltz, R. K. 1991. International accounting harmonization: The impossible (and unnecessary) dream. *Accounting Horizons*, 5 (1): 85–88.

Grinyer, J. R., and Russell, A. 1992. National impediments to international harmonization: Evidence of lobbying in the U.K. *Journal of International Accounting Auditing & Taxation*, 1 (1): 13–31.

Guenther, D. A., and Hussein, M. E. 1995. Accounting standards and national tax laws: The IASC and the ban on LIFO. *Journal of Accounting and Public Policy*, 14 (1): 115–141.

Herrmann, D., and Thomas, W. 1995. Harmonisation of accounting measurement practices in the European Community. *Accounting and Business Research* (Autumn): 253–265.

Hoarau, C. 1995. International accounting harmonization: American hegemony or mutual recognition with benchmarks? *European Accounting Review*, 4 (2): 217–233.

Houston, C. O., and Jones, R. A. 1999. The multijurisdictional disclosure system: Model for future cooperation? *Journal of International Financial Management and Accounting*, 10 (3): 227–248.

Kenny, S. Y., and Larson, R. K. 1993. Lobbying behaviour and the development of international accounting standards: The case of the IASC's joint venture project. *European Accounting Review*, 2 (3): 531–554.

Meek, G. K., and Saudagaran, S. M. 1990. A survey of research on financial reporting in a transnational context. *Journal of Accounting Literature*, 9: 145–182.

Mueller, G. G. 1997. Harmonization efforts in the European Union. *International Accounting and Finance Handbook*, edited by F. D. S. Choi, Second Edition, New York: John Wiley & Sons.

Nobes, C. 1992. *Accounting Harmonization in Europe: Process, Progress and Prospects.* London: Financial Times.

Nobes, C. 1995. International accounting harmonization: A commentary. *European Accounting Review*, 4 (2): 249–254.

Nobes, C., and Parker, R. 1991. *Comparative International Accounting.* London: Prentice-Hall.

Purvis, S. E. C., Gernon, H. and Diamond, M. A. 1991. The IASC and its Comparability Project: Prerequisites for Success. *Accounting Horizons*, 5 (2): 25–44.

Samuels, J. M., and Oliga, J. C. 1982. Accounting standards in developing countries. *International Journal of Accounting*, 17 (Fall): 69–88.

Saudagaran, S. M. 1991. The SEC and the globalization of financial markets. *Research in Accounting Regulation*, 5: 31–54.

Saudagaran, S. M., and Biddle, G. C. 1992. Financial disclosure levels and foreign stock exchange listing decisions. *Journal of International Financial Management and Accounting*, 4 (2): 106–148.

Saudagaran, S. M., and Biddle, G. C. 1995. Foreign listing location: A study of MNCs and stock exchanges in eight countries. *Journal of International Business Studies*, 26 (2): 319–342.

Saudagaran, S. M., and Diga, J. G. 1997. Accounting regulation in ASEAN: A choice between the global and regional paradigms of harmonization. *Journal of International Financial Management and Accounting*, 8 (1): 1–32.

Saudagaran, S. M., and Diga, J. G. 2003. Economic integration and accounting harmonization options in emerging markets: Adopting the IASC/IASB model in ASEAN. *Research in Accounting in Emerging Economies*, 5: 239–266.

Securities and Exchange Commission. 1991. *Securities Act Release No. 6902*, Multijurisdictional disclosure and modifications to the current reporting and registration system for Canadian issuers. (June 21): 56 FR 30036.

Street, D. L., Gray, S. J., and Bryant, S. M. 1999. Acceptance and observance of international accounting standards: An empirical study of companies claiming to comply with IASs. *International Journal of Accounting*, 34 (1): 11–47.

Tay, J. S. W., and Parker, R. H. 1990. Measuring international harmonization and standardization. *Abacus*, 26 (1): 71–88.

Van der Tas, L. G. 1992. Evidence of European Community financial reporting practice harmonisation: The case of deferred taxation. *European Accounting Review*, 1 (1): 59–104.

Van Hulle, K. 1992. Harmonization of accounting standards: A view from the European Community. *European Accounting Review*, 1 (1): 161–172.

Wallace, R. S. O. 1990. Survival strategies of a global organization: The case of the International Accounting Standards Committee. *Accounting Horizons*, 4 (2): 1–22.

Wallace, R. S. O., and Briston, R. J. 1993. Improving the accounting infrastructure in developing countries. *Research in Third World Accounting*, 2: 201–224.

Walton, P. 1992. Harmonization of accounting in France and Britain: Some evidence. *Abacus*, 28 (2): 186–199.

Wyatt, A. 1997. International accounting standards and organizations: Quo vadis? *International Accounting and Finance Handbook*, edited by F. D. S. Choi, Second Edition, John Wiley & Sons: New York.

Zeff, S. 2002. "Political" lobbying on proposed standards: A challenge to the IASB. *Accounting Horizons*, 16 (1): 43–54.

CHAPTER 3

ACCOUNTING FOR CURRENCY EXCHANGE RATE CHANGES

LEARNING OBJECTIVES

- Provide an overview of foreign exchange markets and define related terminology.

- Describe the different types of foreign exchange exposure.

- Differentiate between foreign currency transaction and translation.

- Compare the different methods of accounting for foreign currency translation.

- Describe the main features of FASB Statement No. 52 and compare it with earlier standards.

- Present the translation methodology under IAS 21.

- Discuss the impact of the introduction of the euro on financial reporting.

As business becomes increasingly global, more companies are affected by fluctuations in currency exchange rates. The manner and extent to which a company is affected naturally depends on the level of its global involvement. However, even the purely domestic firms are exposed to the effects of currency fluctuations. Consider, for example, a U.S. furniture manufacturer that sources only domestic raw materials and sells exclusively in the U.S. domestic market, with no foreign currency transactions. Even this seemingly purely domestic company is affected by foreign currency fluctuations if it competes against furniture imports from, say, Sweden. When the dollar strengthens against the Swedish krona, the imports from Sweden cost less in U.S. dollars, thereby enabling the importers to sell Swedish furniture cheaper in the United States and hurting the U.S. manufacturer. Thus, substantially all businesses are affected to at least some degree by fluctuation in currency exchange rates.

OVERVIEW OF FOREIGN CURRENCY MARKETS AND EXCHANGE RATES

This section explains essential terminology related to foreign currency markets. It provides a background of foreign currency markets including a discussion of the main participants in the market, the role of the market, and the different exchange rate regimes.

Foreign exchange is the money of another country. It may come in a variety of forms such as paper money and coins, bank drafts, and other commercial paper. A *foreign exchange transaction* is one where two parties agree to exchange one currency for another at a specified rate of exchange (e.g., US$1 = Indian Rupees 48.25). Different types of exchange transactions include spot transactions, forward contracts, currency swaps, and currency options. The *foreign exchange market* is the mechanism through which the money of one country is exchanged for that of another, the exchange rate between currencies is set, and foreign exchange transactions are completed. In terms of its physical location, the foreign currency market spans the globe and exists wherever individuals or institutions exchange the currencies of different countries among each other. The foreign exchange market is vast in terms of the volume of activity. In the late 1990s, it was estimated that daily trading activity was about US$1,400 billion compared to US$600 billion per day in the late 1980s.

In terms of timing, foreign exchange transactions can occur in the spot market or the forward market. The *spot market* involves the almost immediate purchase or sale of foreign currency. Typically, settlement (exchange of currencies between the two parties involved in the transaction) is immediate for smaller transactions in the retail market, and takes up to two business days for larger transactions in the wholesale market. In the *forward market*, participants contract today for the future delivery of foreign currency. For example, a company might choose to buy a million British pound sterling three months forward to settle a payable account that is due in three months to a supplier in the United Kingdom. While the exchange rate under the forward contract is set today, the settlement of the forward contract will occur at the maturity date in three months. The difference between the spot rate and the forward rate is called a *premium* when the forward rate is more expensive than the spot rate, and a *discount* when the forward rate is less expensive than the spot rate. A *currency option* is a contract that provides the right but not the obligation to trade a foreign currency at a set exchange rate on or before a given date in the future. A *currency swap* is a transaction that involves a simultaneous purchase and sale of two different currencies. The purchase is effective at once, with the sale back to the same party at a price agreed upon today but to be completed at a specified future date. The table below illustrates how exchange rates are reported in the financial media.

	U.S. $ Equiv.	Currency per U.S. $
Britain (Pound)—spot	1.5875	0.6299
1 month forward	1.5880	0.6279
3 months forward	1.5890	0.6293
6 months forward	1.5905	0.6287

In this example, the first column of rates is a direct quote from the U.S. perspective (and an indirect quote from the U.K. perspective). The direct quote represents the price of one unit of the foreign currency priced in the domestic currency. Thus, in the illustration above, it costs US$1.5875 to purchase one British pound in the spot market. The second column of rates is an indirect quote from the U.S. perspective (and a direct quote from the U.K. perspective). The indirect quote represents how much of the foreign currency can be purchased for one unit of the domestic currency. In the illustration above, one U.S. dollar will purchase 0.6299 British pounds in the spot market. The illustration also provides forward rates for one, three, and six months. For the sake of simplicity, the illustration used a single rate; however, foreign currency price quotations are stated as bid and ask rates. The *bid* rate (or buy rate) represents the price at which a financial institution is willing to buy a currency, while an *ask* rate (or sell rate) is the price at which it is willing to sell a currency. The difference between the bid and ask rates is the *spread*. It represents the gross margin for the exchange trader. Thus, if a U.S. bank quoted a bid rate for British pounds of 1.5895 and an ask rate of 1.5995, the spread would be 0.01.

The main *participants in the foreign exchange market* are central banks and treasuries of countries, commercial banks and other financial institutions, companies that are engaged in international business, speculators and arbitrageurs, and individuals who buy or sell foreign currencies for their personal needs. As with most other products and commodities, the foreign exchange market has a wholesale market and a retail market. The wholesale market is characterized by transactions that are relatively large in size (i.e., millions of U.S. dollars or the equivalent value in other currencies), and the participants are generally banks and other financial institutions. The transactions generally occur at the inter-bank rate and are characterized by high volume and low spreads. In the retail market, the foreign currency transactions are considerably smaller in size (e.g., buying $500 worth of Thai currency when you arrive in Bangkok for a short vacation) and generally have higher spreads.

The world's monetary system is comprised of many national currencies. Each country establishes, defines, and manages its own currency, which impacts its value against currencies of other countries. The fluctuation in the relative values of currencies creates foreign exchange risk in doing business globally. In a climate of volatile exchange rates, it is important for managers to be aware of exchange risk and to take adequate steps to manage it. The competitiveness of firms engaged in international business is likely to be affected by fluctuation in exchange rates. The next section discusses the different types of foreign currency exposures and their implications.

FOREIGN EXCHANGE EXPOSURE

Foreign exchange exposure is a measure of the potential for a firm's profitability, cash flow, and market value to change due to a change in exchange rates. Sound financial management requires that foreign exchange exposure be monitored and managed so as to maximize the profitability, cash flow, and market value of the firm. Foreign exchange exposure has conventionally been classified into three main types:

- translation (or accounting) exposure,
- transaction exposure, and
- economic (or operating) exposure.

Translation exposure, also referred to as accounting exposure, arises when foreign currency financial statements of foreign affiliates must be restated into the parent's currency in order to prepare consolidated financial statements. The external reporting department within a U.S. corporation must restate the financial statements of foreign affiliates from their local currency into U.S. dollars so these amounts can be added in order to prepare U.S. dollar-denominated financial statements. This accounting process is referred to as *translation* and, hence, the terms translation exposure or accounting exposure. Translation exposure is defined as the potential for an increase or decrease in the parent's net worth and reported net income, caused by a fluctuation in the exchange rates since the previous period's consolidated financial statements.

Although the main purpose of translation is to prepare consolidated financial statements, it also facilitates performance evaluation across the affiliates globally by converting the numbers into a common currency (i.e., that of the parent's country). While any yardstick might facilitate comparison, using the parent's currency is most appropriate since a majority of the stockholders are generally in the parent country and, therefore, require that performance be measured in the home country's currency. We will discuss the details of the various methods available for accounting for foreign currency translation in the next section. However, it is important to reiterate that translation is purely an accounting issue and arises because of the need to prepare consolidated financial statements.

Transaction exposure relates to the sensitivity of the firm's contractual cash flows denominated in foreign currency to exchange rate changes as measured in the firm's domestic currency. Transaction exposure measures gains or losses that arise from the settlement of existing financial claims and obligations that are set in a foreign currency. Transaction exposure can arise from any of the following:

1. buying or selling on credit any goods or services whose prices are contractually denominated in foreign currencies,
2. borrowing or lending funds in a foreign currency,
3. engaging in contracts to buy or sell foreign currency at a future date, or
4. other economic transactions to acquire assets or incur liabilities denominated in foreign currencies.

A common example of transaction exposure arises when a transaction to buy or sell goods or services on credit is denominated in a foreign currency. The potential fluctuation of exchange rates between the initiation of the transaction and the settlement of the invoice amount is the transaction exposure. Total transaction exposure consists of quotation exposure, backlog exposure, and billing exposure, in that order. From the time the seller quotes a price to the time when the buyer orders the goods is called the period of the *quotation exposure*. From the moment that the order is placed to the point of shipment (and invoicing) is considered the period of *backlog exposure*. Finally, the lag between the point of shipping to the payment of the invoice is the period of *billing exposure*. Though quotation exposure, backlog exposure, and billing exposure are all measurable, only billing exposure is accounted for in financial reporting.

Economic exposure, also known as operating exposure, can be defined as the extent to which the value of the firm would be affected by unexpected changes in currency exchange rates. An expected rate change in currency exchange rates is not included in the definition of operating exposure because both management and investors should have factored this information into their evaluation of anticipated operating results and market value. Economic exposure analysis assesses the impact of future changes in exchange rates on a firm's operations and its competitive position relative to other firms. The aim is to identify strategic steps that the firm might take to enhance or preserve its value in the face of unexpected currency rate changes. Economic exposure can have much more serious ramifications on the long-term financial health of a business than changes caused by translation or transaction exposure. However, economic exposure is also subjective given the greater uncertainty of economic variables over a long-term horizon. Planning for economic exposure involves the entire organization (as opposed to translation and transaction exposure, which mainly involve the treasury and accounting managers) because it affects the interaction of strategies over virtually every functional area of the company including accounting, finance, marketing, personnel, and production.

ACCOUNTING FOR EXCHANGE RATE FLUCTUATIONS

Foreign Currency Transaction versus Translation

As discussed above, companies engaging in global business face the risk of incurring gains or losses from fluctuations in exchange rates. However, we must distinguish between a foreign transaction and a foreign currency transaction since not every foreign transaction is denominated in a foreign currency. Thus, if a U.S. company is exporting to an Australian company with the invoice denominated in Australian dollars, the U.S. company has a foreign currency transaction and faces transaction exposure. The Australian company does not have a foreign currency transaction, in this example, even though it is engaged in a foreign transaction since the invoice is denominated in its own currency. It is important to understand that there is a difference between transaction gains and losses and translation gains and losses. Transaction gains and losses are realized and affect the cash flows of the company. Consider a U.S. company that sells some products to a customer in Australia with an invoice amount of A\$16 million when the exchange rate is A\$1.60 per U.S. dollar. The customer in Australia is allowed 60 days' credit. When the Australian company pays the U.S. company in 60 days, the amount of U.S. dollars received by the U.S. company will depend on the exchange rate at the time.[1] If the Australian dollar has weakened relative to the U.S. dollar (e.g., A\$1.65 = US\$1), then the U.S. company will receive fewer U.S. dollars. On the other hand, if the Australian dollar has strengthened relative to the U.S. dollar (e.g., A\$1.55 = US\$1) since the invoice date, then the U.S. company will receive more U.S. dollars. The former scenario results in a foreign currency transaction loss for the U.S. company, while the latter scenario results in a foreign currency transaction gain for the U.S. company. In this example, since the invoice was denominated in Australian dollars, the U.S. company bears the risk of exchange rate fluctuations. The

---

[1] In this example, we assume that the U.S. company has not taken any steps to hedge the transaction exposure. Management of foreign currency exposure is discussed in Chapter 7.

Australian company was not affected by exchange rate fluctuations because its cash flow in Australian dollars was locked in by virtue of the transaction being denominated in its currency. As is evident from this example, transaction gains and losses are actual and realized. The accounting treatment of foreign exchange transaction gains or losses is fairly straightforward—they must be included in the company's income statement and affect its earnings for the period in which they occur.

In foreign currency transactions, one accounting issue relates to how the transactions should be recorded in the reporting currency at the transaction date. There is general agreement that the transaction should be recorded using the spot exchange rate at the transaction date. If credit terms are not granted, there are no other accounting issues in recording the transaction. However, in the event of a credit transaction, there are two more accounting issues that arise:

1. how to report exchange rate adjustments, and
2. whether to make adjustments at balance sheet dates for changes in exchange rates.

The first question refers to whether the transaction should be considered as a single transaction or as two transactions. Under the single-transaction approach, a company's foreign currency receivable or payable is considered an essential part of the economic transaction to sell or buy goods or services. The amount initially recorded is considered an estimate until the final settlement. As a result, the original cost or revenue is subsequently adjusted for any difference between the amount recorded at the transaction date and the amount at the settlement date. Under the single-transaction approach, the entries in the books of the U.S. company for the example cited above would be as shown in Illustration 3-1.

ILLUSTRATION 3-1

Entry at transaction date:		
Accounts Receivable	10,000,000	
Revenues		10,000,000
(A$16,000,000/1.6 = US$10,000,000)		
Entry at settlement date (assuming an exchange rate of A$1.65=US$1)		
Cash	9,696,970	
Revenues	303,030	
Accounts Receivable		10,000,000
(A$16,000,000/1.65 = US$9,696,970)		

Under the two-transaction approach, a company's foreign currency receivable or payable is considered a second transaction which is distinct from the original transaction to buy or sell goods or services. As a result, any difference between the amounts in the reporting currency on the settlement date from the transaction date is treated as a foreign currency transaction gain or loss. The original amount recorded for the cost or revenue is not subsequently adjusted even though the exchange rate may have changed between the transaction date and the settlement date. Under the two-transaction approach, the entries for the example cited above would be as shown in Illustration 3-2.

There is no global consensus as to which of these two approaches is preferable. The FASB has adopted the two-transaction approach in SFAS No. 52 on the basis that the effects of exchange rate exposure of foreign currency transactions should be kept

ILLUSTRATION 3-2

Entry at transaction date:		
Accounts Receivable	US$10,000,000	
Revenues		US$10,000,000
(A$16,000,000/1.6 = US$10,000,000)		
Entry at settlement date (assuming an exchange rate of A$1.65=US$1)		
Cash	US$9,696,970	
Loss on Foreign Exchange	US$303,030	
Accounts Receivable		US$10,000,000
(A$16,000,000/1.65 = US$9,696,970)		

separate from the original transaction for goods or services. Under the requirements of SFAS No. 52, a U.S. entity would account for transactions denominated in a foreign currency as follows: 1) at the transaction date, measure and record in U.S. dollars the asset, liability, revenue, or expense using the spot exchange rate on the transaction date; 2) if financial statements are prepared between the transaction date and the settlement date, adjust the receivable or payable amount to reflect the exchange rate at the balance sheet date; and 3) report in the income statement a foreign currency transaction gain or loss resulting from a) adjustments made at the balance sheet date, and b) adjustments from settling the transaction at an amount different from the transaction date or the balance sheet date (in the case of intervening balance sheets between the transaction date and the settlement date).

On the second question, most accountants agree that any foreign currency receivable or payable amounts at the balance sheet date should be adjusted to reflect the exchange rate at that date. Illustration 3-3 demonstrates the appropriate accounting treatment of outstanding foreign currency assets or liabilities at the balance sheet date.

It is worth noting the following points for Illustration 3-3. First, foreign exchange gains and losses recognized in the income statement at intervening balance sheet dates are unrealized. The FASB decided that recognizing unrealized gains and losses in the period in which they occur would better serve financial statement users even though reversals might occur in subsequent periods. This is the only area of SFAS No. 52 in which unrealized gains and losses can be recognized in the income statement. Second, when one of the parties to a foreign transaction incurs a foreign exchange gain or loss, the other party does *not* incur an opposite, offsetting foreign exchange loss or gain because that other party does not transact in a foreign currency. Accordingly, foreign currency transaction gains and losses are one-sided.

Foreign currency translation gains or losses are generally regarded as unrealized or "paper" gains and losses since they do not have direct cash flow effects, but simply change the carrying amounts of assets and liabilities from one period to the next. There are a number of alternative accounting methods used to record translation gains and losses. The treatment of translation gains and losses varies based upon the accounting method used, affecting: 1) the exchange rates used to translate foreign currency amounts into the currency of the parent country, and 2) in which financial statement—income statement or balance sheet—the translation gains and losses are recorded. Next, I provide an overview of the four translation methods and how they affect the two items discussed above.

ILLUSTRATION 3-3

Assume that a U.S. company has the following transaction with a supplier in Japan:

1. On November 15, 2000, inventory was acquired from Satoh & Co. for 10,000,000 Japanese Yen. Payment is due on January 15, 2001.

Payments are made as required. The indirect spot exchange rates for the relevant dates in November and December 2000 and in January 2001 (when the yen was strengthening) are as follows:

November 15, 2000 US$1 = 125 yen
December 31, 2000 US$1 = 115 yen
January 15, 2001 US$1 = 112.5 yen

Entries Related to Purchase from Satoh & Co.

November 15, 2000

Inventory (or Purchases)	$80,000	
Accounts Payable		$80,000
To record purchase of Inventory (10,000,000 yen @125 yen per dollar)		

December 31, 2000

Foreign Exchange Loss	$ 6,957	
Accounts Payable		$ 6,957
To adjust foreign currency payable to the current spot rate.		
(10,000,000/115 = $86,957) ($86,957 – $80,000 = $6,957)		

January 15, 2001

Foreign Exchange Loss	$ 1,932	
Account Payable		$ 1,932
To adjust foreign currency payable to the current spot rate.		
(10,000,000/112.5 = $88,889) ($88,889 – $86,957 = $1,932)		

Accounts Payable	$88,889	
Cash		$88,889
To record payments to vendor		

Combined entry at the settlement date. Companies can combine the two entries on the settlement date. Thus, the following lone entry can be made at the settlement date (rather than the two entries shown for January 15, 2001):

Accounts Payable	$86,957	
Foreign Exchange Loss	$ 1,932	
Cash		$88,889

Translation Methods

The four main methods of foreign currency translation are the current rate method, the current/non-current method, the monetary/non-monetary method, and the temporal method. Since these methods stipulate the exchange rate to be used for translation, one needs to know the definition of the different exchange rates available. The *current rate* is the exchange rate prevailing at the balance sheet date. The *historical rate* is the exchange rate that prevailed at the date on which a specific transaction occurred. The *average rate* is a weighted average of the exchange rates that prevailed during the period for which financial statements are being prepared. Exhibit 3-1 summarizes the exchange rates to be used for translating the main balance sheet and income statement items under each of the four translation methods. At this stage, it is useful to draw a distinction between conversion and translation in the foreign currency context. Actually exchanging one currency for another is called *conversion* (e.g., when you convert your U.S. dollars into Japanese yen upon landing at Osaka airport). By contrast, *translation* is the process of restating numbers in a financial statement applying an appropriate exchange rate (e.g., when you translate the revenues of your subsidiary in Japan for purposes of preparing a consolidated income statement).

EXHIBIT 3-1 Translation Methods

	Current Rate Method	Current/ Non-current Method	Monetary/ Non-monetary Method	Temporal Method
Cash	C	C	C	C
Current receivables	C	C	C	C
Inventories				
Cost	C	C	H	H
Market	C	C	H	C
Long-term receivables	C	H	C	C
Long-term investment				
Cost	C	H	H	H
Market	C	H	H	C
Property, plant, and equipment	C	H	H	H
Intangible assets (long-term)	C	H	H	H
Current liabilities	C	C	C	C
Long-term debt	C	H	C	C
Paid-in capital	H	H	*H	H
Retained earnings	B	B	B	B
Revenues	A	A	A	A
Cost of goods sold	A	A	H	H
Depreciation expense	A	H	H	H
Amortization expense	A	H	H	H

A = Average exchange rate for the current period   H = Historical exchange rate

C = Current exchange rate at balance sheet date   B = Balancing (residual or plug) figure

*Assumes no nonconvertible preferred stock

CURRENT RATE METHOD. Under this method, all balance sheet items (except owners' equity) are translated at the current exchange rate. The common stock and additional paid-in capital accounts are carried at the historical exchange rate—the date at which the stock was issued. The year-end shareowners' equity includes a cumulative translation adjustment which serves as a plug to make the balance sheet balance. Under the current rate method, foreign currency translation gains and losses do not affect the income statement. In the income statement, all revenues and expenses that need to be translated use the average exchange rate for the period.

This is the simplest of all translation methods to apply. Since a constant exchange rate is used in the balance sheet, the current rate method preserves the original financial statement relationships of the individual entities included in the consolidation. It also assumes that all foreign currency assets are exposed to currency exchange risk. However, this is not always true since the fair market value of physical assets, such as inventory and fixed assets, generally rises due to inflation in countries with weakening currencies. Thus, translating a historical cost foreign currency amount by a current exchange rate results in a number that is not representative of the historical cost or the current fair market value. This approach does not consider differences in the nature of assets and liabilities (monetary versus non-monetary) or their duration (current versus non-current). There is no attempt to understand reasons for the exchange rate change. Distortions in the foreign currency financial statements are perpetuated and carried over to the translated financial statements.

TEMPORAL METHOD. Under this method, the measurement basis of an asset or liability determines the exchange rate to be used for translation. Accordingly, monetary accounts such as cash, receivables, and payables are translated at the current exchange rate. Non-monetary items such as inventories and fixed assets are translated at the current exchange rate if they are carried on the books at current value, and they are translated at the historical exchange rate if carried on the books at historical cost. This preserves the original measurement bases for the non-monetary items after translation. In situations where inventories and fixed assets are carried at historical cost, the temporal method and the monetary/non-monetary method will provide essentially the same results upon translation. Under the temporal method, most revenues and expenses are translated using the average exchange rate for the period. Depreciation and cost of goods sold are translated at historical exchange rates if the related fixed assets and inventories are carried at historical costs.

In the temporal method, a foreign currency measurement is translated to a dollar measurement without changing the basis. Since the accounting principles are not changed as a result of translation, the temporal method can handle any measurement basis (historical cost, current replacement price, or current market price). The flexibility afforded by the temporal method, which was developed in 1968 by Leonard Lorenson, received such wide support that the FASB mandated this as the only permissible translation method under SFAS No. 8 in 1975.

CURRENT/NON-CURRENT METHOD. The underlying principle of the current/non-current method is that assets and liabilities should be translated based on their maturity. A foreign subsidiary's current assets and liabilities are converted at the current exchange rate. Non-current assets and liabilities are translated at the historical exchange rate that prevailed when the assets or liabilities were first acquired. Most income statement items, except for those associated with non-current assets and liabilities, are translated at the average exchange rate for the accounting period. Income statement items such as depreciation or amortization expenses, related to non-current balance sheet items, are translated at the historical rates in effect when the related assets were acquired.

This method was widely used in the United States from the 1930s until the 1970s when SFAS No. 8 became effective. The current/non-current method is based on a classification of assets and liabilities that is entirely unrelated to the economic effects of exchange rate fluctuations on the assets and liabilities. Using the current rate to translate current assets and liabilities is based on the false premise that they are similarly affected by exchange rate changes. For example, it is clear that foreign currency cash, payable, and inventories are not equally exposed to exchange risk. Thus, the local price of inventory can be increased as the local currency weakens to protect its value from the decline in the local currency. Naturally, that is not the case with foreign currency cash positions.

MONETARY/NON-MONETARY METHOD. Under this method, all monetary items (such as cash, receivables, and payables) in the balance sheet of a foreign subsidiary are translated at the current exchange rate because this method perceives such items as subject to exchange rate risk. Non-monetary items such as inventories and fixed assets are translated at historical exchange rates. Most income statement items are translated at the average exchange rate for the period. However, income statement items such as cost of goods sold and depreciation that relate to non-monetary balance sheet accounts such as inventories and fixed assets are translated using the historical exchange rate applicable to the corresponding balance sheet account.

This method differs from the current/non-current method in that for translation purposes, it separates accounts into two categories based on the similarity of attributes rather than on the similarity of maturity. However, this method also suffers from weaknesses. Translating all non-monetary assets by a historical exchange rate is not appropriate for those assets restated to current market value in accordance with the lower of cost or market principle (such as inventories or fixed assets). Multiplying the current market value of such assets by a historical exchange rate provides an amount in the parent's currency that is neither its current market value equivalent nor its historical cost. Another weakness of this method is that it translates foreign subsidiaries' revenues at average exchange rates and cost of goods sold at historical exchange rates.

The results obtained under the monetary/non-monetary method and the temporal method are similar except for the translation of non-monetary assets (primarily inventories) carried at market (below cost), which are translated using the current rate under the temporal method and the historical rate under the monetary/non-monetary method. In such a situation, the underlying philosophies behind the two methods are rather different. The temporal method has the added advantage of flexibility since it adjusts to the valuation method used in the financial statements. Consequently, the temporal method accommodates current market valuation of non-monetary assets while the monetary/non-monetary method does not.

In summary, all four methods have been used at various points in time in many countries including the United States. The current rate method, current/non-current method, and monetary/non-monetary method are based on determining which assets and liabilities are subject to foreign currency exposure. The current rate method treats all assets and liabilities as subject to currency risk and translates them using the current exchange rate. The current/non-current method assumes that only the current items are exposed, while the monetary/non-monetary method assumes that only the monetary items face currency risk. The temporal method is different in that it adjusts balance sheet items according to the valuation basis used in the financial statements. Along a different dimension, the current rate method of translation adopts the foreign currency unit of measure approach, while the temporal method, current/non-current method, and monetary/non-monetary method adopt the domestic currency unit of measure approach.

FOREIGN CURRENCY TRANSLATION IN THE UNITED STATES

In March 1973, when the Bretton Woods Agreement stipulating fixed exchange rates collapsed, foreign currency translation emerged as a significant accounting issue with the advent of floating exchange rates. This period coincided with severe pressure on the U.S. dollar despite devaluations in 1971 and 1973. The accounting standard-setting structure in the United States was also in a state of flux during this period with the dissolution of the Accounting Principles Board (APB) and the establishment of the new Financial Accounting Standards Board (FASB) in 1973. At the time, there was considerable divergence in foreign currency translation methods used in the United States. Exhibit 3-2 summaries the extant practice on foreign currency translation in the United States before there was an accounting standard for foreign currency translation.

EXHIBIT 3-2 Translation Methods Used in the U.S. Prior to SFAS No. 8

Translation Methods	Respondent Firms	
	Number	Percent
Current/non-current method	54	34.6
Current/non-current method with non-current receivables and payables translated at the current rate	10	6.4
Monetary/non-monetary method	22	14.1
Monetary/non-monetary method with inventories translated at the current rate	41	26.3
Temporal method	7	4.5
Current rate method	4	2.6
Other	3	1.9
No response	15	9.6
	156	100.0

Source: Thomas G. Evans, William R. Folks, Jr., and Michael Jilling, *The Impact of Statement of Financial Accounting Standards No. 8 on the Foreign Exchange Risk Management Practices of American Multinationals: An Economic Impact Study* (Stamford, Conn.: FASB, 1978), p. 147. Copyright by the Financial Accounting Standards Board. Reprinted with permission. Copies of the complete document are available from the FASB.

FASB Statement No. 8 (SFAS No. 8)

The FASB issued its Statement of Financial Accounting Standards No. 8, "Accounting for the Translation of Foreign Currency Transactions and Foreign Currency Financial Statements," in October 1975, to be effective January 1, 1976. According to SFAS No. 8, the objective of translation was to measure in U.S. dollars and in conformity with U.S. GAAP an enterprise's assets, liabilities, revenues, and expenses that are denominated in a foreign currency. SFAS No. 8 essentially mandated that U.S. companies use the temporal method to translate foreign currency amounts in preparing consolidated financial statements. One needs to appreciate the subtleties of the temporal method in order to understand the controversy it generated.

The temporal method required that most revenues and expenses be translated at the average exchange rate for the year. In practice, multinational companies translate and prepare the income statement monthly. The current month's numbers are added to the cumulative total of previous months to get the year-to-date totals. Accounts such as costs of goods sold and depreciation are translated at historical exchange rates.

A major criticism of SFAS No. 8 was that it required foreign currency translation gains and losses to be included in the income statement. This introduced considerable volatility in the reported earnings of corporations independent of their operating performance. The experience of ITT, as relates to its reported earnings under SFAS No. 8, was symptomatic of the volatility that resulted from the temporal method.

	Change in Reported Earnings	
	With TGL*	Without TGL*
First quarter	– 45%	–
Second quarter	+109%	–29%
Third quarter	–119%	+ 2%

*Translation gains/losses

Corporate managers were very unhappy about this volatility and lobbied extensively to overturn SFAS No. 8. They argued that the volatility caused by SFAS No. 8 had little to do with their operating performance and made their companies appear more risky than they really were. This, in turn, had the potential to adversely affect their stock prices and their cost of capital. A number of U.S. companies strongly opposed having to include translation gains and losses in the income statement.

Many companies also objected to having to translate inventory at historical exchange rates if they carried it at historical cost, as most companies do. One reason for the objection was simply the bookkeeping costs involved in having to track the old historical exchange rates for translating inventory balances. Companies deemed it less costly to compute inventory values based on current exchange rates. A second problem arising from translating inventory at the historical rate was that it was possible for the exchange rate from one period to affect earnings in a subsequent period when the inventory flowed through the cost of goods sold. Thus, critics argued that it made more practical sense for inventory to be translated at current rather than historical exchange rates.

A third major criticism of SFAS No. 8 related to the disposition of the gain or loss on long-term debt. Recall that the temporal method requires long-term debt to be translated using the current exchange rate. Given that the dollar was weakening against the major foreign currencies in the 1970s, U.S. firms faced considerable translation losses from their foreign currency denominated long-term debt. U.S. managers complained that there was no real foreign currency exposure because the foreign currency debt was being repaid from foreign currency earnings. They also argued that the foreign assets purchased from the foreign currency financing were a natural hedge since they were generating foreign currency earnings. They wanted to be able to write off the losses over the life of the assets.

In response to the barrage of criticism directed at SFAS No. 8, the FASB felt pressured to find an acceptable alternative. In 1979, it formed the largest task force to that time to address what was proving to be the most contentious accounting issue in its rather brief history. There was a sense in certain quarters that the FASB faced tremendous pressure to produce a politically acceptable alternative to SFAS No. 8 in order to ensure its own survival. It is important to recognize that this was the environment under which the subsequent standard on foreign currency translation was generated.

FASB Statement No. 52 (SFAS No. 52)

The considerable criticism directed at SFAS No. 8 by U.S. multinational companies and the accounting profession forced the FASB to include on its agenda in January 1979 a proposal to reconsider all aspects of SFAS No. 8. In February 1979, a task force was formed with representatives of the FASB, the IASC, and accounting standard-setting bodies in Canada and the United Kingdom. After deliberations spanning almost three years, FASB Statement No. 52 was issued in December 1981. SFAS No. 52 superseded SFAS No. 8 and was effective for fiscal years starting on or after December 15, 1982. The stated objectives of SFAS No. 52 are to:

1. provide information that is generally compatible with the expected economic effects of a rate change on an enterprise's cash flows and equity, and
2. reflect in consolidated statements the financial results and relationships of the individual consolidated entities as measured in their functional currencies in conformity with U.S. generally accepted accounting standards.[2]

The approach to foreign currency translation under SFAS No. 52 differs considerably from that under SFAS No. 8. By requiring that foreign currency financial statements be prepared as though all transactions occurred in U.S. dollars, SFAS No. 8 took a parent company perspective. SFAS No. 52 allows for both the parent company and the local perspective based on determining the primary economic environment of the foreign subsidiary. SFAS No. 52 does this through the concept of functional currency, which it defines as the currency of the primary economic environment in which the foreign subsidiary operates and generates cash flows. SFAS No. 52 offers three possibilities for the choice of functional currency. If the foreign subsidiary is a relatively independent entity that is the product of its local environment, then the local currency is the functional currency (e.g., pound sterling for a subsidiary in the United Kingdom). If a foreign subsidiary is merely an extension of its U.S. parent (e.g., a Nike factory in Indonesia that assembles sportswear and ships it back to the United States), then the U.S. dollar is the functional currency. A third possibility is that the functional currency is neither the U.S. dollar nor the local currency but rather a third currency (e.g., Hong Kong dollar for a U.S. company's assembly operations in China). The FASB laid out a number of criteria in SFAS No. 52 to help determine the functional currency of foreign subsidiaries, which are summarized in Exhibit 3-3. The fact that there are several criteria and that there are no specific quantitative tests provides considerable latitude to companies in the selection of functional currency for their foreign subsidiaries. Since the functional currency determines the translation method to be used under SFAS No. 52, companies can effectively select the translation method they use by their choice of functional currency.

Next, we will discuss translation under each of the three functional currency scenarios. When the U.S. dollar is deemed to be the functional currency of the foreign subsidiary, its financial statements are converted to U.S. dollars using the temporal method. With this scenario, translation under SFAS No. 52 is essentially the same as in SFAS No. 8. All translation gains and losses are included in the income statement and thus affect the company's earnings for the period.

When the local currency is determined to be the foreign subsidiary's functional currency, its financial statements are translated to U.S. dollars using the current rate method. As discussed previously, under the current rate method, translation gains and losses appear as a separate line item called cumulative translation adjustment (CTA) in the stockholders' equity section of the consolidated balance sheet. Since the translation gain or loss bypasses the income statement under the current rate method, choice of the local currency as the functional currency avoids the earnings volatility which companies complained about under SFAS No. 8.

In certain situations, the functional currency is neither the U.S. dollar nor the local currency of the country where the subsidiary is located but rather the currency of a third country. In that situation, SFAS No. 52 requires a two-step translation process. First, the subsidiary's financial statements are to be converted from the local currency

---

[2]Financial Accounting Standards Board, Statement of Financial Accounting Standards No. 52, "Foreign Currency Translation," paragraph 4 [Stamford, CT: FASB, 1981].

EXHIBIT 3-3 Functional Currency

Economic Indicators	Foreign Currency	Parent's Currency
a. Cash Flows	Cash flows related to the foreign entity's individual assets and liabilities are primarily in the foreign currency and do not directly impact the parent company's cash flows.	Cash flows related to the foreign entity's individual assets and liabilities directly impact the parent's cash flows on a current basis and are readily available for remittance to the parent company.
b. Sales Price	Sales prices for the foreign entity's products are not primarily responsive on a short-term basis to changes in exchange rates but are determined more by local competition or local government regulation.	Sales prices for the foreign entity's products are primarily responsive on a short-term basis to changes in exchange rates; for example, sales prices are determined more by worldwide competition or by international prices.
c. Sales Market	There is an active local sales market for the foreign entity's products, although there also might be significant amounts of exports.	The sales market is mostly in the parent's country, or sales contracts are denominated in the parent's currency.
d. Expenses	Labor, materials, and other costs for the foreign entity's products or services are primarily local costs, even though there might also be imports from other countries.	Labor, materials, and other costs for the foreign entity's products or services, on a continuing basis, are primarily costs for components obtained from the country in which the parent company is located.
e. Financing	Financing is primarily denominated in foreign currency, and funds generated by the foreign entity's operations are sufficient to service existing and normally expected debt obligations.	Financing is primarily from the parent or other dollar-denominated obligations, or funds generated by the foreign entity's operations are not sufficient to service existing and normally expected debt obligations without the infusion of additional funds from the parent company. Infusion of additional funds from the parent company for expansion is not a factor, provided funds generated by the foreign entity's expanded operations are expected to be sufficient to service that additional financing.
f. Intercompany Transactions and Arrangements	There is a low volume of intercompany transactions, and there is not an extensive interrelationship between the operations of the foreign entity and the parent company. However, the foreign entity's operations may rely on the parent's or affiliate's competitive advantages, such as patents and trademarks.	There is a high volume of intercompany transactions, and there is an extensive interrelationship between the operations of the foreign entity and the parent company. Additionally, the parent's currency generally would be the functional currency of the foreign entity is a device or shell corporation for holding investments, obligations, intangible assets, and the like, that could be readily be carried on the parent's affiliate's books.

Source: Financial Accounting Standards Board, *Statement of Financial Accounting Standards No. 52, Foreign Currency Translation* (Stamford, Conn.: FASB, December 1981), pp. 26–27.

to the functional currency using the temporal method and then translated from the functional currency to the U.S. dollar using the current rate method. Exhibit 3-4 contains a flow chart of the steps for selecting the translation method under SFAS No. 52.

SFAS No. 52 made three major changes that were aimed at correcting the perceived weaknesses of SFAS No. 8. First, it allowed multiple units of measure so that differing economic situations can be accounted for differently. It did so by retaining the U.S. dollar unit measure of approach (under the temporal method) and introducing the foreign currency unit measure of approach (under the current rate method), contingent on the designation of functional currency. Second, it required translation gains/losses under the current rate method to be taken directly to shareholders' equity in the balance sheet, completely bypassing the income statement. In doing so, the FASB has placated companies that were concerned about earnings volatility under SFAS No. 8. Third, it created the concept of functional currency as the determining factor of the translation method to be used. SFAS No. 52 has its own "chicken and egg" question. It is not clear whether the FASB first created the functional currency concept in the process of trying to distinguish between economic situations which, in turn, led to the decision to use multiple units of measure, or whether the FASB first decided to allow multiple units of measure as a solution to SFAS No. 8 and then came up with the functional currency concept as a mechanism to determine when the different translation methods ought to be used. In light of the end result of SFAS No. 52, which has been to give management considerable latitude in the choice of translation method, the FASB could just as easily have allowed companies to judgmentally select the translation method they preferred. Thus, it is hard to fathom the conceptual need for the functional currency concept. Politically, it may have given the FASB the fig leaf to argue that it had not capitulated to the preparers of financial statements on this issue.

SFAS No. 52 and the Functional Currency Concept

A review of Exhibit 3-3 indicates that, under SFAS No. 52, most foreign subsidiaries of U.S. companies are deemed to fit into two main categories. One category is the

EXHIBIT 3-4 Translation Method Choices Under SFAS No. 52

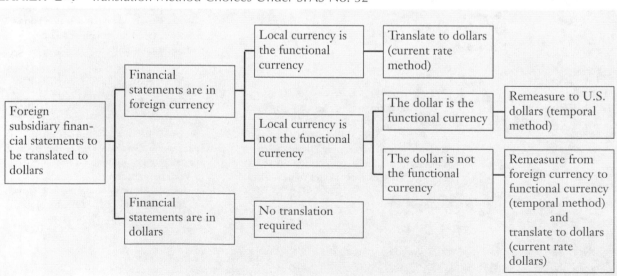

subsidiaries whose primary operating environment is the country where they are located. These relatively independent and self-sustained entities conduct most of their operating, financing, and investing activities in the currency of the country where they are located, and hence the local currency is their functional currency under SFAS No. 52. The second category is the subsidiaries that are an extension of the parent in that their operating, financing, and investing decisions are dollar denominated and are a product of business conditions in the United States. Though they are located outside the United States, the primary operating environment for these subsidiaries is still the United States and hence the U.S. dollar is their functional currency.

Under SFAS No. 52, the determination of functional currency is based on the economic facts of each foreign entity and cannot be arbitrary. Given that the choice of functional currency can result in significant differences in the reported earnings of the parent company, management ought not to be able to influence earnings by choice of functional currency. However, recall that there are six variables in the FASB's criteria to determine functional currency and all of them are rather judgmental and lack any specific quantitative measures. The result is that, in practice, management has considerable latitude to choose whatever translation method it prefers via the choice of functional currency. If the FASB had hoped that the independent auditors would police the choice of functional currency, that has certainly not been the case. An article in *Forbes* magazine on the choice of functional currency by U.S. firms was aptly titled "Plenty of Opportunity to Fool Around."[3] The article focused on the oil and gas industry to demonstrate the arbitrary choice of functional currencies by U.S. firms and the lack of oversight by the independent auditors. The six largest oil companies were evenly divided as to the functional currencies of their foreign subsidiaries. Three of them—Texaco, Occidental, and Unocal—chose the U.S. dollar as the functional currency, while the other three—Exxon, Mobil, and Amoco—chose the foreign currency as the functional currency. This is puzzling given that these companies are in the same industry and often have subsidiaries in the same countries (i.e., OPEC member countries). The fact that they opted for different functional currencies raises legitimate questions as to whether their foreign operations are that different or whether they simply use the functional currency criteria to choose the translation method that portrays them in the best light. The arbitrary choice of translation methods concerns users of financial statements in that it adversely affects comparability of company performance.[4] For example, Compaq Computers has determined that the functional currency of its foreign subsidiaries is the U.S. dollar, while IBM uses the local currency as the functional currency in selecting the translation method for its foreign subsidiaries. To add insult to injury, firms using the temporal method (i.e., U.S. dollar as the functional currency) seldom disclose the amount of foreign currency translation gain/loss that has been included in net income. Disclosing this amount separately either in the income statement or the notes to the financial statements would at least permit users to "back out" the transaction gain/loss from the net income amount and compare the earnings of companies using different translation methods. Below is an example of such disclosure from the 2000 annual report of The Gillette Company (page 30):

---

[3]*Forbes*, June 2, 1986, p. 139.

[4]See Mehta and Thapa [1991] for a detailed discussion of the adverse effects on the comparability of financial statements from SFAS No. 52.

Notes to Consolidated Financial Statements
Foreign Currency Translation
Net exchange gains or losses resulting from the translation of assets and liabilities of foreign subsidiaries, except those in highly inflationary economies, are accumulated in a separate section of stockholders' equity. Also included are the effects of exchange rate changes on intercompany transactions of a long-term investment nature and transactions designated as hedges of net foreign investments. The change in accumulated foreign currency translation adjustment in 2000 was a loss of $249 million, with the United Kingdom accounting for $115 million of the loss. Losses in 1999 were $205 million, with Brazil accounting for approximately half of the loss. Losses in 1998 were $36 million. Included in other charges in the Consolidated Statement of Income are a net exchange gain of $8 million in 2000 and losses of $35 million and $23 million in 1999 and 1998, respectively.

Another interesting note in the actual implementation of SFAS No. 52 and the application of the criteria for determining functional currency is the frequency with which companies decide that all their foreign subsidiaries have the U.S. dollar or the foreign currency as the functional currency. Surely there must be differences in the type of activity and, therefore, the primary operating environment of various foreign subsidiaries of the same company. For example, a subsidiary in a developing country might mainly assemble products for re-export (to use the low labor costs) while a subsidiary in a developed country might manufacture to meet the demand in that country. It is hard to justify how both these subsidiaries could have the same functional currency, and yet that is what many U.S. multinationals implicitly claim via their choice of a uniform translation method for their subsidiaries worldwide.

Given the potential for abuse and arbitrary selection of translation methods (and plenty of anecdotal evidence to that effect), it is rather curious that the FASB has not commissioned a study on corporate practices related to the choice of functional currency under SFAS No. 52.

SFAS No. 52 Translation in Highly Inflationary Economies

The application of the translation methods discussed above has the potential for causing serious distortions in highly inflationary situations, especially when the current rate method is used. Recall that SFAS No. 52 requires the use of the current rate method when the local currency is the functional currency and that, under the current rate method, assets and liabilities are translated using the current (i.e., year-end) exchange rate. In the early 1980s, in a relatively short period, the exchange rate between the Bolivian peso and the U.S. dollar went from 25 pesos per U.S. dollar to 1.13 million pesos per U.S. dollar due to annual inflation of over 20,000 percent in Bolivia! To understand why the FASB had to include an exception to translation procedures for subsidiaries located in highly inflationary economies, consider an example. Say a U.S. company's Bolivian subsidiary, which has the local currency as its functional currency, acquired a factory for 250 million pesos when the exchange rate was 25 pesos to a U.S. dollar. Under SFAS No. 52, using the current exchange rate, the carrying amount of the factory would be approximately US$10 million (250 million pesos/25 pesos). After the onset of hyperinflation, if the current rate method was still used for translation, the carrying value of the factory in the consolidated financial statements of the U.S. parent would be a paltry $221 (250 million pesos/1.13 million pesos). This phenomenon is sometimes referred to in the literature as the "disappearing property, plant, and equipment problem." This is a nonsensical result because the market value of the manufacturing facility in Bolivia will have also risen with inflation.

To avoid such anomalies in the translated financial statements, SFAS No. 52 requires that in hyperinflationary situations ("cumulative inflation of 100 percent or more over a three-year period"), the reporting currency of the parent (i.e., the U.S. dollar for U.S. companies) must be designated as the functional currency. This, in turn, requires such companies to use the temporal method of translation in highly inflationary situations, meaning that balance sheet items are translated using the historical exchange rate that prevailed when the items were acquired. In our Bolivian example, the factory would still be carried at US$10 million using the temporal method rather than US$221 using the current rate method. It should be clear by now that the purpose of including the exception in FASB No. 52 for hyperinflationary situations is to prevent significant balance sheet items, carried at historical values, from having insignificant values after they are translated into the parent's currency using the current exchange rate. Finally, what happens when a country that was previously experiencing high inflation is able to bring inflation under control such that it no longer qualifies as hyperinflationary under the SFAS No. 52 definition? Assume that the U.S. company with the Bolivian subsidiary was able to switch back from the temporal method to the current rate method on January 1, 1992, because of low inflation in Bolivia. According to the Emerging Issues Task Force (EITF) Issue No. 92-4, the reporting currency amounts on January 1, 1992, should be translated into the local currency at the spot rate on that date, and these amounts become the functional currency values of the non-monetary assets and liabilities from that date on.

SFAS No. 133—Accounting for Derivatives and Hedging Activities

A derivative is a contract whose value is derived from that of another underlying security or commodity.[5] Foreign exchange derivatives deal with future foreign exchange transactions. Accounting for derivative instruments has reflected the technical complexity of these instruments. In June 1998, the FASB issued Statement of Financial Accounting Standards No. 133, "Accounting for Derivative Instruments and Hedging Activities." SFAS No. 133 has been very controversial. It attempts to standardize the accounting rules for all derivatives. It applies to all entities and to all types of derivatives and was originally intended to be effective for all fiscal periods beginning after June 15, 1999. However, due to considerable criticism and opposition from the business community, the implementation date of SFAS No. 133 has been postponed to periods beginning after June 15, 2000.

A detailed discussion of the requirements of SFAS No. 133 is beyond the scope of this book.[6] The PricewaterhouseCoopers (1998) implementation guide for SFAS No. 133 provides the following brief synopsis of the main features of the standard:

- All derivatives must be carried on the balance sheet at fair value. No exceptions.
- Generally, changes in the fair value of derivatives must be recognized in income

[5]An article in the *Economist* (February 10, 1996) provided a straightforward explanation of what a derivative is: "Although derivatives can sometimes be complex and can require mathematics doctorates to design and price, what they do is actually quite simple: They provide a low-cost and precise method of transferring risk from those that are exposed to it but would rather not be to those that are not but would like to be."

[6]Most of the large international accounting firms have published guides to assist their clients with the implementation of SFAS No. 133. The complexity of this accounting standard is reflected in the fact that these guides are very voluminous. For example, PricewaterhouseCoopers' "A Guide to Accounting for Derivative Instruments and Hedging Activities: Understanding & Implementing Statement of Financial Accounting Standards No. 133" is over 600 pages long!

when they occur. The only exception is for derivatives that qualify as hedges in accordance with the standard.

■ If a derivative qualifies as a hedge, a company can elect to use "hedge accounting" to eliminate or reduce the income-statement volatility that would arise from reporting changes in a derivative's fair value in income. The type of accounting to be applied varies depending on the nature of the exposure that is being hedged. In some cases, income-statement volatility is avoided by an entity's recording changes in the fair value of the derivative directly in shareholder's equity (thereby creating "equity volatility"). In other cases, changes in the fair value of the derivative continue to be reported in earnings as they occur, but the impact is counterbalanced by the entity's adjusting the carrying value of the asset or liability that is being hedged.

■ There are extensive disclosure requirements.

■ No grandfathering is allowed. When SFAS No. 133 is first applied, all existing derivatives must be recognized on the balance sheet at fair value. The transition rules, therefore, focus on what to do with previously unrecognized changes in the fair value of both derivatives and hedged items.

THE INTERNATIONAL ACCOUNTING STANDARD ON FOREIGN CURRENCY TRANSLATION

International Accounting Standard No. 21, "The Effects of Changes in Foreign Exchange Rates," deals with foreign currency. It was originally issued in 1983 and was revised and reissued in 1993 as part of the IASC's Comparability Project. The original IAS No. 21 (along with the corresponding standards in Canada and the United Kingdom) was issued shortly after SFAS No. 52 in the United States. It is therefore not surprising that it adopts the same basic approach to foreign currency translation as SFAS No. 52. However, there are differences in the terminology used in the two standards. IAS No. 21 does not use the term *functional currency*. Rather, it uses terms such as *foreign entity* and *foreign operations* that are integral to the operations of the reporting enterprise. Under IAS No. 21, a foreign entity is one that "accumulates cash and other monetary items, incurs expenses, generates income, and perhaps arranges borrowings, all substantially in its local currency." Thus, a foreign entity under IAS No. 21 is essentially similar to those entities under SFAS No. 52 for whom the local currency is the functional currency. Similarly, foreign operations that are integral to the operations of the reporting enterprise under IAS No. 21 are similar to those foreign subsidiaries for which the functional currency is the U.S. dollar under SFAS No. 52.

IAS No. 21 requires the use of the temporal method of translation for foreign operations that are integral to the operations of the reporting enterprise. Translation gains or losses are included in the income statement. Under IAS No. 21, the current rate method of translation is required for a foreign entity. The translation gains and losses are transferred to reserves and reported in shareholders' equity.

There is at least one important difference between IAS No. 21 and SFAS No. 52. Under IAS No. 21, the financial statements of subsidiaries in highly inflationary economies must be adjusted to reflect changes in general price levels before translation. This approach, often referred to as "restate/translate," is similar to that followed in the United Kingdom. The approach adopted under SFAS No. 52 in the United States is "translate/restate." The FASB did consider the "restate/translate" approach while working on SFAS No. 52 but decided against it. Many regard the "restate/translate" approach as being the more accurate of the two because it actually accounts for changes in purchasing power. The "translate/restate" approach, on the other hand, assumes that the effects of inflation are captured by the change in the exchange rate.

As with a number of other international accounting standards that are criticized for allowing alternative accounting treatments, IAS No. 21 also permits alternative treatments in two situations. The first situation relates to exchange losses on a liability for the recent acquisition of an asset purchased in a foreign currency. Similar to SFAS No. 52, the benchmark treatment under IAS No. 21 requires that the exchange losses be charged to expense. However, the alternative treatment under IAS No. 21 allows exchange losses to be added to the cost of the asset when the related liability cannot be settled and there is no practical means of hedging.

Another area where IAS No. 21 permits alternative treatments is in translating goodwill and fair value adjustments to assets and liabilities that arise from purchase accounting for the acquisition of a foreign entity for which the local currency is the functional currency. When the local currency is the functional currency, SFAS No. 52 requires use of the current exchange rate to translate all balance sheet items, including goodwill and fair value adjustments. IAS No. 21 allows the use of either the current exchange rate or the historical exchange rate. There could be significant differences in the results of current rate translation relative to historical rate translation of goodwill, fair value adjustments of balance sheet items, and related depreciation, amortization, and other expenses.

ACCOUNTING ISSUES RELATED TO THE EURO

The European Union (EU) launched a new currency named the euro in January 1999. Of the 15 member nations of the EU, 11 joined the European Economic and Monetary Union (EMU). The 11 countries adopting the euro as their currency are Austria, Belgium, Finland, France, Germany, Ireland, Italy, Luxembourg, the Netherlands, Portugal, and Spain. These countries are collectively referred to as Euroland. Of the other four EU countries, Britain, Denmark, and Sweden chose not to relinquish their national (legacy) currencies and Greece did not meet the criteria for the euro. The euro was phased in over a three-year transition period—from January 1, 1999, to January 1, 2002. Euro coins and bank notes were only issued on January 1, 2002, and the national currencies of the participating countries became obsolete on July 1, 2002. There are a number of accounting issues that arise as a result of the introduction of the euro. They are discussed briefly in this section.

For the years 1999–2001, companies in Euroland had a choice of preparing financial statements in either the national currency or euros. As of 2002, all Euroland companies must prepare their financial statements in euros. In some non-euro countries such as the United Kingdom, companies will have a choice of reporting in the euro or in their national currency depending on the firm's functional currency. In order to meet the euro functional currency criterion, a company will be expected to have a majority of its assets, liabilities, revenues, and expenses denominated in euros. For U.S. companies that conduct a significant amount of their business in Euroland, conversion to the euro could have a material effect on their financial statements which, in turn, might require them to make euro-related disclosures.[7] Such disclosures might

---

[7]SEC Legal Staff Bulletin No. 6 discusses related disclosure obligations.

relate to the changes in the company's competitive environment or significant costs related to euro conversion.

In Europe, companies are generally permitted to expense all conversion costs related to the euro. The exception is Germany where companies are required to capitalize conversion costs in certain situations. In the United States, the accounting for conversion costs should be consistent with the company's existing accounting practice for similar costs. Losses resulting from the impairment of fixed assets as a direct result of conversion to the euro (e.g., coin-operated vending machines) must be recognized in accordance with SFAS No. 121.[8] In the United Kingdom, the cost of converting assets to make them euro-compliant can be expensed. Future obligations related to conversion costs must be disclosed in the balance sheet.

Finally, euro-denominated financial statements must also deal with the issue of comparative figures. In countries where comparative figures for the previous year are required to be included in financial statements and for the previous five years in the notes, the preferred method for translating the comparative figures is using the fixed conversion rate stipulated by the European Commission. Translation of the figures using historic exchange rates is not possible since the euro did not exist prior to 1999. The European Commission expressly prohibits the use of the European Currency Unit (ECU) because some of the currencies in the ECU are not in the euro. Additional information on the euro can be obtained from the web sites of a number of organizations, including the Council of the European Union, the European Commission, the European Federation of Accountants, and the European Central Bank.[9]

SUMMARY

1. Most companies engaged in international business are affected by the fluctuation in the value of currencies (relative to other currencies). Currencies can be traded in the spot market or the forward market. The exchange rate of currencies can be quoted direct (the price of one unit of a foreign currency in your currency) or indirect (the units of the foreign currency available for one unit of your currency).

2. There are three main types of foreign exchange exposure: 1) translation exposure, 2) transaction exposure, and 3) economic exposure.

3. There is a distinction in the accounting treatment of foreign currency translation gains and losses and foreign currency transaction gains and losses. Foreign currency transaction gains and losses are required to be included in the income statement. The treatment of foreign currency translation gains and losses depends on the accounting method used.

4. The four methods of accounting for foreign currency translation are the current rate method, the current/non-current method, the monetary/non-monetary method, and the temporal method.

5. In the United States, FASB Statement No. 52 introduced the concept of functional currency to be used in determining the foreign currency translation method to be used.

---

[8]This standard deals with accounting for the impairment of long-lived assets and for long-lived assets to be disposed of.

[9]Their web site addresses are: Council of the European Union (**www.ue.eu.int**); the European Commission (**www.europa.eu.int/euro/**); the European commission (**www.europa.eu.int/euro/**); the European Federation of Accountants (**www.euro.fee.be**); and the European Central Bank (**www.ecb.int/**).

6. With the introduction of the euro on January 1, 1999, companies doing business in Europe or with European entities must deal with certain foreign currency financial reporting issues related to the euro. These include a new method of translating among the national currencies of the 11 participating countries and financial reporting issues for conversion and compliance costs related to the euro.

QUESTIONS

1. What are the different types of foreign exchange exposure faced by companies engaged in international business? Explain what causes each type of exposure.
2. What are the accounting issues related to gains or losses from foreign currency transactions? What are the alternatives for foreign currency transaction accounting?
3. Why is translation exposure also referred to as accounting exposure? In what respects is translation exposure different from transaction exposure?
4. Explain the different foreign currency translation methods. What are the pros and cons of each of the translation methods?
5. Which foreign currency translation method did the FASB mandate under SFAS No. 8? What was the reaction of the U.S. business community to SFAS No. 8?
6. How did the FASB respond to the criticism of SFAS No. 8?
7. Describe the requirements for foreign currency translation under SFAS No. 52.
8. Discuss the concept of functional currency under SFAS No. 52. What purpose does the functional currency serve? In your view, was it really necessary to include functional currency in SFAS No. 52?
9. In choosing the foreign currency translation method under SFAS No. 52, the FASB included an important exception. What was this exception, and why was it necessary?
10. What are the requirements for foreign currency translation accounting under IAS No. 21? Do they differ significantly from SFAS No. 52?
11. Select three U.S. companies from the same industry and review their annual reports to determine their accounting policy on foreign currency translation. Given their practice on this issue, are their financial statements comparable? Explain.

EXERCISES

1. As multinational companies continue to expand globally, managing the risk related to fluctuating currency exchange rates has become a strategic challenge usually resulting in the use of financial derivatives. Obtain the annual report of a company and describe the different types of derivative financial instruments the company utilizes.
2. Obtain both the 1997 annual report for Chrysler Corp. before its 1998 merger with Daimler Benz, and the 1998 Daimler/Chrysler annual report. Determine the functional currency Chrysler used for its foreign subsidiaries under SFAS No. 52 before the merger and what Daimler/Chrysler subsequently used as the functional currency for its foreign subsidiaries. Does this make sense to you? Explain.
3. The four main foreign currency translation methods are the current rate method, the current/non-current method, the monetary/non-monetary method, and the temporal method. Research the foreign currency translation methods/standards in your home country. Which method is used by most multinationals based in your country?
4. Important financial data for the British subsidiary of Millette Company (U.S.) for the 2000 fiscal year is shown on the following page.

	British pound sterling (millions)
a) Net Sales	2,056
b) Gross Profit	1,203
c) Income before Taxes	669
d) Net Income	481

Assume the following average exchange rates for the year (U.S. dollars per British pound sterling):

1. $1.71   2. $1.65   3. $1.69   4. $1.59

Using each exchange rate, make a table converting a), b), c), and d) into U.S. dollars. Determine which exchange rate produces the most favorable results in U.S. dollars.

5. Gator Corporation (U.S.) purchased equipment worth 2 million Swiss francs from Holdstet (Switzerland) at the beginning of the year. The transaction was denominated in Swiss francs. The exchange rate at that time was US$0.65 = 1 SFr. However, due to a stronger economy, the Swiss franc had strengthened against the U.S. dollar resulting in an exchange rate of US$0.70 = 1 SFr at year end.

   a) Determine the transaction gain/loss that Gator Corporation will report in its year-end income statement.

   b) Determine the transaction gain/loss Holdstet will report in its year-end income statement.

CASES

Case

Cupid's Corner

Angelica Corporation is headquartered in the United States and is owned entirely by U.S. investors. However, a large portion of Angelica's manufacturing operations are located in Singapore.

"Since all of our shares are owned entirely by U.S. investors, in addition to our corporate office being here in the States, the company's functional currency for financial reporting purposes should be the U.S. dollar," proclaims Brent Reed, the company's CEO, to the CFO, Alexis Pidcu.

"But Brent, our Singapore subsidiary's primary operating environment is Singapore since we source our raw materials there, set our prices based on market conditions in Singapore, and finance the operation from loans in Singapore dollars obtained from local banks. That is why we must use the Singapore dollar as our functional currency."

1. Do you agree with Mr. Reed or Ms. Pidcu? Explain.
2. What are the consequences to Angelica Corporation's reported income numbers of choosing the U.S. dollar or the Singapore dollar as the functional currency of its Singapore subsidiary?
3. Do the auditors of Angelica Corporation have a role in the functional currency that the company chooses? Given the facts of this case, as the auditor, would you agree with Mr. Reed or Ms. Pidcu? Explain.

Case

Euro-Fusion

In the Financial Review section of its 1998 annual report, Coca-Cola explains the Euro Conversion as follows:

In January 1999, certain member countries of the European Union established permanent, fixed conversion rates between their existing currencies and the European Union's common currency (the Euro).

The transition period for the introduction of the Euro is scheduled to phase in over a period ending January 1, 2002, with the existing currency being completely removed from circulation on July 1, 2002.

Assume that the costs of all Coca-Cola products are U.S.-dollar based, and the exchange rates for the euro relative to the U.S. dollar in 2002, 2003, and 2004 are:

For the Years Ended December 31,	2002	2003	2004
U.S. dollars per euro (weighted average)	1.07	1.15	1.10
U.S. dollars per euro (year-end)	1.10	1.12	1.11

1. With the strengthening of the euro in 2003 and the weakening of the euro in 2004, would you expect exchange gains/losses in Coca-Cola's Consolidated Statements of Income for the years 2003 and 2004? Explain.
2. Operating in nearly 200 countries, Coca-Cola is affected by inflation in many markets around the world. Often weaknesses in some currencies are offset by strengths in others. List a few strategies that multinationals can use to protect themselves against fluctuation of exchange rates.

Case

Tag-sale

DSM's (Netherlands) 1998 corporate annual report included important financial data in both the Dutch guilder (NGL) and the euro (EUR). Excerpts from the company's ten-year summary figures for the year 1998 are shown below.

Income Statement

	in NGL million	in EUR million
net sales	14,018	6,361
operating result	1,290	586
financial income and expense	(156)	(71)
result from ordinary activities before taxation . . .	1,134	515
tax on result from ordinary activities	(237)	(108)
result of non-consolidated companies	42	19
result from ordinary activities after taxation	939	426
extraordinary result after taxation	(21)	(9)
result after taxation	918	417
minority interests' share in result	(4)	(2)
net result	914	415
per ordinary share in NGL:		
result from ordinary activities after taxation	27.19	12.34
net result	26.43	11.99
cash flow	57.55	26.12

1. Comment on the differences resulting from DSM's conversion to the euro for the 1998 fiscal year.
2. Referring to your answer above, how will the conversion to the euro affect DSM's balance sheet for the year?
3. In your opinion, with the introduction of the euro, what is the management at DSM likely to use to measure operating performance, NGL or EUR or both? Support your answer.

REFERENCES

Brankovic, M., and Madura, J. 1990. Effect of SFAS No. 52 on profitability ratios. *International Journal of Accounting*, 25 (1): 19–28.

Coopers and Lybrand. 1994. *Foreign Currency Translation and Hedging*. New York: Coopers & Lybrand.

Evans, T. G., Folks, W. R., and Jilling, M. 1978. *The Impact of Statement of Financial Accounting Standards No. 8 on the Foreign Exchange Risk Management Practices of American Multinationals: An Economic Impact Study*. Stamford, CT: FASB.

Financial Accounting Standards Board. 1975. *Accounting for the Translation of Foreign Currency Transactions and Foreign Currency Financial Statements, Statement of Financial Accounting Standards No. 8*. Stamford, CT: FASB.

Financial Accounting Standards Board. 1981. *Foreign Currency Translation, Statement of Financial Accounting Standards No. 52*. Stamford, CT: FASB.

Glaum, M., Brunner, M., and Himmel, H. 2000. The DAX and the Dollar: The economic exchange rate exposure of German corporations. *Journal of International Business Studies*, 31 (4): 715–724.

Goldberg, S. R., and Godwin, J. H. 1994. Foreign currency translation under two cases—integrated and isolated economies. *Journal of International Financial Management and Accounting*, 5 (June): 97–119.

Griffin, P. A. 1983. Management's preferences for FASB Statement No. 52: Predictive ability results. *Abacus*, 19 (2): 130–138.

Hooper, P., and Liao, L. M. 1990. Foreign currency accounting: A review and critique of major empirical studies. *International Journal of Accounting*, 25 (2): 113–126.

Hosseini, A., and Rezaee, Z. 1990. Impact of SFAS No. 52 on performance measures of multinationals. *International Journal of Accounting*, 25 (1): 43–52.

Houston, C. O. 1989. Foreign currency translation research: Review and synthesis. *Journal of Accounting Literature*, 8: 25–48.

International Accounting Standards Committee. 1993. *The Effects of Changes in Foreign Exchange Rates, International Accounting Standard 21 (revised)*. London: IASC.

Kirsch, R. J., and Evans, T. G. 1994. The implementation of SFAS 52: Did the functional currency approach prevail? *International Journal of Accounting*, 30 (1): 20–33.

Mehta, D. R., and Thapa, S. B. 1991. FAS-52, functional currency, and the non-comparability of financial reports. *International Journal of Accounting*, 26 (2): 71–84.

Pantzalis, C., Simkins, B. J., and Laux, P. A. 2001. Operational hedges and the foreign exchange exposure of U.S. multinational corporations. *Journal of International Business Studies*, 32 (4): 793–812.

Pinto, J. A. M. 2001. Foreign currency translation adjustments as predictors of earning changes. *Journal of International Accounting, Auditing, and Taxation*, 10 (1): 51–69.

PricewaterhouseCoopers. 1998. *The New Standard on Accounting for Derivative Instruments and Hedging Activities*. New York. PricewaterhouseCoopers.

Sigel, P. H., Theerathorn, P., and Joaquin, C. A. 1992. The determinants of systematic risk in multinational corporations after SFAS 52. *International Journal of Accounting*, 27 (4): 324–341.

Soo, B. S., and Soo, L. G. 1994. Accounting for the multinational firm: Is the translation process valued by the stock market? *Accounting Review*, 69 (October): 617–637.

Ziebart, D. A., and Kim, D. H. 1987. An examination of the market reactions associated with SFAS No. 8 and SFAS No. 52. *Accounting Review*, 62 (April): 343–357.

CHAPTER 4

SELECTED FINANCIAL REPORTING AND DISCLOSURE ISSUES IN THE GLOBAL CONTEXT

LEARNING OBJECTIVES

- Identify the effect of inflation on financial reporting and discuss the two main inflation-adjusted accounting models.

- Examine the issues related to accounting for goodwill and intangible assets, and discuss the main accounting approaches related to them.

- Highlight the costs and benefits of geographic segmental disclosure and review the new U.S. and international accounting standard on segmental reporting.

- Discuss the growing demand for social reporting including employee and environmental disclosures.

This chapter covers a number of financial reporting and disclosure issues that have particular relevance in the international arena. The topics covered are 1) accounting for changing prices, 2) accounting for goodwill and other intangible assets, 3) geographic segment reporting, and 4) social disclosure. These topics are relevant to financial statement users for several reasons. First, they relate to fundamentally important aspects of a company's business and represent critical items of decision-relevant information. Second, in certain countries there has traditionally been very little transparency on some of these items (e.g., effects of inflation, geographic segments, social reporting). Third, there is considerable diversity of practice resulting in non-comparability of financial statements across countries and even within countries.

ACCOUNTING FOR CHANGING PRICES

We all know that inflation can significantly affect the purchasing power of money. In recent history, there have been numerous instances of countries suffering dramatically from high inflation.[1] However, it is important to recognize that, over an extended period, inflation corrodes the purchasing power of money even in countries that have relatively modest inflation. For example, annual inflation of just 5 percent over 15 years would result in a doubling of prices, thereby causing a currency to lose half its purchasing power.

Yet the historical-cost accounting model, which dominates financial reporting practice in most countries, does not account for changes in the purchasing power of the currency that is used in the financial statements. As is evident in any historical-cost-based financial statement, when monetary amounts from different time periods are added there is an implicit assumption that these amounts are homogeneous and are additive. For example, GE's consolidated balance sheet at December 31, 2001, shows the Property, Plant, and Equipment (net) balance as US$42.1 billion. What is the information content of this number from a decision-making perspective? Those who understand the principles underlying the historical-cost accounting model know that this number does not represent the current fair market value of GE's fixed assets. Nor is this number a representation of the historical cost of these assets in 2001 dollars. Rather, it is simply an arithmetical sum of the historical cost of the Property, Plant, and Equipment (PP&E) that GE owns today, regardless of when these assets were purchased. However, since GE has been in existence for almost 100 years, the PP&E balance includes assets (particularly land and buildings) that were acquired by GE at various points over its existence.

To understand how inflation can distort the information content of historical-cost financial statements, let us review the recent history of general changes in purchasing power in the United States. As indicated in Exhibit 4-1, the consumer price index (CPI) in the United States rose from 24.1 in 1950 to 172.2 in 2000. Thus, consumer prices increased sevenfold in the United States over the past 50 years. Stated differently, the purchasing power of one U.S. dollar in 1950 was equal to more than seven U.S. dollars in 2000. How much sense does it make then to add a 1950 dollar to a 2000 dollar and treat them as if they are homogeneous units? And yet, that is exactly what occurs under the historical-cost model. When global inflation was relatively high in

---

[1]For example, in the early 1980s, Bolivia experienced inflation of over 20,000 percent annually which resulted in the Bolivian peso declining in value from 25 pesos per U.S. dollar to 1.13 million pesos per U.S. dollar in a relatively short period.

EXHIBIT 4-1   U.S. Consumer Price Index, 1950–1995

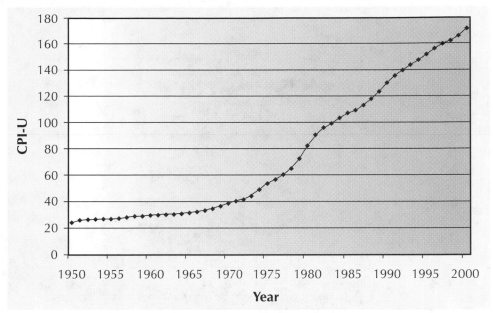

the 1970s, accounting standard-setters in various countries, including the United States and the United Kingdom, issued standards that required companies to provide inflation-adjusted financial statements as supplements to the main historical-cost financial statements. However, these requirements were relatively short-lived. Based on a combination of reduced inflation and widespread opposition by corporations, these requirements were eliminated in most countries in the 1980s. The result is that users of financial statements only receive historical-cost-based financial statements with nary a word in corporate annual reports on the effects of inflation on accounting numbers. Exhibit 4-2 contains a sample of the inflation-adjusted disclosure that was provided in the United States by Weyerhaeuser in 1985 when companies were still required to provide financial statements adjusted for both general price level changes and specific price changes as supplementary disclosure. In the United States, inflation-adjusted disclosure was no longer required after 1985. This will be discussed further below.

While the failure to provide an indication of the effects of inflation on financial statements is problematic enough from a decision-making perspective in a purely domestic context, it becomes a more serious problem in international financial reporting when users of financial statements need to compare accounting numbers from different countries that have different rates of inflation. Comparability and relevance of the accounting numbers both suffer as a result. For instance, how can a user make sense of an Indonesian company's 1997 historical-cost rupiah-denominated financial statements when inflation during the year was over 100% and the exchange rate of the rupiah ranged from 2,600 per U.S. dollar to 16,000 per U.S. dollar! And yet, because many developing countries follow the lead of developed Western countries on financial reporting standards, most of them do not have any requirements for reporting the effects of changing prices on their financial position and performance. The exceptions are countries like Mexico that have experienced high inflation rates and have retained the requirement to provide inflation-adjusted financial disclosure.

EXHIBIT 4-2 Weyerhaeuser 1985 Supplementary Financial Information

Net Assets Adjusted For Changing Prices

Year ended December 29, 1985	As Reported	Current Cost
Product inventories	$ 379,399	$ 561,744
Materials and supplies	167,376	167,376
Property and equipment	3,432,377	4,862,705
Timber and timberlands	645,630	1,880,105
Leased property under capital lease	58,750	103,382
All other assets, net	596,253	596,253
	5,279,785	8,171,595
Deduct net monetary liabilities	1,955,734	1,927,026
Net assets	$3,324,051	$6,244,569

Consolidated Earnings Adjusted for Changing Prices

Year ended December 29, 1985	As Reported	Specific Prices
Net sales	$5,205,579	$5,205,579
Real estate and financial services	111,914	111,914
Other income, net	30,419	(7,910)
	5,347,912	5,309,583
Operating costs and expenses:		
Other than depreciation, amortization, and fee stumpage*	4,583,822	4,602,437
Depreciation, amortization, and fee stumpage	350,155	611,530
Interest expense	110,219	110,219
	5,044,196	5,324,186
Earnings before income taxes	303,716	(14,603)
Income taxes	103,600	103,600
Net earnings	$ 200,116	$ (118,203)
Gain from decline in the purchasing power of net amounts owed		$ 70,401

*Fee stumpage is the cost of standing timber and is charged to fee timber disposals as fee timber is harvested, lost as the result of casualty, or sold (Note 4, 1995 Weyerhaeuser Annual Report).

Inflation-Adjusted Accounting Models

There are two main inflation-adjusted accounting models. The General Price Level Adjusted (GPLA) model uses price indexes to adjust for general changes in the purchasing power of the country's monetary unit. The objective is to convert the historical-cost nominal amounts from different time periods to a common point in time, generally at the balance sheet date, so that all numbers in the financial statements are reported in monetary units of the same purchasing power. The Current Cost-Adjusted (CCA) model takes a physical asset perspective to measuring performance and financial position. It focuses on the specific price changes of physical assets owned, used, or sold by the company. Expenses are recorded based on the current replacement cost of the assets employed rather than on their historical cost.

General Price Level Adjusted (GPLA) Model

The GPLA model attempts to account for changes in the general purchasing power of the reporting currency over time. Since it deals with general price changes, the model uses a summary measure of inflation such as a consumer price index (CPI). It aims to address an important weakness of the historical-cost model, which ignores changes in the purchasing power of the reporting currency over time. As discussed above, the historical-cost model requires adding monetary amounts from very different time periods, even though the sum of these amounts has little information content. The following example illustrates the weakness of the historical-cost model and shows how the GPLA model addresses it.

Suppose that an executive has just returned to the United States from a business trip to Asia during which she visited Hong Kong, Indonesia, Japan, and Singapore. While in the Immigration and Customs Hall at San Francisco International Airport, she is approached by a U.S. customs officer who asks the executive how much money she is carrying with her. The executive goes through her purse and finds the following amounts:

U.S. $	100
Japanese Yen	12,100
Hong Kong $	780
Singapore $	180
Indonesian Rupiah	920,000
Total	933,160

If the executive were to add these amounts and respond to the customs officer that the total "money" she had with her was 933,160 we know that this would be a nonsensical answer and, in all likelihood, the customs officer would not be very amused. Yet one could argue that the PP&E amount of $42.1 billion in GE's 2001 balance sheet, and in most corporate balance sheets, is a similarly nonsensical total since the purchasing power of a 1925 dollar is as different from a 2001 dollar as some non-U.S. currencies are from a U.S. dollar.

The sensible approach to responding to the customs officer's question would be to convert the various currencies to a single currency—in this instance, the U.S. dollar— before stating the amount. Thus, as indicated in Illustration 4-1 below, an appropriate response by the executive would be that she has approximately US$500. While the total in the third column makes sense, the total in the first column does not. In the context of inflation, the historical-cost numbers in corporate annual reports are like the totals in the first column. The GPLA model goes through the process of converting the nominal amounts from diverse periods, and therefore in diverse purchasing powers, to a constant purchasing power, typically that at the balance sheet date.

ILLUSTRATION 4-1

	Nominal Amount	Exchange Rate per US$	Converted Amount in US$
U.S. $	100	1.00	100
Japanese Yen	12,100	121	100
Hong Kong $	780	7.80	100
Singapore $	180	1.80	100
Indonesian Rupiah	920,000	9,200	100
Total	933,160		500

ACCOUNTING PROCEDURES UNDER THE GPLA MODEL. Having explained the basic concept behind the GPLA model, we are now in a position to illustrate GPLA procedures. We start by obtaining historical-cost-based financial statements. The nominal numbers become the "first column" in preparing GPLA-based financial statements. Next, we need to label the individual items in the financial statements as either monetary or non-monetary. Monetary items are those items that are contractual obligations, such as cash, accounts receivable, and all payables. Monetary items are not adjusted for inflation in the GPLA model and, thus, appear at their original nominal amounts. All other financial statement items are non-monetary and must be adjusted in the GPLA model to reflect the effect of inflation.

Just as we had an exchange rate that got us from the diverse currencies to a single currency in Illustration 4-1, we need adjustment factors that will get us from the nominal amount to the constant purchasing power amount in the GPLA model. The adjustment factor is comprised of two CPI numbers for each non-monetary item on the financial statement. The numerator in the GPLA adjustment factor is always the CPI at the financial statement date. Thus, in our example, the numerator for all the non-monetary items is 180, which is the CPI on December 31, 2000. The denominator is the CPI at the date of purchase of the asset or occurrence of a transaction (i.e., the CPI at the date of the historical event). For example, if a piece of equipment with a historical cost of $1 million was purchased in 1995 when the CPI was 150, then the adjustment process for it would be:

	Nominal Amount	Adjustment Factor	GPLA Basis
Equipment (Cost)	$1,000,000	180/150	$1,200,000

After all the non-monetary items are restated on a GPLA basis balance sheet, the difference between the GPLA basis assets and the GPLA basis liabilities and stockholders' equity (except the retained earnings) is the GPLA basis retained earnings balance. In effect, the retained earnings account serves as a plug in moving from a historical-cost balance sheet to a GPLA balance sheet.

Similarly, in preparing a GPLA basis income statement, we start with the numbers in the conventional historical-cost income statement as the "first column." Once again our objective is to move from the nominal dollars from different time periods and with diverse purchasing powers to a specific point in time with a constant purchasing power. As with the balance sheet, the numerator in the adjustment factor is the CPI at the end of the current period. The denominator is again the CPI at the date of purchase of the asset or occurrence of a transaction (i.e., the CPI at the date of the historical event).

For most revenue and expense items, the denominator in the adjustment factor is the average CPI for the period since revenues and expenses typically occur throughout the period. However, there are two important exceptions. First, for converting cost of goods sold, the relevant CPI to be used in the denominator of the adjustment factor is the CPI on the date on which the inventory item was purchased since that is the nominal amount reflected in the historical-cost income statement. Second, for converting depreciation expense (as well as amortization and depletion, where appropriate), the relevant CPI in the denominator is again the CPI on the date on which the asset was acquired.

After we have all the adjusted revenue and expense amounts in the third column of the GPLA basis income statement, we subtract the expenses from the revenues to determine the GPLA net operating income. The final step in the GPLA basis income statement is to compute the net monetary gain or loss. This can be computed separately for each monetary asset and liability (as shown in Illustration 4-2) and then computing the net monetary gain or loss on an aggregate basis (as shown in Illustration 4-3).

ILLUSTRATION 4-2

Monetary Loss on Cash			
	Actual Monetary Amounts	**Index**	**December 31, 2000 Purchasing Power Equivalent**
January 1, 2000 balance	$350,000	110/100	$385,000
Net additions during 2000	100,000	110/105	104,800
Totals	$450,000		$489,800
2000 monetary loss			$ 39,800

ILLUSTRATION 4-3

Aggregate Monetary Gain/Loss			
	Jan. 1, 2000	**Dec. 31, 2000**	**Change 2000**
Monetary assets	$ 350,000	$ 690,000	$ 340,000
Monetary liabilities	(740,000)	(1,260,000)	520,000
Net monetary liability position	$(390,000)	$ (570,000)	$ (180,000)
General price-level index:	January 1, 2000	100	
	Average for 2000	105	
	December 31, 2000	110	
		Net Monetary Gain (Loss)	
Monetary gain on beginning monetary liability position $(390,000 \times 110/100) - 390,000$		$39,000	
Monetary gain on change for 2000 $(180,000 \times 110/105) - 180,000$		8,600	
Net monetary gain for 2000		$47,600	

It should be apparent that, in times of rising prices, one incurs monetary losses from holding on to monetary assets. Thus, if one were to keep some currency under one's mattress, it would lose purchasing power in an inflationary period. Holding monetary liabilities, on the other hand, results in monetary gain. For instance, if a business owner received 90 days' credit from a supplier, the business owner would have monetary gains from the accounts payable because the nominal amount paid three months later would have less purchasing power than the same amount at the invoice date. Finally, the net monetary gain (loss) number is added to (subtracted from) the GPLA net operating income to obtain the GPLA basis net income. The computations to convert historical-cost financial statements to GPLA financial statements are shown in Exhibit 4-3 for the income statement and Exhibit 4-4 for the balance sheet.

EXHIBIT 4-3 General Price Level Adjusted Income Statement

For the Year Ending December 31, 2000			
	Historical Cost	Adjustment Ratio	P-L-A Basis
Revenue from sales	$3,000,000	110/105	$3,142,900
Cost of goods sold	(1,200,000)	110/105	(1,257,100)
Rent	(180,000)	110/105	(188,600)
Advertising	(150,000)	110/105	(157,100)
Personnel expenses	(900,000)	110/105	(942,900)
Equipment depreciation	(200,000)	150,000 × 110/100	(165,000)
		50,000 × 110/105	(52,400)
Interest on loan	(60,000)	110/105	(62,900)
Utilities	(50,000)	110/105	(52,400)
Federal income taxes	(130,000)	110/105	(136,200)
Net operating income	$ 130,000		$ 128,300
Add: Net monetary gain	N/A		47,600
Conventional net income	$ 130,000		
P-L-A net income			$ 175,900

EXHIBIT 4-4 General Price Level Adjusted Balance Sheet

December 31, 2000			
	Historical Cost	Adjustment Ratio	P-L-A Basis
Assets:			
Cash	$ 450,000	Not restated*	$ 450,000
Accounts receivable	240,000	Not restated*	240,000
Prepaid expenses	60,000	110/105	62,900
Merchandise inventory	90,000	110/108	91,700
Supplies	40,000	110/105	41,900
Equipment	1,000,000	750,000 × 110/100	825,000
		250,000 × 110/105	261,900
Less: Accumulated depreciation	(200,000)	150,000 × 110/100	(165,000)
		50,000 × 110/105	(52,400)
Total assets	$1,680,000		$1,756,000
Liabilities and Owners' Equity			
Accounts payable	$ 90,000	Not restated*	$ 90,000
Accrued liabilities	70,000	Not restated*	70,000
Bank loan payable	600,000	Not restated*	600,000
Bonds payable	500,000	Not restated*	500,000
Owners' Equity			
Paid-in capital	350,000	110/100	385,000
Retained earnings	70,000	Reconciliation item	111,000
Total liabilities and owners' equity	$1,680,000		$1,756,000

*Monetary Items

EVALUATING THE GPLA MODEL. The GPLA model is an improvement on the historical-cost model in that it addresses the problem of adding "apples and oranges" by converting nominal amounts from different points in time and with different purchasing powers into a constant purchasing power at a specific point in time. However, it does not deal with specific price changes of assets. In the final analysis, companies are affected differently by inflation based on their product line and the type of fixed assets they own. The GPLA model paints all entities with the same broad brush of general levels of inflation. It does not consider the specific price changes in the fixed assets, inventories, and other physical assets owned by the company.

Current Cost-Adjusted (CCA) Model

The Current Cost-Adjusted (CCA) model focuses on the specific price changes of physical assets owned by each business entity. The model requires that the carrying value of physical assets owned by a business be restated to their current value, and the corresponding expenses also be restated to reflect their current cost. Before getting into the mechanical procedures of this model, it is important that one understand a fundamental difference between this model and all the other accounting models.

There are a number of accounting models in addition to the CCA model. These are 1) the cash flow model, 2) the discounted cash flow model, 3) the conventional historical-cost model, and 4) the general price level adjusted (GPLA) model. The common feature of these four models is that they take a monetary approach to measuring income and wealth. While each uses different accounting methods, they all measure income and wealth in monetary terms. Thus, under each of these models, if one started a period with an amount x and ended the period with an amount $x + y$, then one would be considered to be better off by the amount y. So a sole proprietor who started the year with $1 million and ended the year with $1.2 million would be considered to be better off by $200,000. This reflects the monetary approach to measuring income and wealth.

The CCA model, however, takes a physical asset approach to measuring wealth and income. Under this model, money is treated simply as a medium of exchange that facilitates business activity by reducing transactions costs. However, money is not deemed to necessarily have inherent value. Consequently, having more money at the end of a period than at the beginning of a period does not necessarily guarantee that one is better off. (One only needs to consider the situation in the Bolivian example in Footnote 1 to be convinced of this.) Under the CCA model, it is the physical assets that are the measure of income and wealth. In order to be better off at the end of a period, one must have more physical assets than one did at the beginning of the same period. Again, let us use a simple example to explain. Assume that the sole proprietor with the $1 million referred to above was a cattle rancher. Since the CCA model measures income and wealth in physical assets, let us assume that the only physical assets owned by the rancher at the start of the period were 1,000 head of cattle that he had bought at $1,000 each. Also assume that the $1.2 million that the rancher has at the end of the period is a result of selling the 1,000 head of cattle at $1,200 each. While the historical-cost model would tell us that the rancher was $200,000 better off at the end of the year, under the CCA model we need to know the rancher's physical assets at the end of the year in order for us to determine whether he is, indeed, better off. Assuming that he wants to stay in the cattle ranching business, this requires information on the current cost (also referred to as the replacement cost) of the cattle. If the replacement cost of the cattle at year end soars to $1,500 each, then the rancher can only purchase 800 cattle with his $1.2 million. While the historical-cost model considered the rancher to be 20 percent better off at the end of the period because his money had grown from \$1 million to \$1.2 million, the CCA model actually considers the rancher to be 20 percent worse off since his herd has shrunk from 1,000 to 800 head of cattle. While this example is simplistic, it conveys the essence of the physical asset perspective taken by the CCA model which distinguishes it from the other accounting models that take a monetary perspective.

ACCOUNTING PROCEDURES UNDER THE CCA MODEL. The concept of *holding gains and losses* is critical in the CCA model. Holding gains (or losses) arise as a result of an increase (or decrease) in the price of physical assets. Gains occur as a result of inflation, while losses result from deflation in the price of the specific physical assets. The CCA model distinguishes between *realized holding gains* and *unrealized holding gains.*

Realized Holding Gains/Losses occur when the physical asset has been consumed—either through sale of merchandise (as in finished goods inventory) or recognition of depreciation expense (as in fixed assets). The appropriate replacement cost is the replacement cost when the asset was consumed—sales date for merchandise and year end for fixed assets. The difference between Net Operating Income on a replacement cost basis (CCA) and Net Operating Income on a historical-cost basis is realized holding gains/losses. Realized holding gains/losses are reported in CCA income statements.

Unrealized Holding Gains/Losses occur when the physical assets owned by a business at year end have changed in value from the historical cost at which they were originally acquired. The appropriate replacement cost is the cost at year end. Unrealized holding gains/losses are the difference between the current cost and historical cost carrying amounts of the physical assets. The two asset categories typically involved in the computation of unrealized holding gains are inventory and book value of fixed assets. Only the change in unrealized holding gains/losses is reported in the CCA income statement and the Owners' Equity section of a CCA balance sheet. Exhibit 4-5 contains the relationships and formulae for the computation of realized and unrealized holding gains/losses and also indicates where these items appear in CCA financial statements.

Evaluating the CCA model

The CCA model is different from the other accounting models in that it takes a physical asset perspective to measuring wealth and income. This is important in inflationary situations when monetary units often experience a dramatic decline in their purchasing power. It emphasizes the idea that money is neither a good measure nor a store of wealth in an inflationary environment. The main weakness of the CCA model is that for certain types of fixed assets, determining current cost can be highly subjective. For other assets, current costs may be difficult to obtain. However, corporations in equity-oriented capital markets such as the United States are opposed to the CCA model because it tends to understate reported earnings relative to the historical-cost model. In an environment where there is a fixation with earnings numbers and where market valuations of companies fluctuate dramatically when reported earnings diverge from expected earnings, corporate managers are unwilling to have the CCA model earnings number raise doubts in investors' minds as to the accuracy of the historical-cost earnings number. This is ironic because, as indicated in the excerpt from Weyerhaeuser's 1995 Annual Report, the "balance sheet effect" of the CCA model is generally positive since it enables companies to reflect the higher current values of

EXHIBIT 4-5 Current-Cost (Replacement-Cost) Relationships and Formulae

Income Statement

Historical Cost Model

Revenues

– Expenses (*Historical Cost*)

   Net Operating Income

Replacement Cost Model

Revenues

– Expenses (*Replacement Cost*)

   Net Operating Income

+ Realized Holding Gains/Losses

+ Change in Unrealized Holding Gains/Losses

   Net Income

Balance Sheet

Historical Cost Model

Assets (*historical cost*) = Liabilities + Owners' Equity

Replacement Cost Model

Assets (*replacement cost*) = Liabilities + Owners' Equity + Change in Unrealized Holding Gains/Losses

Realized Holding Gains/Losses

Merchandise: COGS (*replacement cost*) - COGS (*historical cost*)

Fixed assets: Depreciation expense (*replacement cost*) - Depreciation expense (*historical cost*)

Unrealized Holding Gains/Losses

Merchandise: Inventory (*replacement cost*) - Inventory (*historical cost*)

Fixed assets: Book Value (*replacement cost*) - Book Value (*historical cost*)

their fixed assets. The attitude of financial statement preparers to the CCA model is further evidence of the dominance of the "income statement effect" in most equity-oriented capital markets.

ACCOUNTING FOR GOODWILL AND INTANGIBLE ASSETS

The growth of the service sector and information technology-related businesses, along with the dramatic increase in the number and size of recent mergers and acquisitions, has made accounting for goodwill and other intangible assets such as brands, trademarks, patents, and research and development very significant. As evidenced by the emergence of software companies such as Microsoft and Oracle in the 1980s and internet companies such as AOL, Amazon, and Yahoo! in the 1990s, it is frequently the case that the intangible assets of companies are valued considerably higher than their tangible assets. According to one estimate, the annual U.S. investment in intangible assets in the late 1990s was roughly US$1.0 trillion, almost equal to the US$1.2 trillion total investment in physical assets.[2] In August 1999, Cisco Systems agreed to acquire networking startup Cerent Corp. for US$6.9 billion in stock. At the time of its acquisition, Cerent had only generated $10 million sales in two and a half years and it had never made a profit.[3] While subsequent events have shown that the valuations

---

[2] See "Intangibles at a Crossroads: What's Next?" by B. Lev, *Financial Executive*, [March/April 2002, pp. 35–39.]

[3] See "Cisco to Acquire Networking Firm Cerent: Deal for $6.9 Billion in Stock Reflects Power of Web over Firms' Valuations," *Wall Street Journal*, [August 26, 1999, pp. A3, A10].

attached to some of these firms were speculative and based on "irrational exuberance," it does not detract from the fact that business entities invest huge amounts in intangible assets such as brands, intellectual property, business processes and software, and employee training.

Accounting for goodwill and intangibles is subjective and complex by virtue of the fact that there are various ways by which they come about. Goodwill can be purchased externally or generated internally, intangibles can be identifiable or unidentifiable, and both goodwill and intangibles can have determinate or indeterminate lives. Historically, there has been a divergence of practices used to account globally for goodwill and intangibles. While this diversity mattered less in the past because these items were relatively small in value, standard-setters, preparers, and users of financial statements are beginning to recognize the need to devise comparable accounting methods for goodwill and intangibles as they become a more significant component in corporate financial statements worldwide.

Goodwill

While the precise definition and nature of goodwill might be elusive, it is generally considered to be the excess of the value of an ongoing business over the value of the individual identifiable net assets of the business. It includes non-quantifiable factors such as management, reputation for quality and/or service, and customer or employee loyalty. Goodwill is the intangible that is supposed to enable a business to generate a higher rate of return than could be earned by the tangible assets alone. Purchased goodwill is measured as the difference between the total price paid for an acquired business and the fair value of its net identifiable assets (i.e., identifiable assets minus liabilities). When the former exceeds the latter, there is positive goodwill, which is the typical case. However, when the fair value of the company's net identifiable assets is more than the purchase price, then the acquired business is deemed to have negative goodwill. Negative goodwill might result from a bargain purchase or a negative image of a company's products, management, or prospects.

There are two main questions related to accounting for goodwill. First, should it be recognized as an asset on a corporate balance sheet? Second, should recognized goodwill be systematically amortized? The first question is answered conceptually by determining whether the goodwill in question will generate future economic benefits for its owners and whether its historic cost can be reliably computed. On this question, there is general agreement that purchased goodwill meets the criteria for asset recognition while internally generated goodwill does not. The willingness of the buyer to pay a price in excess of the fair value of the net identifiable assets is regarded as evidence of the expectation of future economic benefits, and it also provides a reasonable historical cost measure of the goodwill amount.

However, there has been considerable international debate on the question of whether purchased goodwill should be systematically amortized. Proponents of amortization argue that the goodwill purchased at the time of acquisition has a finite life and will likely erode over time as conditions change. The goodwill elements of the purchase price of a business are "used up" over time as the excess profits are earned and, therefore, should be charged against those profits. Proponents of amortization also argue that, over time, even if the total goodwill does not diminish, the purchased goodwill is replaced by internally generated goodwill that does not meet recognition criteria and, therefore, does not belong in the balance sheet. Opponents of amortization, on the other hand, argue that goodwill has an infinite life that can be maintained and even enhanced over time. Since maintaining goodwill requires outlays on advertising, employee training, and product development, opponents of amortization argue that adding amortization as an expense would result in a double hit against future earnings. Goodwill amortization is also criticized on the grounds that it is inherently arbitrary, with no clear measure of its decline or of the appropriate period of amortization. This can lead to financial statements that do not faithfully represent the economic value of goodwill in the balance sheet or its true impact on earnings in the income statement. Opponents of amortization contend that the only reason to charge a write-down of goodwill against earnings is when there is evidence of a permanent impairment in the value of goodwill.

In the United States, the amortization of goodwill had been required since 1970 [APB No. 17, 1970], with a maximum amortization period of 40 years. However, in June 2001, the FASB issued SFAS No. 142 which addresses financial accounting and reporting for acquired goodwill and other intangible assets. Intangible assets that are obtained in an acquisition should be recognized and, if necessary, amortized. It also requires that goodwill and intangible assets with indefinite useful lives not be amortized, but rather tested at least annually for impairment using a fair-value-based test. Companies are required to write down goodwill when there is a discernible impairment in its value. Intangible assets that have finite useful lives are to be amortized over their useful lives. In addition, SFAS No. 142 expands the disclosure requirements about goodwill and other intangible assets in the years subsequent to their acquisition.

The Canadian AcSB, which worked with the FASB on this project, similarly revised its standards to bring them in convergence with those of the United States. The newly restructured International Accounting Standards Board has a project on its agenda to eliminate goodwill amortization. The goodwill impairment approach presents a number of challenges. First, it is necessary to separate goodwill from other intangible assets to ensure representational faithfulness in applying the impairment test. Second, it is very difficult to keep track of goodwill from an acquisition, subsequent to the acquisition, since companies are likely to integrate acquired businesses with other parts of their existing operations. Third, the benefits arising from goodwill occur when the assets of a business work together and, since goodwill does not generate its own revenues and cash flows, it cannot be measured in isolation.[4]

Brands, Patents, and Trademarks

Intangible assets can be classified into three categories for accounting purposes: 1) unidentifiable, 2) acquired identifiable, and 3) internally generated identifiable. Unidentifiable intangible assets are typically included in goodwill since they cannot be separated from goodwill. Acquired identifiable intangibles such as patents, licenses, and trademarks (akin to purchased goodwill) generally meet asset recognition criteria since they are acquired presumably because they have future earnings potential. There is also a clear acquisition price. When patents, licenses, and trademarks are internally generated, it is generally possible to identify and capitalize directly related outlays such as legal fees and registration costs. However, these expenditures generally represent only a very small fraction of the true worth of the asset. Other internally gener-

---

[4]See "An International Bugbear," by M. Jones and H. Mellet, *Accountancy International*, [May 1999, pp. 76–77] for a numerical example comparing the effects of different goodwill methods under various national and international standards and "Tale of Two Standards," by T. Johnson and K. Petrone, for a discussion of SFAS 141 and 142.

EXHIBIT 4-6 World's Most Valuable Corporate Brands

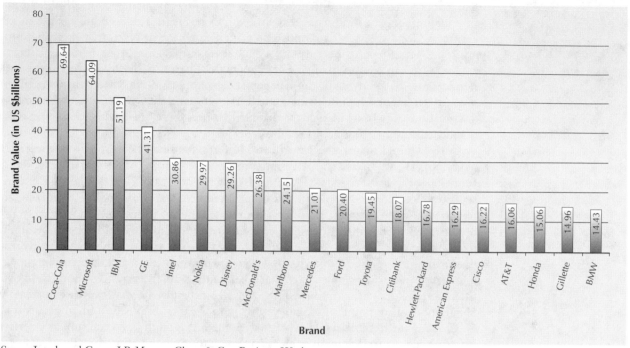

Source: Interbrand Corp., J.P. Morgan Chase & Co., Business Week

ated identifiable intangible assets such as brands are controversial from an accounting standpoint and have resulted in different treatments globally. For example, valuable brands such as Coca-Cola, IBM, or Mercedes were created over decades and it is difficult to arrive at the cost of generating these assets internally. Yet, as indicated in Exhibit 4-6, a recent study estimated that these brands were worth billions of dollars, in several cases more than the tangible assets of these companies.

The amortization of recognized identifiable intangible assets requires the assessment of their remaining useful lives. Where this is clear—as in the case of patents, licenses, and copyrights—there is little argument as to the need to systematically amortize recognized asset balances over their remaining economic or legal life (whichever is shorter). However, when the remaining life of the intangible asset is indeterminate, as in the case of brands, then the arguments for and against amortization are very similar to those for goodwill. Proponents of amortization argue that the matching concept requires that, as the benefits expected from the acquisition of the brand are earned, the asset should be amortized. Opponents of amortization argue that the brand has an indeterminate life and that any amortization is arbitrary. They also argue that since there are costs to maintaining a brand, adding amortization would result in a double count of expenses related to the brand.

There has been considerable debate on the accounting treatment of brands in the United Kingdom and Australia. In the United Kingdom, a number of companies reported internally generated brands as an asset on the balance sheet based on the EU's Fourth Directive which allowed intangibles to be included at their current cost. For certain retail and service companies, this had the effect of substantially improving the financial position and net worth reflected in their balance sheet. The accounting standard-setters in the United Kingdom frowned on this treatment and issued various exposure drafts to prohibit the recognition of internally generated intangibles and to discourage the separate recognition of brand names acquired in a merger or acquisition. In its new standard, the ASB will require similar treatment for the amortization of intangible assets and goodwill. In Australia, there is considerable diversity in accounting for brands. Many companies recognize internally generated brands as assets and often do not even amortize them, arguing that they do not have finite lives and, in fact, appreciate in value. The United States has the most conservative accounting treatment related to the recognition of internally generated intangible assets, including brands. APB No. 17 only permits recognition of assets if the costs are capable of specific identification, assets have determinate lives, and the asset is separable from the continuing business. Consequently, very few internally generated assets ever qualify for recognition under U.S. GAAP. This is rather ironic given that the United States had, by far, the largest number of companies on the list of the most valuable global brands (Exhibit 4-6).

The IASC requires that intangible assets be recorded at their fair values where measurable. IAS No. 38, "Intangible Assets," specifies the criteria under which an outlay can be treated as an intangible asset or must be written off as an expense in the income statement. The rule on the initial recognition and measurement of intangibles under IAS No. 38 comes in two parts: 1) An intangible asset must have the characteristics of an asset in that it must be a resource that the owner controls as a result of past events, and there must be a reasonable expectation of earning future economic benefits from it; 2) An intangible asset can only be recognized if it is probable that it will generate future economic benefits to the owner and the assets can be reliably measured. This rule precludes the recognition of internally generated intangibles as assets.

IAS No. 38 permits two possible treatments for intangibles after they meet the initial recognition criteria. The preferred treatment is to carry the intangible asset at cost, less any reduction due to amortization or impairment. The allowed alternative treatment is to revalue the intangible asset at its fair value, less any subsequent amortization or impairment. Revaluation is only permitted if there is an active market from which to determine the fair value of the asset. IAS No. 38 imposes a rebuttable presumption that the useful life of the intangible asset is 20 years or less. Finally, IAS No. 38 requires companies to undertake annual impairment reviews of intangible assets that have not yet come into use, and those that are in use but are being amortized over more than 20 years.[5]

Research and Development

This is an area of economic activity that is of increasing importance, especially in industries such as pharmaceuticals. The main issue from the accounting perspective is whether to capitalize or expense research and development (R&D) costs as they are incurred. Since the accounting requirements in various countries often distinguish between "research" and "development" activity, it is useful to understand these terms. Research is the activity that is aimed at inventing or creating a new product, method, or system. Development is the activity that converts the result of research into a marketable product.

Accounting for R&D varies across countries. The United States requires that all R&D outlays be expensed when they are incurred because of the inherent uncertainty of the future economic benefits. In the United Kingdom, research expenditures are

---

[5]See "Accounting for the Intangible" by K. Cearns, *Accountancy International*, [July 1999, pp. 82–83] for a detailed discussion of IAS No. 38.

immediately written off against earnings, whereas development costs may be capitalized if they meet certain asset recognition criteria. Deferred development costs must be reviewed each period and be expensed immediately if they no longer meet the asset recognition criteria. In France, research and development outlays may be treated as an asset. Basic research is never reported as an asset but applied research can be treated like development expenditure. In Germany, R&D costs are expensed as incurred unless they are for a specific product and can be related to the start of that product's manufacturing process. Under Dutch law, research and development costs may be treated as an asset if certain conditions are met. Swedish GAAP allows R&D costs to be capitalized and amortized over a five-year period. However, there is a move to expense R&D unless there is clear evidence of future economic benefits from the R&D. In Australia, deferral of R&D costs is allowed only where recovery is probable beyond a reasonable doubt. In Canada, research costs are expensed immediately; development costs can be deferred only if they meet specific criteria. Japan's Commercial Code allows R&D to be amortized over a five-year period; however, immediate expensing is the dominant practice. Brazil is rather liberal in its accounting for R&D, allowing companies to choose to expense or capitalize R&D. Expenditures for new products are typically capitalized when they are material, while expenditures on existing products are expensed. When R&D is capitalized, the company is required to disclose the type and amount of capitalized outlays along with the method and period of amortization. In 1998, the IASC issued IAS No. 38, which addresses accounting for R&D. This standard requires that research costs be expensed immediately and that development costs also be expensed as incurred unless they meet asset recognition criteria. These include the determination of the technical feasibility of the product, the identification of the costs incurred, the probability of an external market or internal use, the ability of the entity to develop the product, and the realistic expectation that there will be sufficient future revenues to cover costs. Under IAS 38, the amount of R&D expenses for the period must be disclosed. If development costs are capitalized, the company must disclose the amortization method and rates used, and provide a reconciliation between the beginning and ending balances of unamortized development costs.

GEOGRAPHIC SEGMENT REPORTING

Over the past three decades, the emergence of large, diversified, transnational companies has prompted national accounting standard-setting bodies and global organizations concerned with financial reporting to address the topic of geographic segment disclosures. As the global activities of such firms have grown, various stakeholders have demanded information disaggregated by geographic segments.

There are several reasons why geographic segment disclosures might be valuable. First, they provide more information on future corporate performance. In a fully integrated market with no restrictions on the flow of capital or physical assets, corporate earnings ought to be valued uniformly regardless of where they are earned. In reality, however, countries erect barriers that affect the mobility of capital and assets. Thus, although earnings increase the net assets of a firm, if these increases are restricted to a geographical area, their availability for subsequent distribution as dividends or reinvestment in countries other than where they were earned may be subject to varying degrees of uncertainty in different countries. If so, different geographical compositions of earnings ought to be valued differently by the stock market.

Further, geographic segment disclosures facilitate investigations of the appropriate economic boundaries of multinational firms. If financial and asset markets are totally integrated and efficient, there is little reason to believe that economic boundaries would be influenced by geographic (political) boundaries. On the other hand, if a firm has location-specific advantages (or disadvantages) such as access (or lack of access) to low cost raw materials and labor, or markets for its products, and significant cost of fixed asset relocation, one could argue that geographic boundaries determine economic boundaries. If so, the financial operations of geographic segments should be assessed and valued by the market before income aggregation.[6] An important step in examining whether equity valuations of firms are affected by geographical segment disclosures is to see if the earnings within a geographical segment behave as if they belong to an independent economic unit. If they do, then forecasting geographical segment earnings and subsequently translating and aggregating these earnings makes more sense than translating and consolidating before forecasting. Finally, firms may have different permanent and transitory components of earnings in different geographical segments because of differing economic prospects.

Research Evidence on Geographic Segment Reporting

Much empirical research on geographic segment disclosures focuses on the usefulness of geographic data in estimating expected returns. One group of studies investigates the effects of geographic disclosure on investors' assessments of expected returns.[7] Another analyzes stock market reactions to geographic data,[8] and a third group studies the effects of geographic data on investors' assessment of risk.[9] There have also been studies that surveyed the practice of international geographic segment disclosure.[10]

Roberts [1989] addresses the question of whether geographically disaggregated sales and earnings data can enhance the ability of earnings forecasts models to predict future consolidated earnings, compared to models that use historical consolidated data only. She finds that models based upon geographic data outperform other models, and that forecast models using segment sales data were generally more accurate than models incorporating segment earnings. Balakrishnan, Harris, and Sen [1990] find also that relative to consolidated data alone, geographic data can improve the accuracy of earnings forecasts and, to a lesser extent, revenues forecasts. Their results suggest that earnings forecasts should be revised as macroeconomic factors (e.g., currency exchange rates, GNP growth rates) change.

Senteney and Bazaz [1992] find a reduction in the unexpected security price revisions associated with unexpected earnings subsequent to implementation of SFAS No. 14 geographic segment disclosures. They regard this as evidence that SFAS No. 14 meets the predictive ability criterion set by SFAC No. 1 and provides investors with important price-relevant information not available from other sources. Ahadiat [1993] found that geographically segmented earnings improve the accuracy of predictions and that the predictive ability of foreign earnings is improved with more

---

[6]See Saudagaran [1993].

[7]See Roberts [1989]; Balakrishnan, Harris, and Sen [1990]; Senteney and Bazaz [1992]; Ahadiat [1993]; and Nichols, Tunnell, and Seipel [1995].

[8]See Senteney [1990]; and Boatsman, Behn, and Patz [1993].

[9]See Prodhan [1986]; Prodhan and Harris [1989]; and Doupnik and Rolfe [1989, 1990].

[10]See Tonkin [1989]; and Van Offeren [1989].

disaggregation. Nichols, Tunnell, and Seipel [1995] found that, post-SFAS No. 14, financial analysts' forecasts of earnings did become more accurate after adjustment for earnings variability. Two stock-pricing studies, Senteney [1990] and Boatsman, Behn, and Patz [1993], find that aggregate market revisions of expected returns are associated with the disclosure of geographic data. Both studies provide evidence that geographic segment data affect stock prices.

Practical ways of improving segment disclosure might include narrowing segment definition and increasing the extent and frequency of disclosure. Narrower geographic segments are relatively inexpensive to provide (in terms of record-keeping costs) and are likely to be perceived as more useful than the existing disclosure, which permits companies a great deal of discretion in defining segments. Users have also been asking for quarterly disclosure of geographic data. There is some evidence to suggest that quarterly segment data improve analysts' forecasts and reduce return variability.[11] One study found that analysts' published earnings forecasts generally were more accurate for the providers of quarterly segment data than for the non-providers. Stock return variability surrounding earnings announcements dates was lower for the providers during the year of initial disclosure of quarterly segment data than during the preceding year.

Over the years, a number of survey studies have compared segment reporting practices across countries. While the level of geographic segment disclosure has varied between the countries studied, there is a broad consensus that geographic segment disclosure in the various countries is inadequate. In evaluating the quality and usefulness of geographic disclosure, the question generally is how bad—rather than how good—the disclosures are.

Some samples of geographic disclosure are presented in Exhibits 4-7 to 4-11. These exhibits demonstrate the wide range in the level of transparency present in corporate geographic segment disclosure. Moving from least disclosure to most, in Exhibit 4-7, Gillette uses just two segments for its net sales (i.e., U.S. and foreign),

EXHIBIT 4-7   Gillette 2001 Geographic Segment Disclosure

Net Assets

Years ended December 31, (millions)	2001	2000	1999
Foreign	$5,204	$5,510	$5,509
United States	3,757	3,715	3,565
	$8,961	$9,225	$9,074

Long-lived assets

At December 31, (millions)	2001	2000	1999
Germany	$ 508	$ 519	$ 546
Other Foreign	1,013	1,145	1,178
Total Foreign	1,521	1,664	1,724
United States	2,027	1,886	1,743
	$3,548	$3,550	$3,467

[11]See Fried, Schiff, and Sondhi [1992].

EXHIBIT 4-8 Ford Motor 2000 Geographic Segment Disclosure

	Geographic Areas			Total Company
	United States	Europe	All Other	
2000				
External revenues	$118,373	$ 32,132	$ 19,559	$170,064
Income from continuing operations	6,009	(862)	263	5,410
Net property	25,930	13,614	6,260	45,804
1999				
External revenues	$111,423	$ 32,709	$ 16,526	$160,658
Income from continuing operations	6,008	376	118	6,502
Net property	24,146	13,098	6,719	43,963
1998				
External revenues	$ 99,879	$ 26,795	$ 16,676	$143,350
Income from continuing operations	20,856	445	67	21,368
Net property	22,266	9,774	6,608	38,648

while in Exhibit 4-8, Ford Motor splits revenues into three segments (i.e., U.S., Europe, and All Other). In Exhibit 4-9, McDonald's provides disclosure where the geographic segments are aggregated mainly by continent. It provides geographic segment disclosure for revenues, operating income, assets, capital expenditures, and depreciation and amortization. If investors use geographic segments to make a probability assessment of the company's future performance, then one must question whether aggregating by continents is helpful since the economic condition of individual countries within the same continent may differ greatly. Companies that provide this type of segment disclosure are essentially trying to comply with the disclosure requirement without divulging what they consider to be proprietary information to their competitors. While users cannot realistically expect a company to provide detailed segment disclosure for every country where it does business, they ought to be able to expect information on the main foreign markets of the company. Exhibit 4-10 provides an example of such disclosure. The Norwegian company, Norsk Hydro, provides geographic segment disclosure on its assets, investments, and operating revenues for over a dozen countries. It provides information on the main countries where it conducts business and aggregates the other countries where it has a less important presence. This is a reasonable level of geographic disclosure in that it enables investors to estimate a company's future performance based on what they know of the economies of countries where the company is doing most of its business. Finally, in Exhibit 4-11, the Swedish company, Esselte, provides geographic segment disclosure on its net sales, capital employed, investment, and depreciation for each of the 28 countries where it does business. This is an example of the most transparent geographic segment disclosure that investors could ask for. The fact that many companies are starting to provide segment disclosure by country suggests that the competitive concerns are not as great as some "low-disclosure" companies make them out to be.

Recent Developments in Geographic Segment Reporting

Organizations representing financial statement users in the United States and abroad [e.g., Association for Investment and Management Research (AIMR) 1991; Robert Morris Associates 1992; British Bankers' Association 1993] have regularly expressed dissatisfaction with the geographical segment disclosures provided by multinational

EXHIBIT 4-9 McDonald's Geographic Segment Disclosure

IN MILLIONS	2000	1999	1998
U.S.	$ 5,259.1	$ 5,093.0	$ 4,868.1
Europe	4,753.9	4,924.9	4,466.7
Asia/Pacific	1,987.0	1,832.3	1,633.2
Latin America	949.3	680.3	814.7
Other	1,293.7	728.8	638.7
Total revenues	$ 14,243.0	$ 13,259.3	$ 12,421.4
U.S.	$ 1,773.1	$ 1,653.3	$ 1,201.4(1)
Europe	1,180.1	1,256.5	1,167.5
Asia/Pacific	441.9	421.9	359.9
Latin America	102.3	133.0	189.2
Other	94.1	117.4	120.3
Corporate	(261.8)	(262.5)	(276.4)
Total operating income	$ 3,329.7	$ 3,319.6	$ 2,761.9(1)
U.S.	$ 7,876.7	$ 7,674.3	$ 7,397.8
Europe	7,083.7	6,966.8	6,932.1
Asia/Pacific	2,789.7	2,828.2	2,659.7
Latin America	1,855.6	1,477.5	1,339.6
Other	1,069.3	979.3	678.7
Corporate	1,008.5	1,057.1	776.5
Total assets	$ 21,683.5	$ 20,983.2	$ 19,784.4
U.S.	$ 468.6	$ 426.4	$ 392.4
Europe	797.6	881.8	870.2
Asia/Pacific	224.4	188.4	224.0
Latin America	245.7	213.2	236.8
Other	161.2	112.3	102.8
Corporate	47.6	45.7	53.1
Total capital expenditures	$ 1,945.1	$ 1,867.8	$ 1,879.3
U.S.	$ 417.6	$ 399.7	$ 375.9
Europe	296.5	305.2	268.0
Asia/Pacific	120.5	114.9	97.3
Latin America	69.4	45.5	42.9
Other	60.8	46.2	40.6
Corporate	45.9	44.8	56.4
Total depreciation and amortization	$ 1,010.7	$ 956.3	$ 881.1

(1) Includes $161.6 million of Made For Your costs and the $160.0 million special charge related to the home office productivity initiative.

companies. Groups such as the AIMR (formerly the Financial Analysts Federation) and Robert Morris Associates have repeatedly lobbied the SEC and the FASB for more disaggregated geographical disclosures. One AIMR report described the general level of segment information reporting in U.S. annual reports as "inconsistent, jumbled, or meaningless" [Pacter 1993, p. 73].

EXHIBIT 4-10 Norsk Hydro 2000 Geographic Segment Disclosure

Amounts in NOK million	Assets		Long-lived assets		Investments		Operating revenues		
	2000	1999	2000	1999	2000	1999	2000	1999	1998
Europe:									
Norway	113,375	101,406	79,931	85,307	8,080	42,180	14,238	10,745	9,058
EU:									
Great Britain	6,754	12,308	2,114	7,132	464	5,697	19,311	12,063	10,658
Germany	3,121	3,022	1,258	1,321	63	237	18,503	11,572	11,900
France	9,260	9,277	1,595	1,764	122	402	16,538	11,104	9,809
Sweden	7,364	8,434	1,985	1,981	246	223	13,494	10,024	9,558
Denmark	8,391	7,427	3,054	2,883	651	568	7,256	6,729	6,614
Italy	3,125	2,715	790	583	120	151	6,562	5,624	6,071
Spain	732	390	160	76	89	12	3,751	2,693	2,408
The Netherlands	6,612	4,134	2,093	1,307	1,113	108	3,163	2,533	2,894
Other	4,671	4,417	588	1,022	111	268	8,139	6,015	6,377
Total EU	50,030	52,124	13,637	18,069	2,989	7,666	96,717	68,357	66,289
Switzerland							5,550	3,792	2,887
Other Europe	885	1,184	258	305	37	93	5,434	4,056	4,524
Total Europe	164,290	154,714	93,826	103,681	11,106	49,939	121,939	86,950	82,758
Outside Europe:									
USA	8,137	4,042	2,179	1,536	1,678	175	16,849	11,721	9,990
Asia	4,386	3,035	2,266	1,734	456	427	7,377	5,854	5,723
Other Americas	5,785	3,346	2,742	1,280	1,334	104	5,099	3,330	3,210
Africa	4,164	3,775	2,484	1,752	881	1,218	3,811	2,204	2,418
Canada	9,454	8,387	7,446	6,220	1,078	1,085	1,231	1,520	1,295
Australia and New Zealand	138	120	105	83	32	77	555	376	390
Total outside Europe	32,064	22,705	17,222	12,605	5,459	3,086	34,922	25,005	23.026
Total	196,354	177,419	111,048	116,286	16,565	53,025	156,861	111,955	105,784

In an apparent response to the persistent criticism by user groups, several standard-setting organizations have revisited the subject of reporting financial information by segment. Recently, the International Accounting Standards Committee (IASC), the Accounting Standards Board (AcSB) of the Canadian Institute of Chartered Accountants, and the United States Financial Accounting Standards Board (FASB) have all developed new financial reporting standards on this subject. The IASC's revised standard on segment reporting (revised IAS No. 14), which became effective on July 1, 1998, takes the "risks and rewards approach." Under this IAS, business segments are identified based on differences in risks and rewards among either products/services or geographical areas. The United States and Canada worked jointly to revise their existing segment reporting standards and issued exposure drafts in January 1996. The FASB's Statement of Financial Accounting Standards No. 131, "Disclosures about Segments of an Enterprise and Related Information" (which supersedes SFAS No. 14, the previous standard on segment reporting), became effective on December 15, 1997. It adopts the "management approach," requiring that segments be determined based entirely on the way that management disaggregates the enterprise for making internal operating decisions. IASC has worked closely with the North American standard-setters in the area of segment reporting and views the two standards as being quite similar. Both look to a company's organization structure and internal reporting

EXHIBIT 4-11 Esselte 2000 Geographic Segment Disclosure

Information by Country

SEK millions	Net Sales 2000	Net Sales 1999	Capital Employed 2000	Capital Employed 1999	Capital Investment 2000	Capital Investment 1999	Cost Depreciation 2000	Cost Depreciation 1999
Europe								
Germany	1,910	2,134	2,400	2,560	45	79	219	236
France	628	793	312	237	4	24	19	32
UK	570	730	122	272	43	106	47	184
Belgium	417	422	323	309	32	37	27	49
Netherlands	414	413	52	43	1	1	2	1
Italy	384	397	135	125	4	18	7	6
Sweden	347	419	92	22	1	5	4	9
Denmark	337	362	172	179	13	7	13	15
Spain	295	303	107	108	8	5	8	10
Norway	219	240	40	27	1	1	1	1
Turkey	172	144	112	88	3	4	5	5
Poland	153	121	214	174	16	39	11	9
Austria	145	146	11	8	1	1	1	8
Finland	109	119	24	12	1	1	2	3
Hungary	51	44	12	10	1	1		
Portugal	44	26	9	5	1			
Czech Republic	36	25	7	5	1	1	1	1
Russia	13		5		1			
Europe	**6,244**	6,838	**4,149**	4,184	**177**	330	**367**	569
Americas								
USA	3,928	3,431	1,173	1,040	84	60	92	130
Canada	408	345	−7	68	1	5	3	3
Mexico	85	60	18	26	1	1	1	1
Brazil	12	24	2	−3				
Americas	**4,433**	3,860	**1,186**	1,131	**86**	66	**96**	134
Asia/Pacific Rim								
Australia	256	297	81	116	1	2	6	7
China/Hong Kong	87	71	52	55	1		3	3
New Zealand	55	58	22	23		1	1	2
Singapore	20	17	7	5				
Japan	–	50	−4	−2				1
Malaysia	–	1	−1	−1				
Asia/Pacific Rim	**418**	494	**157**	196	**2**	3	**10**	13
Total	**11,095**	11,192	**5,492**	5,511	**265**	399	**473**	716

system in order to identify its reportable business and geographic segments. Both call for primary and secondary bases of segmentation, with considerably less disclosure required for secondary segments. Both standards only apply to publicly traded companies. While the required disclosures for primary and secondary segments in the international and North American standards are similar, there remain significant differences between the two standards that are the result of slightly different objectives.

First, the FASB standard uses the management approach without modification, while the international standard accepts the internal financial reporting system as a starting point for determining reportable segments but only as long as it provides useful information. Analysts remain concerned about situations in which an irrational management structure groups disparate units together. While this fact may itself be useful information, the price it exacts (in its lack of useful segment data) is too high. Second, the international standard defines reportable segments using sales to external customers only, while the FASB standard considers sales to all segments. Users have expressed preference for the FASB approach on this aspect because it better illuminates the operations of vertically integrated organizations when an entity is managed that way. The international standard does not require such disclosure. Since most companies are unwilling to disclose the separable results of vertically integrated operations if given a choice, this is another area where the reporting between the two standards is likely to differ significantly. Third, the IASC requires that all segment data be reported using IASC GAAP; the FASB rule permits the use of segment data from the internal reporting system and explicitly states that the segment reporting need not be in accordance with domestic accounting principles (i.e., U.S. GAAP for U.S. companies). A related difference is that the FASB only requires disclosure of data already available in the internal financial reporting system, whereas the international standard has specific minimum reporting requirements. In its response to the FASB Exposure Draft, AIMR argued that disclosure ought to be driven at least as much by the investor needs as by management choice since past experience demonstrates that managements are not infallible judges of the usefulness of financial data. AIMR points out that many firms chose not to account for (and manage) such important areas as post-retirement health care, foreign currency effects, and leases until they were required to do so by accounting standards.

The response of financial statement users, research evidence, and recent developments at the AcSB, FASB, and the IASC suggest that the highly aggregated geographical segment disclosures currently provided are not as useful as the more finely disaggregated and more frequent information that is presently provided voluntarily by a small fraction of firms with foreign operations. There is some doubt as to whether the new standards on segment reporting as set out by the AcSB, FASB, and IASC are likely to result in relevant and meaningful geographic segment disclosure for users. The discretion permitted management could once again result in segments that are vague and lack comparability across firms. In fact, there is some early anecdotal evidence to suggest that the disclosure emerging from the new standards on geographical segments is not necessarily an improvement.[12] This is borne out by the highly aggregated disclosures provided by a sample of U.S. multinational companies such as Gillette, Ford Motor, and McDonald's. Users had hoped that the standard-setters would require companies to define the country as the unit of analysis with reasonable materiality thresholds which allowed for regional segments where a company does substantial business in a region but where no single country meets the materiality threshold. However, under the new standards, it is unlikely that financial statements users will receive the level of disaggregated geographic segment information that they consider essential for their investment decisions from either the FASB/AcSB or the IASC standards.

---

[12]See "A New Era of Segment Reporting" by S. Gray, D. Street, and N. Nichols, *Accountancy International*, [April 1999, pp. 76–78].

ENVIRONMENTAL AND SOCIAL DISCLOSURES

This section focuses on corporate disclosures that are likely to be of interest to a wide range of stakeholders in a company including investors, employees, customers, environmentalists, government agencies, labor organizations, and the public at large. This section considers three types of corporate disclosures: 1) environmental disclosures, 2) employee disclosures, and 3) value-added statements.

Environmental Disclosures

Environmental disclosure is no longer just for environmentalists. Increasing public consciousness, high-profile environmental disasters, and strict government regulations in a number of countries have resulted in a growing demand for corporate environmental reporting. Environmental disclosures vary between countries based on a combination of the strength of government environmental regulations and the level of enforcement of these regulations, as well as societal pressures on corporations. The motivations for a company to provide environmental disclosure include an attempt to present itself as a good corporate citizen, particularly in light of the increasing number of socially conscious investors; to garner positive attention from the media; and to demonstrate compliance with existing environmental laws. Critics often complain that most corporate environmental disclosure is predominantly a public relations exercise by companies and contains little substance. However, as various constituents, including investors, demand greater disclosure of companies' environmental impact and any resulting liabilities, companies will have to take this aspect of financial disclosure more seriously. Indeed, there is evidence that a number of companies are already beginning to do just that.[13]

Though environmental concerns have been heightened in recent years, partly due to high-profile disasters such as the Union Carbide chemical leak in Bhopal, India, and the Exxon Valdez oil spill in Alaska, very few countries have specific financial reporting requirements on environmental disclosure. We will focus on the United States in this discussion because it probably has the strictest environmental regulations and the situation in the United States may serve as a precursor of developments on environmental issues in other countries.[14] The major piece of environmental legislation in the United States is the Comprehensive Environmental Response, Compensation, and Liability Act (CERCLA) of 1980, also popularly referred to as the Superfund law. The passage of the Superfund law made environmental disclosure relevant to investors because of the magnitude of liability that a company doing business in the United States might face under this law. The financial reporting issues are significant because estimates of clean-up costs of the sites identified by the U.S. Environmental Protection Agency (EPA), which enforces CERCLA, range as high as $500 to $750 billion. This clean-up estimate does not include liabilities that companies might face under other U.S. federal, state, or local environmental laws. The EPA has identified hundreds of companies as potentially responsible parties (PRPs) under the Superfund law. The PRPs are jointly and severally liable for response and remediation costs, for damage to natural resources, and health assessment and monitoring costs. The law is retroactive, in that the liability is imposed after the fact, for actions that

---

[13]See Beets and Souther [1999].

[14]In many European countries, the sea is a preferred dumping spot. This might explain the absence of a Superfund-type law in European countries.

may not have violated the law at the time that the damage to the environment occurred. Under joint and several liability, any PRP can be held liable by the EPA for the full clean-up cost with the possibility of suing other PRPs subsequently for their share of the clean-up costs. Given the huge amount of potential liability faced by large numbers of U.S. corporations, an important issue for investors is whether the existing financial reporting requirements are sufficiently unambiguous to force companies to provide full disclosure of their obligations for environmental clean-ups.

The main accounting rules for recognizing liabilities which apply to companies, identified as PRPs under the Superfund law, are contained in Statement of Financial Accounting Standards (SFAS) No. 5, "Accounting for Contingent Liabilities," SFAS Interpretation No. 14, and SEC disclosure requirements. SFAS No. 5 requires that a loss contingency must be accrued by a charge to income if it is probable that an asset has been impaired or a liability has been incurred and the amount of loss can be reasonably estimated. SFAS No. 5 requires footnote disclosure of the contingency if the loss is both possible and can be reasonably estimated. SFAS Interpretation No. 14 provides that if there is a range of estimates of the loss and if all estimates in a range are equally likely, then the minimum loss should be recognized. There are three items under the SEC's Regulation S-K that may affect environmental disclosures. Item 101 requires disclosure of material effects of compliance with federal, state, and local environmental laws on capital expenditures, earnings, and competitive position. Item 103 requires disclosure of pending legal proceedings arising under environmental laws if they involve potential monetary sanction. Item 303 requires inclusion in the Management Discussion and Analysis section, and disclosure of any known trends, demands, commitments, events, or uncertainties that may have a material effect on the company's liquidity or capital resources.

There are a number of issues that affect the reasonable estimation of clean-up costs and thus the nature of compliance with SFAS No. 5. Even after a company is identified by the Environmental Protection Agency as a PRP on a Superfund site, it can claim that it is unable to reasonably estimate its liability for any or all of three reasons: 1) that the total clean-up cost of the site is in question, 2) that its share of the total clean-up cost is in dispute, and 3) that the amount of insurance recovery of its share of the clean-up cost is indeterminate. A Price Waterhouse survey (1992) found a wide range of treatments of Superfund law liability by U.S. companies. Fifty-six percent of respondents indicated that they often accrued a liability upon internal discovery of a problem site; 22 percent accrued upon notification by regulatory authorities; 16 percent when they consented to conduct a Remedial Investigation and Feasibility Study (RIFS); 80 percent said they often accrue during or at completion of an RIFS; and 20 percent only accrue at the point when they make a settlement offer. In the same Price Waterhouse survey, 80 percent of respondents indicated that they consider insurance recoveries in recording their liability, and only 13 percent recorded liabilities gross of potential insurance recoveries.

The situation in the United States should make it clear that environmental disclosures are important to investors because they can include very significant liabilities. Disclosures on liabilities under the U.S. Superfund law also indicate that there is a wide divergence in disclosure practices, therefore the comparability of financial statements is in question. While many countries may not currently have strict environmental laws such as those in the United States, it is entirely possible that they may adopt such laws in the future. Given that such legislation can be retroactive, prudent investors need environmental disclosures to make informed economic choices regardless of the location and nationality of the company.

A number of countries have taken other approaches to environmental disclosure. In 1994, France revised its laws to make companies accountable for polluting their surrounding communities. The law contains provisions that deal with "environmental terrorism" including deliberate pollution. Norway requires the inclusion of environmental disclosure in the directors' report. Its regulations require that companies disclose whether the business pollutes the external environment and the measures that have been implemented or are planned to address the problem. Environmental disclosure practices in Norway range from brief statements indicating compliance with the laws, to separate environmental reports that are often as long as the annual report. In Japan, the Keidanren—an influential business roundtable that includes the largest corporations—has issued a Global Environment Charter. It calls for companies to provide disclosure on their recycling programs and on the proper use and disposal of their products. Given the global presence of many Japanese companies, it calls on companies to be environmentally sensitive both at home and abroad. All companies listed on the Australian Stock Exchange must prepare an annual directors' report that includes detailed information about compliance with environmental laws.

A number of multilateral organizations have also expressed concern for environmental reporting and sustainable development. The United Nations' Intergovernmental Working Group of Experts on International Standards of Accounting and Reporting (ISAR) has issued a series of detailed recommendations on environmental reporting which go considerably further than present practice. The European Union's (EU) Fifth Action Program on the Environment lays out the EU's policy on environmental protection and sustainable development. The EU is currently working on a detailed set of reporting requirements related to environmental costs.[15] The International Chamber of Commerce (ICC) has initiated the World Industry Council for the Environment (WICE), which has also issued a series of recommendations for environmental disclosure to various constituents. Reflecting its business focus, it appeals to corporate self-interest in advocating environmental disclosure.

A number of professional accounting organizations in European countries have instituted the European Environmental Reporting Awards. The Association of Chartered Certified Accountants (ACCA) in the United Kingdom started this award in 1991. They were joined by the Dutch Koninkiljik Nederlands Institut van Register Accountants (NIVRA) and the Danish Foreningen af Statsautoriserede Revisorer (FSR) in 1995, and the Belgian Institut des Reviseurs d'Enterprises (IRE) in 1997. Professional accounting organizations in a number of other European countries have announced their intent to join this group. Their objective is to identify and recognize innovative examples of corporate environmental reporting. By doing so, the sponsoring bodies seek to popularize and improve environmental reporting practices in Europe. A summary of the criteria used for evaluating environmental reports under this program is presented in Exhibit 4-12.

Companies from the Scandinavian countries typically provide a great deal of environmental disclosure. Many of these companies provide an environmental report separate from the annual report. Selected extracts from the environmental report of MoDo, a Swedish firm in the forest products industry, appear in Exhibits 4-13 and 4-14. As evidenced from these exhibits, MoDo provides very detailed information on its environmental policies, impact, and goals. This type of environmental disclosure is rare in most other parts of the world. Recently, companies have also started to

---

[15]See Piet [1999] for a detailed discussion of environmental reporting initiatives and prospects in Europe.

EXHIBIT 4-12   Summary Criteria for European Environmental Reporting Awards

1 **Disclosure of environmental policies** (or reference to ICC, CEFIC, PERI, Responsible Care Guidelines) and identification of target audience

2 **Evidence of top management commitment / environmental management systems in place** (description of management systems and structure plus reference to environmental audits, reviews, EMAS, ISO, 7750, etc.)

3 **Description (narrative or other format) of impact of core business** (significant environmental impacts)

4 **Factual emissions data (good + bad news)** at global and/or site level

5 **Historical trends in emissions data plus commentary and explanations of trends** at global and/or site level

6 **Performance targets established** (again, global and/or site) preferably quantified so as to be capable of verification

7 **Comparison of actual performance against previously established targets plus explanations of variances**

8 **Financial linkages:** financial statement links via cross-references or by inclusion of environmental data in the full financial statements or summary financial statements themselves (costs, capital expenditures, provisions, long-term liabilities, etc); disclosure of financial/business benefits flowing from environment-related activities

9 **Overall completeness:** nothing significant excluded from the environmental report/application of national standards world-wide

10 **External verification of the environmental statement:** from the auditor or the consultant: should contain details as to auditing standards applied and scope of examination

11 **Eco-efficiency or sustainability:** some discussion of sustainability and the company's attitude toward it; plus, data regarding eco-efficiency

12 **Life cycle, mass balance, eco balance sheet:** alternative methods of communicating the entity's environmental impact and commitments

13 **Computer discs, Internet availability, newsletters, videos, etc.:** Do they add to/detract from/adequately substitute for the overall environmental reporting package?

commission audits of their social (including environmental) performance. An example of such an audit report for Statoil, a Norwegian company, appears in Exhibit 4-15.

Employee Disclosures

Like environmental disclosures, the level of specificity and detail in corporate employee disclosures is a function of business conditions and other societal pressures in countries. Employee disclosure does have a longer history and, until the recent burgeoning interest in environmental disclosure, was the main item of social disclosure in corporate annual reports.

Employee disclosure is not just for unions and other labor organizations. Investors are interested in employee disclosure because how a company treats its employees is likely to impact the quality of its labor relations, which, in turn, is likely to affect its current and future performance. As we transition from the industrial age to the information age, employees become even more important to the success of business entities. Among the specific items of employee disclosure that stakeholders are likely to be interested in are the company's investment in training its workforce; the size, cost, and productivity of its workforce; employee absenteeism and turnover rates; work days lost due to strikes and other labor disputes; and health, safety, and accident statistics.

In the case of multinational companies, host governments also have considerable interest in employee disclosure. Part of this interest stems from a desire to make sure that the employment practices of these companies are consistent with local laws and norms. Part of it is also aimed at being able to compare salaries and wages globally.

EXHIBIT 4-13 MoDo's Environmental Policy

Environmental policy

The environment is the concern of the entire Group. It is essential for the development of MoDo that full account is taken of environmental constraints.

ENVIRONMENTAL PROTECTION. MoDo's business operations shall be managed in a manner which ensures the protection of the environment, the efficient use of raw materials and energy, and the promotion of sustainable development. Our work in this sphere will be guided by a careful assessment of technical feasibility, economic viability and ecological acceptability. This means that our environmental protection measures will be characterised by a holistic approach and will be pursued with the aim of achieving continuous improvements. In order to guarantee sound environmental standards, environmental audits are performed at the individual units within MoDo.

In order to ensure our freedom of action, our aim shall be to comply with environmental legislation and official standards by a safe margin.

Environmental measures involve costs. Effective environmental protection requires healthy profitability. This in turn calls for products which are competitive on international markets.

RESPONSIBILITY. Overall responsibility for the environment is shared by Group management and business area managers together with the Group Board. The primary responsibility for day-to-day environmental activities rests on the managers of our mills and the corresponding managers of other units. When major decisions which influence MoDo's business are to be made on the environment, the mill manager or the corresponding manager shall confer with the Group's Environmental Director.

The allotment of responsibility at each of MoDo's units shall be clearly defined in writing. Our personnel shall exhibit a personal sense of responsibility for the environment in the course of their normal duties, and follow instructions and procedures.

Any risk of breakdowns or disturbances which could influence the environment shall be reported, so that preventive action may be taken. In the event of serious disturbances or breakdowns that could harm the environment, the environment shall be given priority over production.

FORESTRY. MoDo's forests and forestry activities will be managed to ensure a high yield and a sustainable supply of wood, subject to the fullest consideration being given to the needs of the environment. Forestry will be practised in such a way as to protect vital ecological processes. The methods used must ensure biological diversity.

PRODUCTS. Our products shall be harmless to humans and to the environment. Functional and environmental demands shall be considered in an overall perspective.

MoDo shall allow the needs of the market to determine product development.

MARKETING. Marketing with the use of environmental arguments shall be factual and based on a comprehensive approach.

DEVELOPMENT. MoDo shall have a long-term environmental strategy, and keep abreast of the development of environmental requirements within its areas of operation. In connection with investments in new plants, and the modernisation and rebuilding of existing plants, all opportunities shall be taken to combine efficient production with effective environmental protection.

Methods, processes and products which cause a reduced impact on the environment shall be given priority over other comparable alternatives.

The results of research and development shall be used so that measures to protect the environment may be applied to the greatest possible effect.

MoDo shall keep itself fully informed about the environmental impact of the Group's operations, and on measures required to reduce unwanted environmental effects. MoDo shall continue to contribute towards the development of environmental improvements, through its own research and by participating in joint projects.

PURCHASING AND DEMANDS ON SUPPLIERS. Environmental considerations shall be taken into account in connection with the purchase of goods and services. MoDo's environmental requirements shall be satisfied by suppliers.

INFORMATION. Our approach shall be characterised by openness and objectivity. Our personnel, customers and other relevant parties shall be kept comprehensively informed on environmental matters.

Bengt Pettersson,
Bengt Pettersson,
President and CEO

OVERALL ENVIRONMENTAL GOALS

- Naturally occurring plant and animal life shall be given conditions to ensure their long-term survival in the forest landscape.

- The environmental impact of production shall be as low as possible. In connection with investments and rebuilding projects the aim shall be to install equipment which produces a lower overall environmental impact.

- The specific use of resources shall be minimised by the application of the latest scientific research results and by operating as efficiently as possible.

- The quantity of waste shall be reduced by means of sorting at source, recycling and reuse.

- The environmental impact of transport shall be reduced by closer cooperation to improve transport efficiency and by making more stringent demands when purchasing transport services.

- The ISO 14001 environmental management system shall be introduced within all MoDo's units during 1999.

EXHIBIT 4-14 MoDo's Environmental Impact

MoDo's environmental impact

Emissions of environmentally hazardous materials from MoDo's mills have been reduced significantly during the last decades. This process involved several stages, with the initial focus being on local effects, followed by regional effects.

Environmental activities at MoDo's mills started already during the 1960s. Among the first measures taken was to reduce the emissions that had a noticeable effect on the local environment close to the mills. These measures have been successful. The quality of water and the biological life in the water alongside the mills have improved. The difference in comparison with completely unaffected areas is in most cases slight.

The next step was to deal with emissions having regional or national effects.

A broader perspective on the environment

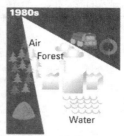

When the forest products industry began to take an interest in the environment at the beginning of the 1970s it focused on water quality, where the problems were most evident. Since then it has gradually broadened into today's holistic perspective.

Emissions of sulphur dioxide and chlorinated organic substances were reduced, for example.

Today, MoDo's environmental activities are also being focused on what might be called our contribution to the global environmental effect. We look at the way we use various raw materials and energy and what effect this has on biodiversity in nature and on the global climate. The presentation on these two pages is based on the ISO 14001 registers at each of MoDo's units. The section entitled "All the Facts" on pages 28-37 presents the most recent figures.

Impact on air

Climate change
The growing amount of carbon dioxide and other greenhouse gases in the atmosphere threatens to endanger the global climate. A higher average temperature could cause significant changes in the direction of winds, sea-currents and rainfall patterns, for instance.

MoDo's impact
Carbon dioxide is formed during incineration and also by the degradation of organic substances. At MoDo, this is primarily a matter of carbon dioxide from boilers and transportation. The carbon dioxide that is released from biofuels is part of nature's carbon cycle and is sufficient to build up an equivalent volume of wood in the forest. In contrast to oil and coal, biofuel does not contribute to the greenhouse effect.

MoDo's measures
MoDo endeavours to use energy as efficiently as possible and to utilise biofuels to the greatest possible extent. It is advantageous that the volume of wood in forests is increasing as this means that they are able to absorb more carbon dioxide.

Ground-level ozone
Ground-level ozone affects human health and plant life, for instance.

MoDo's impact
Ground-level ozone is formed by reactions between volatile organic substances, nitrogen oxides and sunlight. Volatile organic substances are emitted as a result of incomplete combustion in engines, for instance. As the forest industry is a heavy user of transport, MoDo contributes indirectly to such emissions. Emissions from MoDo's mills are low.

MoDo's measures
Numerous measures are being taken to reduce transportation and improve its efficiency. For example, transportation is co-ordinated with the aim of loading ships and trucks as fully as possible. Environmental demands are gradually becoming more stringent in connection with the purchase of transport services.

Ozone-destroying substances
The ozone layer in the atmosphere is broken down by certain substances, such as freons.

MoDo's impact
Leakage of volatile organic substances from refrigerating plants. MoDo's impact is minor.

MoDo's measures
Replacement of cooling agent.

EXHIBIT 4-14 MoDo's Environmental Impact (continued)

Impact on water

Eutrophication and oxygen depletion

Aquatic plant and animal life are adversely affected by the eutrophication and oxygen depletion that occur when nutrients and organic substances leach from the ground or are emitted by communities and mills and factories. Another important cause is that nitrogen oxides that are emitted into air end up in the ground and water from precipitation.

MoDo's impact

Humus and nutrients leach from the forests land. Despite properly closed processes and effective treatment at the mills, some quantities of fibres and dissolved organic substances are emitted together with the effluent. The mills also emit nutrients in the form of various nitrogen and phosphorus compounds. Emissions of nitrogen oxides from mills and transport vehicles also contribute.

MoDo's measures

Harvested areas are re-forested as quickly as possible to prevent leaching of nutrients from the forest land. Protective zones are being created along the shores of lakes and river banks, and more careful methods are being developed for soil scarification.

Mill processes are being closed even further. Wood is being put to efficient use – as a raw material or as a biofuel. Effluent is treated. When biological treatment is used, the dosages of nutrients is minimised. *The measures being taken to reduce the emissions of nitrogen oxide are discussed under "Ground-level ozone" and "Acidification" respectively.*

Acidification

Acidification is a natural phenomenon that is accelerated by human activity, mainly by emissions of nitrogen oxides and sulphur dioxide. Acidic gases, if highly concentrated, can cause direct damage to trees and buildings, for instance. They can also have indirect effects on shellfish and fish, for example, as acidic rain leaches heavy metals from the ground.

MoDo's impact

The fuels used in the mills and for transportation – oil, natural gas, recovered liquor, effluent treatment sludge, and diesel fuel – contain sulphur and generates sulphur dioxide emissions.

All incineration of organic materials, including biofuel, produces emissions of nitrogen oxides.

MoDo's measures

MoDo endeavours only to use fuels with a low sulphur content at mills and for transportation. Fumes are cleaned when necessary. However, nitrogen oxides cannot be removed to any significant extent by flue gas cleaning. Instead, MoDo tries to limit the formation of nitrogen oxides by making effective use of energy, effective process control, and by the addition of various chemicals in the boilers. MoDo is developing knowledge within this area by participating in a variety of industry-wide projects.

Impact on land

Waste and environmentally-hazardous residues

Waste that cannot be reused or used to produce energy for instance, is sent to landfill. This causes risks of leaching of substances that can be harmful to the environment.

MoDo's impact

Certain types of waste cannot be used and must therefore be sent to landfill. They include bulky refuse, ash of various types, sludge and slag. The hazardous waste from MoDo's activities consists mainly of oil spills.

MoDo's measures

Sorting at source is used at MoDo's mills in order to recover as much waste as possible. A permit and a control programme are required to maintain industrial landfill sites. Several developmental projects are taking place to utilise ash and chemical sludge.

All forest machines operated by MoDo use environmentally-adapted oils, as do certain types of mill equipment. Authorised recycling companies take care of spill oils.

Acidification and Eutrophication (see above)

Impact on forest biodiversity

Several centuries of forestry have changed the natural conditions in the forests in some respects. Compared with virgin forests, there is a lack of dead wood, very old trees, burnt ground and wood, as well as of deciduous forests and wet coniferous forests. One effect of this is that many species have been forced away. Several of them are therefore taken up on the "red lists" of endangered species or of those requiring particular consideration.

MoDo's impact

MoDo's units process wood from cultivated forests, mainly in Sweden, the Baltic states, Russia, France and Great Britain.

MoDo's measures

MoDo has established environmental targets as a means of reducing the difference between cultivated forests and virgin forests. The company refrains from harvesting ten per cent of the potential volume on environmental grounds. MoDo's forests were certificated in accordance with the FSC forestry standard in 1998. MoDo's guidelines for wood procurement mean that wood may not be procured from certain biologically valuable types of forest.

EXHIBIT 4-15 Statoil's 2001 Social Audit Report

Report from Ernst & Young AS

We have reviewed the annual health, safety and environment accounting for Statoil ASA in 2001, as presented in the annual report and accounts for 2001 on pages 31–36. The HSE accounting is the responsibility of the corporate executive committee.

Our review has covered the following:
- meetings and discussions with the corporate management for health, safety and the environment on the contents of the HSE accounting, including a review of the group's management system for health, safety and the environment.
- interviewing personnel responsible for collecting the figures in the HSE report, with a focus on consistency in measuring emissions and on the processes governing the collection and collation of data. In this context, we have visited 10 reporting entities.
- verifying that figures from the reporting entities visited have been correctly incorporated in the HSE accounts, and performing overall analyses of the figures compared with earlier reporting periods.
- assessment of whether the overall information is presented in an appropriate manner in the HSE accounting.
- random checks to verify that the HSE figures presented are based on consistent and recognised methods for measuring, analysing and quantifying data.

On this basis, we can confirm that:
- Statoil has established a well-functioning management system for health, safety and the environment. In our opinion, the HSE accounting deals with information on matters relating to health, safety and the environment which are important from a group perspective. This information appears to be appropriately presented in the HSE accounts.
- the HSE performance indicators and environmental charts on pages 31–36 are based on consistent measuring methods and are in accordance with information submitted by the various reporting entities.

Our review was conducted in accordance with standard of auditing no 920 on agreed-upon procedures. As a consequence, our report is confined to the aspects specified above.

Stavanger, 8 March 2002
ERNST & YOUNG AS

Gustav Erikson
State authorised public accountant

Jostein Johannessen
State authorised public accountant

Thus, governments like to see disclosure that provides a detailed breakdown of employees and total compensation in each country where a multinational company has operations. In instances where there is a divergence between the aspirations of the host government and the employment practices of a multinational company (e.g., the former wants to develop a skilled workforce while the latter wants to use cheap labor in that country), the government could change regulations and incentives to appropriately influence the behavior of foreign firms. In other instances, the demand for more transparency on matters relating to employees originates in the company's home country rather than the host country. Nike, the U.S. sports equipment and apparel company, has been subjected to a firestorm of criticism for the working conditions in factories in developing countries where its products are manufactured. Interestingly, most of the criticism has come from the United States and not countries such as Indonesia where the factories are located. This pressure has resulted in Nike devoting much more space to employee disclosure in its annual report.

In 1977, the UN Group of Experts on International Standards of Accounting and Reporting issued the most detailed requirements for employee disclosures by multinationals. Since the UN requirements are voluntary in nature, very few companies have implemented these requirements in their entirety. The European Union's rather limited requirements for employee disclosure are contained in its Fourth (1978) and Seventh (1983) Directives. Companies are required to disclose the average number of employees in total and by categories, and to provide a breakdown of employee costs by categories. Perhaps the most extensive employee disclosures at the national level exist in France. These requirements, which emerged after the social unrest in France in the 1960s, are for French companies to publish a social balance sheet called a Bilan Social. Among the items required to be disclosed by French companies are employees' gender and age, pay structure, health and security conditions, training and development programs, and labor relations.

Despite the extensive requirements in France, a research study that examined employee disclosure by companies in six European countries found that German companies devoted the most space to employee-related disclosures, followed by companies from the United Kingdom, Switzerland, Sweden, Netherlands, and France [Adams, Hill, and Roberts, 1995]. German, Swedish, and Swiss companies provided the most information on the numbers of employees. Swedish companies tend to provide the most detailed breakdowns of employees and costs by geographic area. An example of such a disclosure is contained in Exhibit 4-16. The employee disclosure provided by Industrivarden focuses on the number of employees that it has in each country. Industrivarden also provides a detailed breakdown of the personnel costs in each country. This permits interested readers to determine the average cost per employee in each country. The same study also found that German companies provided the most disclosure on training, while Swedish and Dutch companies provided the least. German companies also revealed the most in the areas of health and safety, with the Swiss companies disclosing the least on this aspect of employee disclosure. Similarly, German companies also gave the most information on accidents, with Dutch and Swedish companies providing the least. However, on the subject of sickness, it was the Dutch and the Swedish companies that provided most disclosure, while companies from France, Switzerland, and the United Kingdom provided no disclosure. The overall superiority of employee disclosures by German firms suggests that it is likely that legal requirements and the political clout wielded by labor organizations significantly affect the level of employee disclosure practices across countries.

In contrast to the continental Europeans, companies from the United States, United Kingdom, and Japan provide very little employee disclosure. Apart from statements indicating that they are an equal opportunity employer, most U.S. firms do not provide detailed employee disclosure comparable to that provided by continental European firms. The only employee disclosure provided by corporations based in the United Kingdom is the compensation of the top executives (see Exhibit 4-17). Japanese firms typically include a brief statement thanking employees for their dedicated service. One can only surmise that most U.S., U.K., and Japanese managers do

EXHIBIT 4-16 Industrivarden's Employee Disclosures

Average Number of Employees	2001		2000	
	Number of employees	Of whom, women	Number of employees	Of whom, women
Parent Company	26	7	25	7
Subsidiaries in Sweden	1,338	393	1,173	358
Total, Sweden	1,364	400	1,198	365
Subsidiaries outside Sweden				
Austria	54	13	53	16
Baltic countries	69	13	48	10
Belgium	45	13	42	10
China	382	210	–	–
Denmark	169	32	159	31
Finland	367	80	197	40
France	394	183	244	104
Germany	268	75	175	40
Italy	28	16	32	17
Netherlands	254	57	239	51
Norway	47	10	10	3
Singapore	28	9	27	9
Spain	39	12	32	8
U.K.	134	28	131	28
USA	302	64	324	68
Other	60	14	36	9
Total	2,640	829	1,749	444
Total, Group	4,004	1,229	2,947	809

Wages, Salaries and Other Remuneration; Social Security Costs	2001			2000		
	Wages, salaries and other remuneration	Social security costs	Of which pension costs	Wages, salaries and other remuneration	Social security costs	Of which pension costs
Parent Company[1]	34	21	8	29	26	10
Subsidiaries in Sweden	395	182	49	318	150	37
Total, Sweden	429	203	57	347	176	47
Subsidiaries outside Sweden						
Austria	18	5	2	17	5	2
Baltic countries	8	2	–	5	1	–
Belgium	13	6	1	10	4	0
China	10	6	5	–	–	–
Denmark	82	4	3	69	3	2
Finland	121	33	23	56	13	9
France	90	33	4	46	18	3
Germany	87	18	7	59	11	5
Italy	9	3	3	9	3	2
Netherlands	77	19	11	69	16	7
Norway	20	2	0	4	0	0
Singapore	7	1	–	6	1	1
Spain	8	2	2	7	2	2
U.K.	51	12	4	46	7	3
USA	165	31	11	160	28	11
Other	10	3	1	9	0	0
Total	776	180	77	572	112	47
Total, Group	1,205	383	134	919	288	94

Of the Parent Company's pension cost, SEK 4 M (5) pertains to the Board of Directors and President. The corresponding amount for the Group was SEK 17 M (17).

EXHIBIT 4-17 Kingfisher's Executive Compensation Disclosure

Directors' remuneration

£000	Salary	Benefits (Note 1)	Annual bonus	Total remuneration 2001	2000	Long-term incentive 2001	2000
Executive							
Sir Geoffrey Mulcahy	967	47	–	**1,014**	1,308	**441**	304
Ian Cheshire[2]	166	26	93	**285**	–	**–**	–
Philippe Francès[3,4]	276	15	–	**291**	527	**–**	–
Roger Holmes[4]	328	99	–	**427**	581	**–**	101
Jean-Noel Labroue[2,3,5]	89	4	58	**151**	–	**–**	–
Jean-Hugues Loyez[3,6]	186	2	170	**358**	474	**–**	–
Anthony Percival[7]	98	26	–	**124**	149	**–**	870
Philip Rowley[8]	346	80	–	**426**	546	**54**	–
Helen Weir[2]	79	16	43	**138**	–	**63**	–
William Whiting[2]	76	3	59	**138**	–	**174**	–
Total	2,611	318	423	**3,352**	3,585	**732**	1,275
Non-Executive							
Sir John Banham (Chairman)[9]	200			**200**	200		
John Bullock[10]	35			**35**	32		
Peter Hardy	32			**32**	32		
Michael Hepher	32			**32**	32		
The Lady Howe[4]	19			**19**	32		
Margaret Salmon[11]	32			**32**	32		
Bernard Thiolon[10]	35			**35**	32		
Total	385			**385**	392		

Notes

1 Benefits incorporate all taxable benefits arising from employment which relate mainly to the provision of a company car and salary supplements where pensionable salary is limited by the Earnings Cap, but also include the cost of medical insurance and, for the Chief Executive, personal tax advice.

2 The 2001 remuneration covers the period since appointment, being 2 June 2000 for Ian Cheshire, 6 October 2000 for Helen Weir and Jean-Noel Labroue and 31 October 2000 for William Whiting.

3 Converted to sterling at an exchange rate of FF10.753 (2000:FF10.083).

4 The 2001 remuneration covers the period to resignation or retirement from the Board, being 2 June 2000 for The Lady Howe, 6 October 2000 for Roger Holmes and 31 October 2000 for Philippe Francès.

5 The salary for Jean-Noel Labroue includes a travel allowance.

6 The annual bonus for Jean-Hugues Loyez includes all his profit sharing arrangements in respect of Castorama Dubois Investissements S.C.A.

7 The 2000 long-term incentive for Anthony Percival relates to the exercise on 29 April 1999 of 126,666 phantom options at 291.5p per share when the market price was 912.0p per share.

8 Philip Rowley left the Company on 31 March 2001.

9 The Company also pays £25,000 per annum for office accommodation and services provided by Sir John Banham through Westcountry Management.

10 The salaries for John Bullock and Bernard Thiolon include the fees payable for their membership of the conseil de surveillance of Castorama Dubois Investissements S.C.A.

11 Margaret Salmon's salary is paid to her current employer.

not feel pressured to provide detailed employee disclosures in their annual reports. Alternatively, they do not consider the benefits of providing this disclosure to justify its costs. The end result is annual reports that are lacking in substantive employee disclosures.

Value-added Statement

The value-added statement is presented voluntarily by companies in a number of Continental European countries (i.e., Germany, Sweden, Netherlands, Norway, and France) as well as the United Kingdom and certain countries in the British

Commonwealth (i.e., Australia, New Zealand, and South Africa). This statement is included under social disclosure because, like environmental and employee disclosures, the value-added statement is of interest to stakeholders beyond just the shareholders of the company. Unlike the income statement, which takes a distinctly shareholder perspective to measuring a company's performance, the value-added statement provides information on the company's performance from the perspective of the many additional groups of stakeholders in the company. It does this by computing the value added by the company to the goods, materials, and services that are the inputs of the company. Thus, the contribution of the company to society as a whole can be considerably greater than just the profit it earns. A complete value-added statement has two parts. In the first part, it computes the wealth (i.e., the value added) created by a company during the reporting period. This is, in effect, the economic pie produced by the company. The remainder of the statement indicates how this wealth is distributed to the various stakeholders of the company, or how big a slice of the economic pie is received by each constituent. By doing so, it provides a clearer picture of the various groups' economic stakes in the company.

The value-added statement is based on the philosophy that the business enterprise makes a contribution beyond simply maximizing the wealth of its stockholders. It is consistent with the idea that a company can also be beneficial to the society in which it exists by creating employment, paying taxes, and making other worthwhile contributions. This is a reasonable perspective if one considers the fact that, when a company ceases to exist, the stockholders are not the only losers. In fact, typically it is the employees (through loss of their livelihood), the government (through a decline in tax revenue and the additional costs of unemployment and welfare payments to laid-off workers), and the immediate communities (through a general decline in the local economy) that stand to lose just as much, and often more, than the stockholders.

The complete absence of the value-added statement in the United States and its recent decline in the United Kingdom suggest the dominance of the shareholder wealth maximization philosophy in these countries. In such a climate, companies do not feel the need or the pressure to provide a statement that focuses on employees and their relatively large stake in the company. By contrast, countries where labor wields greater political clout tend to be the ones where the role of employees as stakeholders is emphasized via the value-added statement.

Given the voluntary nature of the value-added statement, it is not entirely surprising that there is a general absence of comparability between how companies define accounting terms in preparing this statement. Some differences between value-added statements include whether revenues include or are net of sales taxes; whether payroll taxes are shown as distributions to employees or distribution to the government; and whether depreciation is treated as a reinvestment in the business or as a reduction from revenues in computing value added for the period. More often than not, companies do not provide an explanation of these items under the significant accounting policies note to the financial statements. However, despite this drawback, it is clear that companies that include a value-added statement in their annual reports provide more information on their various stakeholders than companies that do not prepare this statement.

A sample of a value-added statement from Barlow Limited, a South African company, is included in Exhibit 4-18. The first part of the statement shows that the wealth created by the company during 1997 was South African Rand 5.1 billion. The second part of the statement indicates how this wealth was distributed among the various stakeholders in the company. As discussed above, the employees were the largest

EXHIBIT 4-18 Barlow's Value-Added Statement

	1997 R'm	%	1996 R'm	%
Turnover	19 387,8		17 810,7	
Paid to suppliers for materials and services	14 876,2		13 740,0	
Value added	4 511,6		4 070,7	
Income from investments*	592,6		387,5	
Total wealth created	5 104,2		4 458,2	
Wealth distribution				
Salaries, wages and other benefits (Note 1)	2 955,9	57,9	2 698,2	60,5
Providers of capital:	751,3	14,7	555,1	12,5
Interest paid on borrowings	419,7		273,8	
Dividends to Barlow Limited shareholders*	268,0		215,5	
Dividends to outside shareholders in subsidiaries	63,6		65,8	
Government (Notes 2 and 3)	357,5	7,0	350,7	7,9
Reinvested in the group to maintain and develop operations:	1 039,5	20,4	854,2	19,1
Depreciation	370,9		314,5	
Retained profit	594,5		510,2	
Deferred taxation	74,1		29,5	
	5 104,2	100,0	4 458,2	100,0

Value added ratios

Number of employees (30 September)	29,681		30,740	
Turnover per employee* (Rand)	641,757		580,153	
Wealth created per employee* (Rand)	168,955		145,218	

Notes

1. **Salaries, wages and other benefits**

Salaries, wages, overtime payments, commissions, bonuses and allowances	2 455,6		2 283,5	
Employer contributions†	500,3		414,7	
	2 955,9		2 698,2	

2. **Central and local government**

Current taxation	253,0		231,0	
Regional Service Council levies	21,5		21,2	
Rates and taxes paid to local authorities	32,6		27,7	
Customs duties, import surcharges and excise taxes	57,1		86,6	
Gross contribution to central and local government	364,2		366,5	
Less: Government cash grants and subsidies	6,7		15,8	
	357,5		350,7	

3. **Additional amounts collected on behalf of government**

Value added tax	451,5		351,4	
Employee tax deducted from remuneration paid	555,7		503,9	
South African withholding taxes	0,7		0,7	
	1 007,8		856,0	

Includes interest received, dividend income and share of associate companies' retained profit.
Includes capitalisation awards and dividends on ordinary shares.
 # Based on average number of employees.
† In respect of pension funds, retirement annuities, provident funds, medical aid and insurance.

stakeholders, receiving 57.9 percent of the total value added; various capital providers (including stockholders) received 14.7 percent; the government received a net of 7 percent; and the remaining 20.4 percent was reinvested in the company. The statement also provides value-added ratios such as the revenue per employee and the wealth created per employee.

SUMMARY

1. The historical-cost model of accounting ignores the effect of inflation on financial statements. This has an adverse effect on the decision usefulness of financial statements. The negative impact on the usefulness is directly related to the level of inflation. Thus, financial statements in countries with high levels of inflation are more negatively impacted than those in countries with low inflation. This makes comparability of financial statements difficult across countries.

2. Due to the compounding effect, even countries with relatively low levels of inflation can experience a significant change in the purchasing power of their currencies. Inflation-adjusted accounting models are a tool in gauging the effect of inflation on financial statements.

3. The two main inflation-adjusted accounting models are the general price level adjusted model (GPLA) and the current cost-adjusted model (CCA). The latter is also referred to as the replacement cost model.

4. The GPLA model focuses on changes in the general level of inflation in a country as measured by a consumer price index. It requires the conversion of historical-cost nominal amounts that are from different periods to a constant point in time, typically the balance sheet date. The CCA model takes a physical asset perspective to measuring wealth and income and focuses on the replacement cost of the tangible assets owned.

5. There are a variety of practices when it comes to accounting for goodwill and other intangible assets. This is relevant to financial statement users since it adversely impacts the comparability of financial statements globally. This is an area that is receiving attention in global harmonization efforts.

6. Financial statement users are increasingly demanding more social disclosure from companies. The two main areas of social disclosure are environmental disclosure and employee disclosure. Environmental disclosures are gaining in economic significance as companies face greater liabilities in light of ever-stricter environmental laws. Employee disclosures are becoming more important as intellectual capital and personnel increase in importance relative to physical assets in the high-tech era. The value-added statement is another element of social disclosure. This statement takes a broader perspective than the income statement in that it considers all stakeholders of the company rather than just the stockholders.

QUESTIONS

1. Discuss why the historical-cost accounting model may not provide decision-relevant information in an inflationary environment.

2. Describe how the general price level adjusted (GPLA) model accounts for changes in the general purchasing power of the reporting currency over time. What are the strengths and weaknesses of the GPLA model?

3. How do monetary items differ from non-monetary items? Indicate whether each of the following is a monetary or non-monetary item:
   a) Cash
   b) Accounts Receivable
   c) Marketable Securities
   d) Merchandise Inventory
   e) Accounts Payable
   f) Obligation to Deliver Goods in the Future
   g) Land
   h) Prepaid Rent
   i) Prepaid Subscription

4. Explain how the current-cost model differs significantly from the other accounting models (i.e., cash, historical cost, and general price level adjusted). What is the physical capital concept? What are the strengths and weaknesses of the current-cost accounting model?

5. Briefly review the recent history in the United Kingdom and the United States on accounting for changing prices. Why do these countries not require companies to disclose the effect of changing prices on their performance and financial position? In your view, who gains and who loses by this "no disclosure" policy?

6. Discuss the main alternatives on accounting for goodwill and explain which one makes the most economic sense to you.

7. A number of Australian and British companies have decided to report internally generated brands as an asset on their balance sheets. Do you agree with this approach? Explain.

8. Why is the accounting treatment for research and development outlays likely to grow more important for firms in certain industries? Explain.

9. Under what circumstances is geographic segment disclosure useful to investors? Examine the geographic segment disclosures in the annual reports of three domestic and three foreign companies from the same industry. Were these disclosures informative in making probability assessments of the companies' future performance?

10. The Financial Accounting Standards Board (FASB) in the United States passed a new accounting standard on segment disclosure, SFAS No. 131, which became effective on December 15, 1997. This is intended to be an improvement on the previous standard, SFAS No. 14, that covered segment disclosure. Select three U.S. companies and compare their geographic segment disclosures under SFAS No. 131 and SFAS No. 14. From an investor perspective, is there a discernible improvement in geographic segment disclosures provided under SFAS No. 131?

11. Why is environmental disclosure relevant to various users of financial statements? What are the specific environmental items you would like to see companies provide?

12. Describe the factors likely to impact employee disclosure by corporations. Relate this to the quality of employee disclosure provided by companies from various countries.

13. Discuss the similarities and differences between an income statement and a value-added statement.

EXERCISES

1. The revolution in information technology has seen the emergence of a large number of high-tech and internet companies. Choose a high-tech company from each of three different countries and compare their accounting policy for research and development costs.

2. Certain countries allow companies to report internally generated brands as assets on the balance sheet. Obtain the annual reports of Fosters (Australia) and Anheuser-Busch (United States), and compare their accounting policy on brand valuation. Which accounting policy better reflects the net worth of the company? Why?

3. As companies continue to expand globally, geographic segment disclosure has become an important disclosure item for financial statement users. Compare the geographic segment disclosures of two domestic companies with two foreign companies in the same industry

and describe any differences. List advantages and disadvantages to a) preparers and b) users of financial statements of including detailed segmental disclosures in company annual reports.

4. Compare the examples of geographic segment disclosures by U.S. and Scandinavian firms provided in Exhibits 4-7 to 4-11. Explain the differences in the level of disclosure provided by the companies.

5. As companies venture into other countries requiring social and environmental reporting, they are subject to greater pressure from various stakeholders, including socially conscious investors, to provide more social disclosures. Below is a brief excerpt from Coca-Cola's 1998 annual report noting the company's commitment to protecting the environment.

> The Coca-Cola Company is dedicated to environmental excellence. While our environmental impact is small, we are committed to managing that impact in a positive manner . . . . We have achieved significant progress in areas such as source reduction, recovery and recycling, water and energy conservation, and wastewater quality . . . . These efforts are helping us protect and advance our business through continued environmental leadership.

In your opinion, are environmental or social disclosures like this informative to financial statements users? Support your answer.

6. Due to the negative publicity in 1997 surrounding allegations that Nike Inc. (United States) was mistreating workers in developing countries (i.e., poor wages, unsafe working conditions), the company turned to public disclosures as one method of combating and repairing its damaged image. Below is an example of a social disclosure from Nike's 1998 annual report regarding its labor practices.

> On May 12, 1998, Phil Knight (Nike's CEO) announced six new initiatives to improve factory working conditions and increase opportunities for people who manufacture Nike products. They are:
> –Expanding Independent Monitoring
> –Raising Minimum Age Requirements
> –Strengthening Environmental, Health, and Safety Standards
> –Expanding Worker Education
> –Increasing Support of the Micro-enterprise Loan Program
> –Building Understanding
> Nike will sever its business relationships with any manufacturer refusing to meet these standards or exhibiting a pattern of violations. In the last year, Nike has terminated business with eight factories in four countries for not meeting our Code of Conduct requirements.

List a few reasons why companies, such as Nike, might voluntarily or involuntarily include social disclosures as part of their financial statements. Do you foresee more companies providing such disclosures in the near future? Explain.

7. The following information is the consolidated balance sheet from Whilips Electronics' (Netherlands) 1999 annual report. Assume that all assets were acquired on January 1, 1999.

General price-level index:	January 1, 1999	100
	Average for 1999	104
	December 31, 1999	110

Using the information given above, adjust Whilips' 1999 balance sheet for inflation using the GPLA model. What is Whilips' GPLA basis retained earnings balance in millions of Euros?

Consolidated Balance Sheet (in millions of Euro)
Year end Dec. 31, 1999

Assets		Equity and liabilities:	
Cash and cash equivalents	2,500	Accounts payable	15,000
Accounts receivables	19,460	Accrued liabilities	8,250
Prepaid expenses	600	Bank loan payable	12,750
Inventory	10,280	Bonds payable	7,340
Supplies	300		
Equipment	24,500	Owner's equity:	
Less: Accumulated dep.	(5,000)	Paid-in capital	7,500
		Retained earnings	1,800
Total assets	**52,640**	**Total equity and liabilities**	**52,640**

8. Latechoc (Switzerland) began its first year of operations on Jan 1, 2000. Below is the company's Statement of Income for the year.

Latechoc
Statement of Income (in millions of Swiss francs)
Year end December 31, 2000

Net sales	7,820
Cost of goods sold	4,000
Selling, general and administrative	850
Rent	400
Advertising	150
Equipment depreciation	1,250
Interest expense	90
Utilities	30
Federal income taxes	65
Net operating income	985

General price-level index:		
	January 1, 2000	100
	Average for 2000	105
	December 31, 2000	108

Assume that equipment was acquired at the beginning of the year and the net monetary gain for the year was 480 (in millions of Swiss francs). What is Latechoc's adjusted GPLA net income for the year ending December 31, 2000? Using the GPLA model, calculate the net monetary gain or loss. What is Latechoc's GPLA-based net income for the year ending December 31, 2000?

CASES

Case

Peanut Corp.

The management at Peanut Corp. is seriously considering an acquisition of one of its two major competitors, Jam Company of Germany or Butter Group of France. Assume that the fair market value of both Jam Company and Butter Group is $450 million and each can be purchased for $560 million. Net assets stated at book value are $400 million. Peanut Corp.'s earnings before any goodwill amortization or depreciation adjustments are $80 million. The company depreciates all its assets over a 5-year period under the straight-line method.

1. Compute Peanut Corp.'s net earnings (in U.S. dollars) after accounting for any additional goodwill or depreciation charges in each of the following countries:

a.   United States (goodwill amortization period of 40 years)
b.   Germany (goodwill amortization period of 15 years)
c.   France (goodwill amortization period of 5 years)
d.   United Kingdom (immediate write-off of goodwill against reserves)

Case

Greenwash's Wish List

The management of Greenwash Company is concerned about the growing demand on the part of investors and the public in general for environmental disclosures in corporate annual reports. In reviewing a number of foreign competitors' annual reports, they have observed a variety of environmental disclosures, including 1) actual and contingent liabilities for the cost of environmental clean-up, 2) corporate programs and policies to protect the environment, and 3) self-assessment reports of the internal goals reached with respect to its environmental protection measures. They have also noticed that some companies include environmental disclosure in their annual report while others prepare a separate environmental report. The management of Greenwash is agonizing over the type and extent of environmental disclosure to provide in the company's next annual report. They have hired you as a consultant to help them establish environmental reporting policies.

1.   In your opinion, are environmental disclosures in company annual reports necessary? Explain.
2.   What specific environmental disclosure should companies provide? Why?
3.   Using examples of two domestic and two foreign annual reports within the same industry as Greenwash, suggest the type of environmental disclosure Greenwash should provide. Explain the costs and benefits of the environmental disclosures you recommend.

REFERENCES

Adams, C. A., Hill, W. Y., and Roberts, C. B. 1995. Environmental, Employee and Ethical Reporting in Europe. *ACCA Research Report # 14.* London: Certified Accountants Educational Trust.

Ahadiat, N. 1993. Geographic segment disclosure and the predictive ability of the earnings data. *Journal of International Business Studies,* 24 (2): 357–371.

Association for Investment and Management Research. 1991. *Report of Association for Investment Management and Research Corporate Information Committee Including Evaluation of Corporate Financial Reporting in Selected Industries for the Year 1990–91.* New York: AIMR (December). [Similar reports were published under nearly identical titles annually since 1948, except that prior to 1990 the name of the organization was Financial Analysts Federation.]

Balakrishnan, H., Harris, T., and Sen, P. K. 1990. The predictive ability of geographic segment disclosures. *Journal of Accounting Research,* 28 (2): 305–325.

Beets, S. D., and Souther, C. C. 1999. Corporate environmental reports: The need for standards and an environmental assurance service. *Accounting Horizons,* 13 (2): 129–145.

Boatsman, J. R., Behn, B. K., and Patz, D. H. 1993. A test of the use of geographical segment disclosures. *Journal of Accounting Research,* 31 (3): 46–64.

British Bankers' Association and Irish Bankers' Federation. 1993. *Statement of Recommended Accounting Practice, Segmental Reporting.* London: BBA and Dublin: IBF.

Burritt, R. 2002. Stopping Australia killing the environment—getting the reporting edge. *Australian CPA,* (April): 70–72.

Davis-Friday, P. Q., and Rivera, J. M. 2000. Inflation accounting and 20-F disclosures: Evidence from Mexico. *Accounting Horizons,* 14 (2): 113–135.

Doupnik, T., and Rolfe, R. 1989. The relevance of level of aggregation of geographic area data in the assessment of foreign investment risk. In *Advances in Accounting*, edited by Bill N. Schwartz, 51–65, Greenwich, Conn.: JAI Press.

Doupnik, T., and Rolfe, R. 1990. Geographic area disclosures and the assessment of foreign investment risk for disclosure in accounting statement notes. *International Journal of Accounting*, 25 (Fall): 252–267.

Fried, D., Schiff, M., and Sondhi, A. C. 1992. *Quarterly segment reporting: Impact on analysts' forecasts and variability of security price returns.* Working Paper, New York University.

Gray, S., Street, D., and Nichols, N. 1999. A new era of segment reporting. *Accountancy International* (April): 76–78.

Herrmann, D. 1996. The predictive ability of geographic segment information at the country, continent, and consolidated levels. *Journal of International Financial Management and Accounting*, 8 (1): 50–73.

Nichols, D., Tunnell, L., and Seipel, C. 1995. Earnings forecast accuracy and geographic segment disclosures. *Journal of International Accounting Auditing & Taxation*, 4 (2): 113–126.

Pacter, P. 1993. *Reporting Disaggregated Information.* Norwalk, Connecticut: Financial Accounting Standards Board.

Piet, J. 1999. Guarding the globe. *Accountancy International*, (August): 62–63.

Price Waterhouse. 1992. *Environmental Costs: Accounting and Disclosure.* Washington: Price Waterhouse.

Prodhan, B. 1986. Geographical segment disclosure and multinational risk profile. *Journal of Business Finance and Accounting*, (Spring): 15–37.

Prodhan, B., and Harris, M. 1989. Systematic risk and the discretionary disclosure of geographical segments: An empirical investigation of U.S. multinationals. *Journal of Business Finance and Accounting*, (Autumn): 467–492.

Roberts, C. 1989. Forecasting earnings using geographic segment data: Some U.K. evidence. *Journal of International Financial Management and Accounting*, 1 (2): 130–151.

Saudagaran, S. M. 1993. Discussion of a test of the use of geographical segment disclosures. *Journal of Accounting Research*, 31 (3): 65–74.

Senteney, D. L. 1990. An empirical analysis of the association between cumulative abnormal security returns prior and subsequent to SFAS 14 geographic segment disclosures of U.S.-based multinational enterprises. *Collected Papers and Abstracts of the Southwest Regional Meeting of the American Accounting Association*, (Feb.–March): 371–377.

Senteney, D. L., and Bazaz, M. S. 1992. The impact of SFAS 14 geographic segment disclosures on the information content of U.S.-based MNEs' earnings releases. *International Journal of Accounting*, 27 (3): 267–279.

Tonkin, D. J. 1989. *World Survey of Published Accounts.* London: Lafferty Publications.

Van Offeren, D. H. 1989. Disclosure Practice of Geographical Segmentation of Net Sales in Annual Reports. *Research Memorandum # 8913.* Amsterdam: Universiteit van Amsterdam.

CHAPTER 5

Using Corporate Financial Reports Across Borders

- Identify the different levels at which corporations respond to foreign financial statement users.

- Recognize how users cope with global diversity in financial reporting.

- Highlight the main issues that users need to consider in conducting international financial statement analysis.

The globalization of capital markets, the increased mobility of firms, the dramatic advances in telecommunications and computer technology, and the resultant decrease in the cost of securities transactions (even at the level of the individual investor) have important implications for financial reporting. Companies can no longer assume a purely domestic audience for their annual reports and other financial disclosures. With the exponential growth in corporate web sites, individuals seeking information about a company's products or its financial statements can access it fairly quickly and inexpensively. This easier access to information on foreign firms could be a mixed blessing for users who are not sensitive to international accounting differences if it leads them to make economic decisions based on inappropriate conclusions. This chapter looks at corporate responses to non-domestic investors and other users of corporate financial reports. It also suggests a variety of approaches for performing international financial statement analysis.

CORPORATE RESPONSES TO FOREIGN USERS OF FINANCIAL STATEMENTS

As long as a company conducts its business and raises purely domestic capital, it may not need to concern itself with financial reporting requirements in other countries or with providing accounting information to users outside its home country. However, once a company's operations or financing become globalized, the company can seldom afford to ignore differences between the financial reporting regime at home and the potentially different reporting practices of foreign countries where it has significant customers or investors. The increased globalization of the company's activities results in an increase in its foreign stakeholders. As a result, such corporations face the responsibility of providing financial reports to investors, financial analysts, and regulatory agencies in other countries in a form that they can understand. This section reviews corporate responses to foreign users of financial statements.

Corporate responses to foreign users range from doing absolutely nothing incremental for their foreign users to preparing country-specific financial statements to comply with the financial reporting regime in the foreign user's country. It is important to recognize that each company will respond based on its own needs and circumstances. Thus, the discussion of the various responses that follows is meant to be a description rather than a judgment of these responses.

Many companies still make no additional effort for the foreign users of their annual reports. Such companies send the same annual report to foreign users as they do to domestic users. While this might appear to be an ethnocentric approach to financial reporting, it can be a perfectly reasonable response for companies that are not looking to attract foreign investors. Companies adopting the **do-nothing** approach apparently do not perceive sufficient benefits to justify incurring the additional costs of catering to foreign users of their financial statements. An example of a do-nothing response appears in Exhibit 5-1. In sending its home-country annual report abroad, this Venezuelan company apparently did not feel the need to make any additional effort for the foreign user. Most U.S. companies also follow the do-nothing approach when it comes to sending annual reports to constituents abroad.

Convenience translations represent a minimal effort on the part of companies to respond to their foreign users. In a convenience translation, the preparer translates the language of the annual report to that of the user's country. However, the currency and the accounting principles are still those of the preparer's country. An example of a convenience translation appears in Exhibit 5-2. Here, the French company has

EXHIBIT 5-1   Do-Nothing Response: Petroleos de Venezuela Consolidated Income Sheet

ESTADOS CONSOLIDADOS
DE RESULTADOS
(Expresados en millones de dólares estadounidenses)

	Años terminados el 31 de diciembre de		
	2001	2000	1999
Ventas netas de petróleo crudo y sus productos derivados:			
Exportaciones y en el exterior	42.682	49.780	30.369
En Venezuela	1.701	2.230	1.450
Productos petroquímicos y otras ventas	1.403	1.224	781
Participación patrimonial en resultados netos de compañías afiliadas	464	446	48
	46.250	53.680	32.648
Costos y gastos:			
Compras de petróleo crudo y sus productos derivados	18.228	19.759	10.959
Gastos de operación	10.882	10.010	8.532
Gastos de exploración	174	169	118
Depreciación y amortización	2.624	3.001	2.821
Gastos de venta, administración y generales	1.853	1.256	1.192
Impuestos de explotación y otros	3.760	4.986	3.008
Gastos de financiamiento	509	672	662
Otros egresos, neto	456	848	6
	38.486	40.701	27.298
Ganancia antes de impuesto sobre la renta e intereses minoritarios	7.764	12.979	5.350
Impuesto sobre la renta	(3.766)	(5.748)	(2.521)
Intereses minoritarios	(5)	(15)	(11)
Ganancia neta	3.993	7.216	2.818

Las notas que se acompañan forman parte de los estados financieros consolidados.

translated the annual report in English while retaining the Euro currency and French accounting principles.

The next step in this progression of responses to foreign users is the **convenience statement.** In the international accounting literature, this term is used to describe annual reports that are prepared in the foreign user's language and currency while retaining the home-country accounting principles. Convenience statements are a mixed blessing in that they have the potential to mislead the foreign user into believing that the accounting principles used in the statements are also those of the user's country. An example of a convenience statement prepared by Toyota Motor Company of Japan appears in Exhibit 5-3. Toyota's financial statements, though written in English and translated into U.S. dollars, are prepared in accordance with Japanese generally accepted accounting principles. Users who are not aware of this fact could make some serious decision errors if they assume that Toyota's financial statements are in U.S. GAAP just because the financial statements are in English and in U.S. dollars.

EXHIBIT 5-2   Convenience Translation: Groupe Bull's Consolidated Balance Sheet

Consolidated balance sheets at December 31

(in EUR millions)

ASSETS	NOTES	2000	1999	1998
» **Intangible assets:**				
Capitalized software costs		148	138	112
Less accumulated amortization		(107)	(91)	(69)
Other intangible assets		6	14	9
Less accumulated amortization		(3)	(9)	(8)
» **Total**		**44**	**52**	**44**
» **Property:**				
Land		24	25	28
Buildings and improvements		204	216	210
Less accumulated depreciation		(134)	(140)	(130)
Machinery and equipment		418	568	638
Less accumulated depreciation		(327)	(441)	(486)
Net		*185*	*228*	*260*
Rental equipment		50	114	155
Less accumulated depreciation		(39)	(91)	(119)
Net		*11*	*23*	*36*
» **Total**	(4)	**196**	**251**	**296**
» **Investments and other non-current assets:**				
Goodwill (net of amortization)	(5)	90	92	68
Investments	(6)	57	51	315
Other	(7)	215	170	141
» **Total**		**362**	**313**	**524**
» **Deferred taxes**	(22)	**74**	**138**	**138**
» **Inventories**	(8)	**246**	**288**	**285**
» **Other current assets:**				
Trade receivables (less allowances for doubtful accounts: 2000, M€ 18 ; 1999, M€ 23 ; 1998, M€ 28)		720	804	885
Other receivables (less allowances for doubtful accounts: 2000, M€ 19 ; 1999, M€ 15 ; 1998, M€ 14)		172	189	216
Marketable securities		214	294	157
Cash		90	154	135
» **Total**		**1,196**	**1,441**	**1,393**
TOTAL ASSETS		**2,118**	**2,483**	**2,680**

See accompanying notes to consolidated financial statements.

EXHIBIT 5-2 Convenience Translation: Groupe Bull's Consolidated Balance Sheet *(continued)*

(in EUR millions)

LIABILITIES AND STOCKHOLDERS' EQUITY	Notes	2000	1999	1998
➤➤ **Stockholders' equity:**				
Common stock	(11)	340	331	252
Additional paid-in capital	(11)	37	17	96
Retained earnings (deficit)		(292)	(49)	239
Accumulated comprehensive income (loss): foreign currency translation adjustments		1	(5)	(30)
➤➤ **Total**		86	294	557
➤➤ **Advance contributions to capital increases**	(12)	-	48	48
➤➤ **Minority interests**	(13)	7	6	18
➤➤ **Market auction preferred stock issued by a consolidated subsidiary**	(14)	107	100	85
➤➤ **Long-term debt**	(15)	345	153	326
➤➤ **Long-term restructuring reserve**	(16)	19	29	30
➤➤ **Provisions and other non-current liabilities**	(17)	176	200	183
➤➤ **Deferred taxes**	(22)	10	8	12
➤➤ **Current liabilities:**				
Trade payables		574	645	614
Customers advances		43	61	46
Provision for corporate income taxes		15	13	5
Deferred income		9	9	11
Other accrued liabilities	(17)	466	475	447
Short-term restructuring reserve	(16)	1	1	15
Current maturities of long-term debt	(15)	51	252	152
Short-term borrowings and notes payable		169	177	97
Bank overdrafts		40	12	34
➤➤ **Total**		**1,368**	**1,645**	**1,421**
TOTAL LIABILITIES & STOCKHOLDERS' EQUITY		**2,118**	**2,483**	**2,680**

Limited restatements represent a further step by corporations to enhance the usefulness of their financial statements for foreign audiences. In addition to translating the language (and often the currency), the company provides supplementary disclosures to reconcile selected financial statements from the company's domestic accounting standards to the user's GAAP. The items selected for adjustment are generally based on the preparer's judgment as to the foreign user's interest. Swedish companies doing business in the United States often prepare limited restatements. Given

EXHIBIT 5-3 Convenience Statement: Toyota's Consolidated Balance Sheet

Consolidated Balance Sheets

Toyota Motor Corporation
March 31, 2002 and 2001

	Yen in millions		U.S. dollars in millions
ASSETS	2001	2002	2002
Current assets:			
Cash and cash equivalents	¥ 1,510,892	¥ 1,657,160	$ 12,436
Time deposits	48,917	19,977	150
Marketable securities	488,096	600,737	4,508
Trade accounts and notes receivable, less allowance for doubtful accounts of ¥33,050 million in 2001 and ¥28,182 million ($211 million) in 2002	1,271,820	1,456,935	10,934
Finance receivables, net	1,633,247	2,020,491	15,163
Other receivables	357,380	508,970	3,821
Inventories	876,252	961,840	7,218
Deferred income taxes	355,051	433,524	3,253
Prepaid expenses and other current assets	323,485	413,211	3,101
Total current assets	6,865,140	8,072,845	60,584
Noncurrent finance receivables, net	2,068,768	2,671,460	20,048
Investments and other assets:			
Marketable securities and other securities investments	1,862,389	1,531,126	11,491
Affiliated companies	1,397,604	1,321,950	9,921
Officers and employees receivables	21,740	21,151	159
Other	346,240	580,188	4,354
	3,627,973	3,454,415	25,925
Property, plant and equipment:			
Land	847,635	1,032,381	7,748
Buildings	2,075,147	2,421,918	18,176
Machinery and equipment	6,213,626	6,959,054	52,225
Vehicles and equipment on operating leases	1,525,164	1,584,161	11,889
Construction in progress	142,278	234,224	1,758
	10,803,850	12,231,738	91,796
Less—Accumulated depreciation	(6,345,948)	(7,124,728)	(53,469)
	4,457,902	5,107,010	38,327
Total assets	¥17,019,783	¥19,305,730	$144,884

The accompanying notes are an integral part of these financial statements.

the well-known U.S. fixation on the net income and earnings per share numbers, most Swedish companies preparing limited restatements for the United States provide these figures in U.S. GAAP. An excerpt from a Swedish company's limited restatement appears in Exhibit 5-4.

Similar to limited restatements are the **reconciliation to a foreign country's GAAP** that are prepared by companies in response to the regulations of those countries where their securities are listed. For example, in the United States, the SEC

EXHIBIT 5-3 Convenience Statement: Toyota's Consolidated Balance Sheet *(continued)*

	Yen in millions		U.S. dollars in millions
LIABILITIES AND SHAREHOLDERS' EQUITY	2001	2002	2002
Current liabilities:			
Short-term borrowings	¥ 1,469,007	¥ 1,825,564	$ 13,700
Current portion of long-term debt	714,674	1,158,814	8,696
Accounts payable	1,290,072	1,420,608	10,661
Other payables	607,170	575,011	4,315
Accrued expenses	814,153	928,160	6,966
Income taxes payable	252,235	327,713	2,459
Other current liabilities	405,976	436,288	3,275
Total current liabilities	5,553,287	6,672,158	50,072
Long-term liabilities:			
Long-term debt	3,083,344	3,722,706	27,938
Accrued pension and severance costs	505,150	754,403	5,662
Deferred income taxes	553,266	467,061	3,505
Other long-term liabilities	62,208	133,669	1,003
Total long-term liabilities	4,203,968	5,077,839	38,108
Minority interest in consolidated subsidiaries	185,117	291,621	2,189
Shareholders' equity:			
Common stock, ¥50 par value in 2001 and no par value in 2002, authorized: 9,815,185,400 shares in 2001 and 9,780,185,400 shares in 2002; issued and outstanding: 3,684,997,492 shares in 2001 and 3,649,997,492 shares in 2002	397,050	397,050	2,980
Additional paid-in capital	488,655	490,538	3,681
Retained earnings	6,479,073	6,804,722	51,067
Accumulated other comprehensive loss	(282,491)	(267,304)	(2,006)
Treasury stock, at cost	(4,876)	(160,894)	(1,207)
Total shareholders' equity	7,077,411	7,264,112	54,515
Commitments and contingencies			
Total liabilities and shareholders' equity	¥17,019,783	¥19,305,730	$144,884

requires companies choosing to file financial statements prepared in their home-country GAAP to provide a reconciliation of income and equity to U.S. GAAP. Thus, a number of non-U.S. companies listed on U.S. stock exchanges provide such reconciliations as part of their Form 20-F filings. An example of such a reconciliation is provided in Exhibit 5-5. It contains the reconciliation from Norwegian GAAP to U.S. GAAP from the annual report of Norsk Hydro—a company listed on the New York Stock Exchange.

Finally, the preparation of **secondary statements** represents the most that a company can be realistically expected to do for its foreign users. In preparing secondary statements, the company translates its home-country annual report (i.e., primary

EXHIBIT 5-4 Limited Restatement: Volvo's Net Income and Shareholders' Equity

Note **33** Net income and shareholders' equity in accordance with U.S. GAAP

A summary of the Volvo Group's net income and shareholders' equity determined in accordance with U.S. GAAP, is presented in the accompanying tables.

Application of U.S. GAAP would have the following effect on consolidated net income and shareholders' equity:

Net income	1999	2000	2001
Net income in accordance with Swedish accounting principles	32,222	4,709	(1,467)
Items increasing (decreasing) reported net income			
Derivative instruments and hedging activities (A)	576	(654)	172
Business combinations (B)	(91)	(91)	(744)
Shares and participations (C)	12	24	–
Interest costs (D)	21	(3)	18
Leasing (E)	39	16	13
Investments in debt and equity securities (F)	253	(548)	(153)
Restructuring costs and income from divestment of Volvo Cars (G)	(1,325)	(281)	(579)
Pensions and other post-employment benefits (H)	40	(170)	456
Alecta surplus funds (I)	–	(523)	111
Software development (J)	370	384	(212)
Product development (K)	–	–	(1,962)
Entrance fees, aircraft engine programs (L)	(22)	(336)	(324)
Tax effect of above U.S. GAAP adjustments	(405)	600	690
Net increase (decrease) in net income	(532)	(1,582)	(2,514)
Net income in accordance with U.S. GAAP	**31,690**	**3,127**	**(3,981)**
Net income per share, SEK in accordance with U.S. GAAP	**71.80**	**7.40**	**(9.40)**
Weighted average number of shares outstanding (in thousands)	441,521	421,684	422,429

Shareholders' equity	1999	2000	2001
Shareholders' equity in accordance with Swedish accounting principles	97,692	88,338	85,185
Items increasing (decreasing) reported shareholders' equity			
Derivative instruments and hedging activities (A)	(632)	(1,286)	(1,114)
Business combinations (B)	1,408	1,317	4,125
Shares and participations (C)	12	36	36
Interest costs (D)	115	112	130
Leasing (E)	(189)	(163)	(149)
Investments in debt and equity securities (F)	(256)	(6,066)	(7,328)
Restructuring costs and income from divestment of Volvo Cars (G)	860	579	–
Pensions and other postemployment benefits (H)	443	109	272
Alecta surplus funds (I)	–	(523)	(412)
Software development (J)	370	754	542
Product development (K)	–	–	(1,962)
Entrance fees, aircraft engine programs (L)	(51)	(387)	(719)
Tax effect of above U.S. GAAP adjustments	(165)	1,941	3,024
Net increase (decrease) in shareholders' equity	1,915	(3,577)	(3,555)
Shareholders' equity in accordance with U.S. GAAP	**99,607**	**84,761**	**81,630**

EXHIBIT 5-5 Reconciliation to Another Country's GAAP: Norsk Hydro's Reconciliation to U.S. GAAP

Reconciliation of US GAAP to N GAAP

Net income:

Amounts in NOK million	Notes	2001	2000	1999
Operating revenues US GAAP		152,835	156,861	111,955
Adjustments for N GAAP:				
Unrealized losses (gains) commodity derivative instruments		134	-	-
Operating revenues N GAAP		152,969	156,861	111,955
Operating costs and expenses US GAAP		131,752	128,395	104,220
Adjustments for N GAAP:				
Unrealized gains (losses) commodity derivative instruments		180	(13)	(19)
Other adjustments		-	(2)	-
Operating income before financial and other income – N GAAP		21,037	28,481	7,754
Equity in net income of non-consolidated investees		566	672	339
Interest income and other financial income		2,847	1,747	1,504
Other income, net		578	3,161	1,350
Earnings before interest expense and taxes (EBIT)		25,028	34,061	10,947
Interest expense and foreign exchange gain (loss)		(3,609)	(3,905)	(3,055)
Income before taxes and minority interest – N GAAP		21,419	30,156	7,892
Current income tax expense		(14,063)	(13,711)	(3,553)
Deferred income tax expense US GAAP		313	(2,467)	(784)
Adjusted to N GAAP deferred tax	10	17	(10)	(6)
Net income - N GAAP		7,686	13,968	3,549
Minority interest		177	18	(90)
Net income after minority interest - N GAAP		7,863	13,986	3,459

Shareholders' equity:

Amounts in NOK million	Notes	2001	2000	1999
Shareholders' equity for US GAAP		74,793	71,227	59,497
Unrealized gains commodity derivative instruments – current and long-term (a)		(106)	(59)	(79)
Cash Flow hedge – current and long-term (a)		(188)	-	-
Unrealized gain on securities (b)	13	(58)	-	(4)
Deferred tax assets and liabilities – current and long-term (c)	10	96	10	24
Dividends payable (d)		(2,576)	(2,470)	(2,094)
Minority Interest (e)		1,051	1,419	1,323
Shareholders' equity for N GAAP		73,012	70,127	58,667

EXHIBIT 5-6 Country-Specific Secondary Statement: Honda's U.S. GAAP Consolidated Balance Sheet

Honda Motor Co., Ltd. and Subsidiaries March 31, 2000 and 2001	Yen (millions)		U.S. dollars (thousands) (note 2)
Assets	2000	2001	2001
Current assets:			
Cash and cash equivalents	¥ 430,587	¥ 417,519	$ 3,369,806
Trade accounts and notes receivable, net of allowance for doubtful accounts of ¥7,077 million in 2000 and ¥7,899 million ($63,753 thousand) in 2001	390,659	440,802	3,557,724
Finance subsidiaries–receivables, net (note 3)	731,580	762,368	6,153,091
Inventories (note 4)	567,705	620,754	5,010,121
Deferred income taxes (note 9)	154,277	151,722	1,224,552
Other current assets (note 7)	180,903	205,771	1,660,783
Total current assets	2,455,711	2,598,936	20,976,077
Finance subsidiaries–receivables, net (note 3)	878,242	1,304,994	10,532,639
Investments and advances:			
Investments in and advances to affiliates (note 5)	175,389	200,625	1,619,250
Other, including marketable equity securities (note 6)	213,705	175,562	1,416,965
Total investments and advances	389,094	376,187	3,036,215
Property, plant and equipment, at cost (note 7):			
Land	296,591	299,984	2,421,178
Buildings	783,055	831,868	6,714,027
Machinery and equipment	1,731,589	1,887,630	15,235,109
Construction in progress	63,408	99,552	803,487
	2,874,643	3,119,034	25,173,801
Less accumulated depreciation	1,753,603	1,864,411	15,047,707
Net property, plant and equipment	1,121,040	1,254,623	10,126,094
Other assets (notes 7 and 9)	54,341	132,669	1,070,775
Total assets	¥4,898,428	¥5,667,409	$45,741,800

See accompanying notes to consolidated financial statements.

statement) into the foreign user's language, currency, and accounting principles. Given their high cost, companies only prepare *country-specific secondary statements* for those countries where the management perceives a sizable investor interest in the company. Users should not be lulled into a false sense of complacency by secondary statements. While this is the most that a company can do for its foreign users, a secondary statement ought not to give the user license to engage in cross-country ratio analysis. As will be discussed in more detail later in this chapter, appropriate use of secondary statements requires users to be aware of and consider differences in the business and economic environments of the countries where the respective companies are based. An example of a country-specific secondary statement appears in Exhibit

EXHIBIT 5-6   Country-Specific Secondary Statement: Honda's U.S. GAAP Consolidated Balance Sheet
(continued)

Liabilities and Stockholders' Equity	Yen (millions)		U.S. dollars (thousands) (note 2)
	2000	2001	2001
Current liabilities:			
Short-term debt (note 7)...	¥ 495,953	¥ 910,417	$ 7,347,998
Current portion of long-term debt (note 7)	343,576	274,481	2,215,343
Trade payables:			
Notes..	19,332	24,372	196,707
Accounts	677,544	795,882	6,423,584
Accrued expenses...................................	483,917	539,348	4,353,091
Income taxes payable (note 9)	53,319	38,633	311,808
Other current liabilities (notes 7 and 9)	128,670	178,124	1,437,643
Total current liabilities.............................	2,202,311	2,761,257	22,286,174
Long-term debt (note 7)	574,566	368,173	2,971,533
Other liabilities (notes 7, 8, 9 and 11)	191,178	307,688	2,483,358
Total liabilities..................................	2,968,055	3,437,118	27,741,065
Stockholders' equity:			
Common stock, authorized 3,600,000,000 shares, par value ¥50 ($0.40); issued 974,414,215 shares at March 31, 2000 and 2001	86,067	86,067	694,649
Capital surplus...................................	172,529	172,529	1,392,486
Legal reserves (note 10)...........................	27,545	27,929	225,416
Retained earnings (note 10)	2,218,848	2,428,293	19,598,814
Accumulated other comprehensive income (loss) (notes 6, 9, 11 and 13)	(574,616)	(484,527)	(3,910,630)
Total stockholders' equity	1,930,373	2,230,291	18,000,735
Commitments and contingent liabilities (notes 16 and 17)			
Total liabilities and stockholders' equity.....................	¥4,898,428	¥5,667,409	$45,741,800

5-6. In this instance, Honda Motors, a Japanese company, has prepared secondary statements for investors in the United States. The Honda Motors financial statements are very similar in appearance to those of Toyota in that both are in English and in U.S. dollars. However, the critical difference is that Honda's secondary statements are in U.S. GAAP while Toyota's convenience statements are in Japanese GAAP.

Another variation of a secondary statement is one that is universal rather than country specific. Firms often prepare secondary statements that are in English, in their domestic currency, and using International Accounting Standards rather than the standards of any particular country. The approach here is one of meeting the investor halfway. Such secondary statements result in considerable cost savings, relative to country-specific statements, since they can be sent to users anywhere in the

EXHIBIT 5-7   "Universal" Secondary Statement: Novartis IAS-based Financial Statements

Consolidated Balance Sheets
(at December 31, 2001 and 2000)

	Notes	2001 CHF millions	2000 CHF millions
ASSETS			
Long-term assets			
Tangible fixed assets	8	9 060	9 030
Intangible assets	9	6 548	5 830
Investments in associated companies	11	6 715	1 531
Deferred taxes	12	3 235	3 265
Other financial assets	13	7 027	5 601
Total long-term assets		**32 585**	**25 257**
Current assets			
Inventories	14	4 112	4 122
Trade accounts receivable	15	5 349	5 283
Other current assets	16	2 895	3 011
Marketable securities	10	10 697	11 720
Cash and cash equivalents		11 147	8 803
Total currents assets		**34 200**	**32 939**
TOTAL ASSETS		**66 785**	**58 196**
EQUITY AND LIABILITIES			
Equity	17		
Share capital		1 443	1 443
Treasury shares		-169	-139
Reserves		40 971	35 558
Total equity		**42 245**	**36 862**
Minority interests		**104**	**78**
Liabilities			
Long-term liabilities			
Financial debts	18	2 492	2 283
Deferred taxes	12	3 885	3 488
Other long-term liabilities	19	3 830	3 845
Total long-term liabilities		**10 207**	**9 616**
Short-term liabilities			
Trade accounts payable		1 809	1 591
Financial debts	21	5 074	3 779
Other short-term liabilities	22	7 346	6 270
Total short-term liabilities		**14 229**	**11 640**
Total liabilities		**24 436**	**21 256**
TOTAL EQUITY AND LIABILITIES		**66 785**	**58 196**

The accompanying notes form an integral part of the consolidated financial statements.

EXHIBIT 5-7 "Universal" Secondary Statement: Novartis IAS-based Financial Statements *(continued)*

Consolidated Income Statements
(for the years ended December 31, 2001 and 2000)

	Notes	2001 CHF millions	2000 CHF millions
Sales	3/4	32 038	35 805
Cost of goods sold		-7 886	-10 242
Gross profit		**24 152**	**25 563**
Marketing & distribution		-11 098	-10 945
Research & development	3	-4 189	-4 657
Administration & general overheads		-1 588	-2 078
Operating income	3/4	**7 277**	**7 883**
Income from associated companies	11	139	98
Financial income, net	5	1 067	1 091
Income before taxes and minority interests		**8 483**	**9 072**
Taxes	6	-1 440	-1 820
Income before minority interests		**7 043**	**7 252**
Minority interests		-19	-42
NET INCOME		**7 024**	**7 210**
Earnings per share (CHF)	7	2.73	2.75
Diluted earnings per share (CHF)	7	2.72	2.75

The accompanying notes form an integral part of the consolidated financial statements.

world. Secondary statements prepared in accordance with International Accounting Standards are also useful in that a number of stock exchanges, including London, accept them from foreign firms seeking to list their stocks in these markets. Exhibit 5-7 shows an excerpt from a Swiss company's annual report containing *a universal secondary statement*. It is in English, denominated in Swiss francs, and has been prepared in accordance with International Accounting Standards.

It is useful to review the different responses by companies to their foreign audiences and to understand why they select the mode of response that they do. The companies that adopt the do-nothing approach to transnational financial reporting are companies that operate almost purely in their home country. While they may export their products, they almost never raise capital abroad. Hence, they do not see the need to incur any additional expenses in responding to foreign users of their financial statements. Companies that translate their annual reports into one or more foreign languages perceive that the public relations benefits from this exercise justify its costs. A convenience translation prepared in the foreign user's language enables the company to communicate with the foreign user not only as relates to its financial performance but also to showcase its products. Since the primary annual report has already been prepared for the domestic audience, the cost of translating it into the foreign reader's language is relatively modest. The convenience statement demonstrates a desire to interest foreign providers of capital and is often an intermediate step for companies that are planning to tap foreign capital markets. As indicated above, because it is essentially similar in appearance to a secondary statement and might be mistaken as such by an unsophisticated foreign user, it is important that the company prominently

EXHIBIT 5-7 "Universal" Secondary Statement: Novartis IAS-based Financial Statements *(continued)*

Consolidated Cash Flow Statements

(for the years ended December 31, 2001 and 2000)

	Notes	2001 CHF millions	2000 CHF millions
Net income		**7 024**	**7 210**
Reversal of non-cash items			
Minority interests		19	42
Taxes		1 440	1 820
Depreciation, amortization and impairments on			
Tangible fixed assets		969	1 196
Intangible assets		780	309
Financial assets		31	--
Income from associated companies		-139	-98
Gains on disposal of tangible and intangible assets		-510	-1
Net financial income		-1 067	-1 091
Interest and other financial receipts		779	1 944
Interest and other financial payments		-391	-1 211
Taxes paid		-1 377	-2 176
Cash flow before working capital and provision changes		**7 558**	**7 944**
Restructuring payments and other cash payments out of provisions		-421	-439
Change in net current assets and other operating cash flow items	23	205	107
Cash flow from operating activities		**7 342**	**7 612**
Investment in tangible fixed assets		-1 351	-1 353
Proceeds from disposals of tangible fixed assets		275	347
Purchase of intangible and financial assets		-7 552	-3 149
Proceeds from disposals of intangible and financial assets		1 550	471
Acquisition/divestment of subsidiaries	24	-169	-1 371
Acquisition of minorities		-1	--
Proceeds from disposals of marketable securities		2 573	4 839
Cash flow used for investing activities		**-4 675**	**-216**
Acquisition of treasury shares		-3 848	-1 165
Proceeds from issue of options on Novartis shares		4 056	--
Change in long-term financial debts		1 258	-124
Change in short-term financial debts		374	-1 402
Dividends paid		-2 194	-2 064
Cash flow used for financing activities		**-354**	**-4 755**
Net effect of currency translation on cash and cash equivalents		31	-119
Net change in cash and cash equivalents		**2 344**	**2 522**
Cash and cash equivalents at the beginning of the year		8 803	6 281
Cash and cash equivalents at end of the year		**11 147**	**8 803**

The accompanying notes form an integral part of the consolidated financial statements.

indicate that the financial statements are in its home-country GAAP and not in the user's GAAP. Limited restatements are often prepared by companies that are either already tapping foreign capital markets or are planning to do so. In situations where capital market regulators accept foreign companies' original financial statements, companies prepare limited restatements voluntarily to accommodate their foreign investors. In the United States, where foreign registrants must either file financial statements in compliance with U.S. GAAP or provide a reconciliation of the differences (between U.S. GAAP and home-country GAAP), companies doing the latter often provide reconciliations to U.S. GAAP in their Form 20-F filings to the SEC. Those companies that prepare U.S. GAAP financial statements for the SEC are likely to provide secondary statements to their U.S. audience since they have already incurred the expense related to preparing U.S. GAAP financial statements. Providing secondary statements obviously makes their financial statements more user-friendly to U.S. readers and might thereby enhance the attractiveness of their shares to U.S. investors. Cost considerations and the need to tap capital providers in several countries sometimes results in companies preparing universal rather than country-specific secondary statements.

COPING WITH TRANSNATIONAL FINANCIAL REPORTING

In a fairly extensive study, Choi and Levich [1991] examined how various groups deal with international accounting diversity. In their research they tried to discern whether and why accounting diversity was perceived to be a problem, how various groups coped with the differences, and whether problems associated with international accounting diversity lead to capital markets effects. They conducted personal interviews with various types of capital market participants such as investors, issuers (i.e., corporations), underwriters, regulators, and rating agencies from five countries—Germany, Japan, Switzerland, the United Kingdom, and the United States. In the next section we discuss their findings related to the corporations that are the preparers of the financial statements. In the following section, we discuss Choi and Levich's findings related to users.

Preparer Response to Transnational Financial Reporting

The nationality of the companies in the study seemed to influence to what extent they were affected by international accounting diversity. U.S. and U.K. firms, which tended to be large and have more experience with international capital markets and international funding arrangements, were relatively less affected by accounting differences. On the other hand, Japanese, German, and Swiss firms seemed to be more affected. The accounting disclosure items that these firms most often mentioned as requiring additional effort on their part were the need to 1) prepare consolidated financial statements, 2) provide more segment information, 3) issue quarterly reports, and 4) explain the nature of various reserves to investors.

Corporate issuers indicated that they used a variety of coping mechanisms to deal with accounting differences. A number of companies restated the GAAP in their financial statements. The restatement took various forms and was selective based on the effect it had on their profitability or their competitiveness. For example, several of the companies in the study did only a partial restatement because they would have looked less well-off if they did a full restatement. A number of other companies would have actually looked better under a full restatement, given the conservative accounting practices used in their home country; however, they indicated that they refrained from doing a full restatement because it would hurt them competitively by revealing proprietary information to their competitors. Many of these companies indicated that they used road shows or hosted conferences for analysts to answer questions arising from accounting differences. The type of response was also affected by the nationality of the companies. U.S. firms adopted the do-nothing approach because non-U.S. regulators accept U.S. GAAP financial statements. Similarly, companies from the United Kingdom, where financial reporting and disclosure standards also tend to be high, appeared to do less restatement for foreign users. On the other hand, firms from Germany, Japan, and Switzerland, where there is less transparency in accounting, appeared to have put more effort into accessing foreign capital markets.

As one might expect, the capital market effects of accounting diversity were also a function of nationality. Choi and Levich found that non-U.S. firms had to incur greater costs for entering U.S. capital markets than did U.S. firms entering non-U.S. markets. Most of the non-U.S. firms indicated that the effect of accounting diversity was that they had refused to list their equity securities in the U.S. markets and had instead 1) bypassed the U.S. market in favor of the Eurobond market, 2) relied on domestic bank financing rather than floating commercial paper in the United States, 3) encouraged foreign investors to buy shares in the company's home market, 4) offered sponsored but unlisted American Depositary Receipts (ADRs) in the United States, and 5) undertaken a U.S. private placement under the SEC's Rule 144A. The last two alternatives do not require non-U.S. companies to provide the high level of disclosure that is required for listed firms.

In the final analysis, corporations presumably respond rationally as to how much additional cost and effort they are willing to undertake for foreign users of their annual reports. The expected benefits of whichever approach they adopt must exceed the cost of undertaking that activity. This equation naturally varies for each company in each foreign country, and hence it is not surprising that there is a great range in the level of resources that companies are willing to devote in communicating with their foreign audiences. As long as it is a product of an appropriate cost-benefit analysis, it is a reasonable response by the company even though it may not always be what the user prefers.

User Response to Transnational Financial Reporting

Just as the responses of preparers (to non-domestic users of their financial statements) are the result of a cost-benefit analysis, so also must users devise strategies on how to deal with financial information that originates in other countries. Again, as with preparers, one can expect a range of responses based on the level of resources that users are able and willing to devote toward a better understanding of foreign financial statements. Thus, small individual investors might adopt a do-nothing approach, simply not investing in the securities of companies that do not provide financial information in the investors' GAAP. Yet others might refuse to invest in individual foreign companies but might be more willing to invest in mutual funds that contain foreign securities on the premise that they are delegating the financial analysis and monitoring function to the professional fund manager. At the other end of the spectrum, large institutional investors might consider it worthwhile to invest in familiarizing themselves with other countries' business environments and developing skills in interpreting foreign financial statements in their original form. It also helps that they have the resources and expect to profit from doing so.

As previously indicated, Choi and Levich [1991] surveyed a number of user groups to determine how they are affected by, and how they respond to, financial information originating in countries other than their own. Their findings as relates to institutional investors, underwriters, and regulators are informative.

Slightly more than half the institutional investors in the study indicated that international accounting diversity affected their investment decisions in that it made it more difficult for them to measure their decision variables. Those institutional investors who did not feel hindered by accounting differences indicated that they focused on the economics of foreign entities, relied on local financial statements, employed the services of local brokers and research institutes, or ignored accounting differences entirely because they used a top-down investment approach. Under this approach, institutional investors rely on macroeconomic data and information on market parameters for their asset allocation decisions and country weights. Upon selecting countries, investment managers typically diversify their stock selections within a country, eliminating the need to engage in detailed cross-country comparisons.

Countries most frequently mentioned by institutional investors as being a source of concern when investing abroad were Germany, Japan, and Switzerland. This is probably reflective of the fact that the study was conducted in the late 1980s when emerging markets were not as "hot" an investment area as they became in the 1990s. Today, one would expect to find a number of emerging markets listed by institutional investors as presenting challenges to financial analysis. This was apparent during the Asian economic crisis. The institutional investors surveyed also identified a number of industries that were difficult to analyze across borders. These included banking, insurance, financial services, semiconductors, and mining. Choi and Levich also asked institutional investors to identify specific accounting measurement and disclosure items that were difficult to analyze in the international context. Among the measurement items that were listed as troublesome were multinational consolidations, discretionary reserves, foreign currency transactions and translation, goodwill, deferred taxes, and inventory valuation. The disclosure items that were identified as being problematic due to their non-comparability were segmental information, frequency and completeness of interim valuation, asset valuation policies, capital expenditures, and hidden reserves.

Institutional investors coped with the accounting differences in a variety of ways. A majority indicated that they restated foreign financial statements into GAAP that they were more familiar with. Some limited their foreign investments to government bonds. Others chose countries they wanted to invest in and then diversified within the selected countries, thereby eliminating (at least, in their view) the need to deal with accounting differences. Almost all the institutional investors surveyed indicated that meetings with company executives were a very important means of obtaining information on companies. This is consistent with the increasing reluctance of financial analysts to downgrade or issue negative reports on companies because such a report often results in the company denying access to the "offending" institutions.[1] Institutional investors indicated that international accounting diversity affected the location of market activity, the types of companies invested in, and the pricing of foreign securities. Given that these were all large investors, they did not consider the information processing costs to be burdensome.

Underwriters were another user group surveyed in the study. A vast majority of underwriters surveyed regarded international accounting diversity as being a problem.

---

[1]In October 1998, *Business Week* did a cover story titled "Corporate Earnings: Who Can You Trust?" The article suggested that financial analysts are reluctant to issue negative reports on corporations they follow for fear of being denied access to companies in the future and for losing the investment banking business from the companies they issue critical reports on (*Business Week*, October 5, 1998).

They indicated that they coped with differences in accounting principles and accounting disclosure in a variety of ways. Their methods of coping with differences in accounting principles included restating foreign financial statements into the underwriter's domestic accounting principles, restating to both domestic and U.S. GAAP (for non-U.S. underwriters), and conducting a time-series financial analysis in the issuer's GAAP. They coped with disclosure differences by requesting additional information from the company, obtaining guarantees from the parent company or some third party, or avoiding the U.S. market in favor of a less demanding one. Other non-accounting coping mechanisms consisted of relying on credit ratings, soliciting only the top-tier companies in each industry, and accessing foreign capital via private placements.

Underwriters indicated that accounting diversity affected their decision-making in a number of ways. It influenced the geographic spread and location of their activity, the types of companies and securities they selected, their information processing costs, and their assessment of securities returns or valuation in different countries. As financial intermediaries between corporate issuers and investors, underwriters' responses are likely to reflect the views of their clients. Underwriters play a role in advising corporate issuers on the types of disclosure policies to be adopted, since these are likely to affect the geographic markets in which firms can issue securities and also the financial terms on which the securities are issued. For some of their investor clients, restating foreign financial statements into the potential investors' GAAP is a useful service that underwriters can provide. For clients that have developed the ability to translate the foreign financial statements, underwriters can provide advice on the business environment and practices in the issuer's country.

Market regulators are another important user category in that they can directly impact the type and volume of foreign securities that can be issued and traded in their jurisdiction. With the increasing globalization of capital markets, regulators face the challenge of balancing their mandate to protect domestic investors without imposing unreasonable barriers to reputable foreign companies desiring to enter the regulator's market. Another challenge facing regulators is to treat domestic and foreign companies evenhandedly when setting financial reporting and disclosure requirements. Because this affects the cost of capital, it is likely to be a determinant in the competitiveness of companies as well as the willingness of foreign companies to enter the regulator's market. This, in turn, affects the investment choices available to domestic investors. How regulators treat foreign firms in their jurisdiction might also affect how their domestic firms are treated in other countries.

Given all of the above, the responses of the regulators surveyed by Choi and Levich were rather surprising. None of the regulators in the survey indicated experiencing significant problems from accounting differences. This may be largely due to the fact that regulators generally have the power to obtain whatever additional information they need directly from the companies that they regulate. Regulators also indicated that in cases where the original auditor's qualifications or procedures were not acceptable to the regulator, they required companies to provide a second audit. Regulators indicated that international accounting diversity had negative effects on the level of capital market activity in their jurisdiction by foreign firms. However, there was also a concern expressed that relaxing domestic requirements for foreign issuers also had a negative effect in that it reduced investor confidence in the market. Thus, regulators have to strive to achieve the optimal disclosure level for foreign private issuers seeking to list securities in their jurisdiction.

INTERNATIONAL FINANCIAL STATEMENT ANALYSIS

Many accounting and finance departments in business schools include financial ratio analysis in a number of their courses in both undergraduate and graduate programs. This sometimes results in calculator-happy business graduates ready to engage in ratio analysis whenever the opportunity presents itself. Ratio analysis based on "apples to oranges" comparisons can lead to highly questionable conclusions and decisions when dealing with transnational financial information. The single most important message in this section is that financial statement analysis can do more harm than good when comparing companies from different countries if the analyst disregards the nationality and the domestic environment of the companies being analyzed. Users of transnational financial information need to consider a number of factors before they can make sensible comparisons between companies from different countries.

In 1998–1999, Morgan Stanley Dean Witter published a series of reports titled *Apples to Apples*.[2] Each report focused on a specific industry and attempted to compare the major multinational companies in that industry from around the world. These reports identified a number of critical variables in each industry that investors might want to adjust in order to make relevant comparisons between firms from a variety of countries. Some of these adjustments related to varying accounting treatments in the firms' home countries while others were industry specific items that needed to be considered in gauging the financial health, performance, and prospects of these companies. They identified six accounting issues as needing the most attention in conducting sensible cross-country comparisons. Their suggestions on dealing with these areas are summarized next.

DEPRECIATION AND REVALUATION OF LONG-LIVED ASSETS Depreciation methods and periods can vary tremendously across countries. For example, in the global automotive industry, firms use both straight-line and accelerated methods (with several instances of the same firm using both methods). The depreciation period ranges from 6 years for Fiat to 15 years for General Motors. It is necessary for investors to factor the cost of capacity required to generate the firm's earnings. If depreciation does not adequately measure this variable then appropriate adjustments must be made to include, in cost of goods sold, the annual expenditure required to generate current revenue. In order to have a reasonable comparison of the firm's financial position, investors need to consider adjustments required to revalue and write off long-lived assets, as appropriate. Finally, all leased assets should be capitalized using their present value. This is particularly important in certain industries such as airlines where the percentage of carriers' aircraft fleets that are carried off the balance sheet (through operating leases) can range from 0% for Ryanair to 42% for United Airlines.

GOODWILL As discussed in Chapter 4, this is another item where there have been varying accounting practices across countries. As goodwill represents a growing percentage of corporate balance sheets, adjusting for these differences becomes more important in conducting international financial statement analysis. For firms that have engaged in acquisitions of other entities, investors must ensure that the full premium is recognized. Since immediate write-off of goodwill, straight-line amortization, and

---

[2]See various issues of *Apples to Apples*, Morgan Stanley Dean Witter (1998–99).

the previously allowed pooling method tend to distort the picture on a firm's profitability for the period, investors are better off using the impairment approach in conducting cross-country analysis. The move towards this accounting treatment in the United States and elsewhere should make financial statement analysis of goodwill easier for investors.

FOREIGN EXCHANGE While we have covered foreign currency translation in detail in Chapter 3, a few observations related to its impact on international financial statement analysis are appropriate here. Differences in the translation method used can have a significant effect on the reported earnings and comparability across firms. In Illustration 5-1, a U.S. company with a fully owned subsidiary in Singapore reports earnings of US $27.78 million when it uses the current rate method (i.e., Singapore dollar as the functional currency), and earnings of US$70.11 million when it uses the temporal method (i.e., U.S dollar as the functional currency). Under the current rate method, net income and equity numbers provide a reasonable picture of the company but changes in cumulative translation adjustment should be treated as a nonrecurring item. Under the temporal method, if a foreign subsidiary finances its long-lived assets with debt in the local currency, the carrying values in the parent's balance sheet are likely to be distorted. Asset values and equity are not likely to be realizable. While analyzing multinational companies, investors need to distinguish operating from financial gains in order to better forecast earnings growth and to use appropriate price earnings multiples. Investors also need to consider companies' foreign exchange hedging policies since they have the potential to impact the firms' operating and financial performance. Finally, investors ought to pay attention to the firms' financing strategy, including the currency in which they raise capital, since this can affect future returns.

PENSION AND OTHER POST-EMPLOYMENT BENEFITS While the extent and importance of post-employment benefits vary from country to country, they generally include all payments due to an employee upon his retirement such as pensions, lump-sum payments, continuing health care and insurance benefits. These obligations can have a significant impact on cross-country analysis. In order to conduct a sensible comparison of firms globally, investors must adjust financial statements to include the cost of health care and pensions without deferrals and treat the companies' net obligations as debt. The net interest portion of the net pension obligation ought to be treated as a financial cost and not an operating expense. Finally, differences between real and reported obligations should be accrued and annual change in the obligation should be treated as a catch-up amount in computing income. A comparison of global telecommunications firms is illustrative of both the potential importance of this item and the dramatic differences across companies. By one estimate, in 1997, for Japan's Nippon Telephone and Telegraph (NTT), cumulative under-expensing of post-employment benefits totaled 16% of equity, while cumulative under-funding was 79% of equity. For the same period, Telstra of Australia had cumulative over-expensing of post-employment benefits amounting to 25% of equity, while its over-funding was 30% of equity.

CONSOLIDATION AND GROUP REPORTING In Japan and many European countries where the shareholder has not traditionally been the main constituent for financial reporting, consolidation accounting is a fairly recent requirement. Often the emphasis by preparers and users in these countries tends to be on the parent's

ILLUSTRATION 5-1   Impact of Differing Foreign Currency Translation Methods

A U.S. parent company owns a Singapore manufacturing company. Assume the exchange rate is US$1 equal to S$1.6 at acquisition on 1/1/2002 and changes to S$1.8 at 12/31/2002, with an average rate for the year of S$1.7. The Singapore company's income is paid as a dividend to the parent and then to shareholders at year end. (Amounts in millions)

In Singapore Subsidiary Statements

	Reported Balance		Reported Balance
1/1 PP&E	S$800	1/1 Long-term loan	S$600
		1/1 Shareholder's equity	200
1/1 Total Assets	S$800	1/1 Total liabilities and equity	S$800
Net income for year	S$50		

In US Consolidated Statements (After Acquisition)

	Reported Balance		Reported Balance
1/1 PP&E at S$800/1.6	$500	1/1 Long-term loan at S$600/1.6	$375
	0	1/1 Shareholder's equity	$125
1/1 Total Assets	$500	1/1 Total liabilities and equity	$500

Case 1 (Translation): S$ as Functional Currency: US Consolidated Report (12/31/2002)
Assets and liabilities are translated at year-end exchange rate; net income is translated at average exchange rate.

	Reported Balance		Reported Balance
12/31 PP&E using year-end rate S$800/1.8	$444	12/31 Long-term loan using year-end rate S$600/1.8	$333
		12/31 Shareholder's equity	125
		Translation loss in equity 200/1.8-200/1.6	(14)
12/31 Total Assets	$444	12/31 Total liabilities and equity	$444

1/1-12/31 Net income before exchange gain/(loss) using average rate S$50/1.7	$29.41
12/31 Loss on dividend receipt from Singapore co. at year-end rate S$50/1.8-S$50/1.7	$(1.63)
1/1-12/31 Reported net income	$27.78

Case 2 (Remeasured): U.S. dollar as Functional Currency: US Consolidated Report (12/31/2002)
Property is translated at exchange rate at acquisition date; liabilities are translated at year-end exchange rate; net income is translated at average exchange rate.

	Reported Balance		Reported Balance
12/31 PP&E using year-end rate S$800/1.6	$500	12/31 Long-term loan using year-end rate S$600/1.8	$333
		12/31 Shareholder's equity	167
12/31 Total Assets	$500	12/31 Total liabilities and equity	$500

1/1-12/31 Net income before exchange gain/(loss) using average rate S$50/1.7	$29.41
12/31 Exchange gain on loan 600/1.6-600/1.8	$42.33
12/31 Loss on dividend receipt from Singapore co. at year-end rate S$50/1.8-S$50/1.7	$(1.63)
1/1-12/31 Reported net income	$70.11

financial statements. Investors need to be mindful of this perspective in using financial statements from these countries. As high technology companies and formerly regulated telecoms and airlines enter into strategic alliances worldwide, investors have to deal with the complexities of consolidation and group reporting. One of the steps analysts can take is to obtain as much geographic and line of business segment information as possible to gain a better understanding of the importance of the various affiliated entities. While one can still use the consolidated equity or net income numbers to conduct an overall analysis of such firms, one needs to exercise caution in using group data for specific income statement and balance sheet items. In order to make meaningful comparisons of companies across countries, it is important to ascertain that they are using consistent consolidation practices. Proportional consolidation might be the best method of comparison for companies that derive a significant portion of their income from equity in affiliates.

TAXATION Deferred taxes are the main issue that investors must contend with in order to estimate a firm's real tax rate in making future projections. While this has always been an issue in countries with dual reporting regimes such as the United States and United Kingdom, until recently deferred taxes were not a consideration in countries such as Germany and Japan, which have a single reporting regime wherein financial reporting coincided with tax reporting. However, the globalization of accounting standards is resulting in the introduction of deferred tax balances in their financial statements also. In adjusting for the effects of taxation while conducting international financial statement analyses, investors need to consider whether certain taxes to be paid in the next few years have not been recorded. The present value of deferred taxes should be computed and changes in net deferred tax balances should be treated as an expense. In order to get a meaningful tax rate for purposes of comparison, current taxes paid should be combined with the tax expense derived from the change in the present value of deferred taxes. In one comparison, the adjustment in the net deferred tax asset ranged from an increase of 217% as a percentage of reported equity for Northwest to a decrease of 3% for British Airways.

As discussed in previous chapters, there is considerable evidence in the international accounting literature that accounting principles in certain countries take a conservative approach to income measurement while other countries take an optimistic approach to income measurement. Thus, in order to enhance comparability, at the very least, the financial statements of firms from different countries must be translated to the same accounting principles. This is the first consideration in making cross-country comparisons. Illustration 5-2 shows the effect on Volvo's return on equity (ROE) in switching from Swedish GAAP to U.S. GAAP. It is evident that the magnitude of the difference in the ROE (from switching GAAPs) is not consistent from one year to the next. However, it is inappropriate to make conclusions even from the ratio analysis based on common GAAP financial statements. The user cannot disregard the business environment in the companies' home country in making decisions as to the leverage, liquidity, or profitability of the companies compared. In this context, a discussion of Japan and Korea[3] is instructive. For instance, while the relatively high leverage in Japan and Korea may alarm the typical U.S. investor, one needs to understand the different capital market orientation in these countries relative to the United States. While the United States has traditionally been an equity-oriented economy,

---

[3]All references to Korea are to the Republic of Korea (i.e., South Korea).

ILLUSTRATION 5-2   Effect of Switching GAAP on Volvo's Return on Equity

Profit for the year	1996	1997	1998
Profit for the year in accordance with Swedish accounting principles	12,477	10,359	8,638
Items increasing (decreasing) reported profit for the year			
Foreign currency translation (A)	(89)	(4,994)	535
Income taxes (B)	494	122	(201)
Tooling costs (C)	(312)	–	–
Business combinations (D)	(529)	(529)	(530)
Shares and participations (E)	176	–	90
Interest costs (F)	15	28	20
Leasing (G)	49	46	(118)
Debt and equity securities (H)	(147)	123	116
Items affecting comparability (I)	–	–	1,178
Pensions and other post-employment benefits (J)	(95)	65	313
Tax effect of above U.S. GAAP adjustments	178	1,336	(609)
Net increase (decrease) in profit for the year	(260)	(3,803)	794
Approximate profit for the year In accordance with U.S. GAAP	**12,217**	**6,556**	**9,432**
Approximate profit for the year per share, SEK in accordance with U.S. GAAP	**26.40**	**14.50**	**21.40**
Weight average number of shares outstanding (in thousands)	463,558	452,540	441,521

Shareholders' equity	1995	1997	1998
Shareholders' equity in accordance with Swedish accounting principles	57,876	60,431	68,056
Items increasing (decreasing) reported shareholders' equity			
Foreign currency translation (A)	3,660	(1,163)	(628)
Income taxes (B)	1,398	1,520	1,319
Tooling costs (C)	–	–	–
Business combinations (D)	2,558	2,029	1,499
Shares and participations (E)	(90)	(90)	–
Interest costs (F)	503	531	551
Leasing (G)	(91)	(51)	(177)
Debt and equity securities (H)	1,604	3,962	133
Items affecting comparability (I)	–	–	1,178
Pensions and other post-employment benefits (J)	786	851	1,548
Other	(203)	(224)	(226)
Tax effect of above U.S. GAAP adjustments	(1,726)	(1,184)	(774)
Net increase in shareholders' acuity	8,399	6,181	4,423
Approximate shareholders' equity in accordance with U.S. GAAP	**66,275**	**66,612**	**72,479**

Return On Equity	1996	1997	1998
Swedish GAAP	$\frac{12477}{57867} = 21.6\%$	$\frac{10359}{60431} = 17.1\%$	$\frac{8638}{68056} = 12.7\%$
U.S. GAAP	$\frac{12217}{66275} = 18.4\%$	$\frac{6556}{66612} = 9.8\%$	$\frac{9432}{72479} = 13.0\%$
Effect of switching GAAP	3.2% Lower	7.3% Lower	0.3% Higher

Japanese and Korean companies have looked less to stockholders and more to lenders for their capital needs.

In the post-World War II era, Japan and Korea have both emerged as predominantly debt-oriented economies, albeit, with a slightly different model in each country. The *keiretsu* (or groups of related companies) that emerged in Japan were formed around Japan's commercial banks. Each keiretsu typically had at its core a bank to which it turned for most of its financing needs. The keiretsu system fostered a close relationship between the borrowing company, related companies, and the bank. Cross-shareholdings became an important characteristic of keiretsu. Consequently, Japanese banks seldom levy penalties on delayed interest payments or call in delinquent loans from related companies; on the contrary, they postpone interest payments and even refinance troubled loans to affiliated companies on more liberal terms. Similarly, related firms within the same keiretsu regularly help each other by prepaying receivables owed to a troubled firm and allowing payables to be delayed. In such an environment, high levels of debt do not pose the same financial threat as they do in countries such as the United States, where bank financing is at arm's length.[4]

Korea is a similarly debt-oriented economy where the government has assumed a major role in corporate finance. In Korea, the government encourages certain business groups, known as *chaebol*, to undertake economic activities that it considers beneficial to the country's economic development. Unlike the keiretsu in Japan, the Korean chaebol consist of groups of related companies with a trading company, rather than a bank, at their core. In Korea, the financing is typically in the form of foreign currency loans guaranteed by Korean banks. Since Korean banks are government controlled, the government was the grantor of credit to the chaebol. Because of its interest in the borrowing firm, the government would make sure that troubled firms were rescued either by additional infusion of capital or via merger with other firms selected by the government. In Korea, corporate debt has traditionally not been classified by the level of risk based on the level of the borrowing company's leverage. On the contrary, the greater the borrower's debt, the more the bank has at stake in the company and the more likely it is to rescue the company. Instead of being a cause for concern, high debt ratios in Korea reflect a company's close ties to its bank, which, in turn, signal a company's close relationship with the government and the greater likelihood that it will be rescued in times of economic difficulty. The Asian economic crisis that started in 1997 has starkly demonstrated the dangers of lending practices that are based on government intervention rather than economic viability.

Similarly, one must be aware of certain environmental differences between Japan, Korea, and the United States in comparing liquidity ratios from these countries. At first glance, the lower liquidity ratios in Japan and Korea might appear alarming to an analyst in the United States or the United Kingdom. In Japan, however, what is a short-term borrowing on the surface (i.e., maturing in a year) is actually more like a long-term debt in that it is typically rolled over rather than repaid at maturity. The lender and borrower both prefer short-term financing over long-term loans. It allows the lender to frequently adjust the interest rates to reflect market rates, and it enables the borrower to obtain capital at a lower cost since the interest rates on short-term loans are typically lower than on long-term financing. Similarly, in Korea, companies

---

[4]The subject of cross-shareholdings among *keiretsu* in Japan has been the subject of much attention recently. Please see Benes [1999], Sapsford [1999], and *Business Week* [1999] for more on this subject.

tend to depend more on short-term borrowings because of the scarcity of long-term debt. Short-term loans are typically rolled over in Korea, also. One could argue that "short-term" is really a misnomer in both these countries since both borrower and lender fully expect to roll over the loan at maturity. Consequently, lower current and quick ratios have not historically been a cause for alarm in Japan and Korea, while they would be in the arm's-length relationship that exists between the borrower and the lender in most equity-oriented countries such as the United States.

Finally, let us examine the cause for possible differences in the profitability ratios between companies in Japan, Korea, and the United States. Related to the debt-orientation and the high level of cross-holdings in Japan, short-run profits and short-run stock market gains are not as important to Japanese managers. The tradition of job security and lifetime employment in Japan are other reasons why Japanese managers are able to take a longer-term perspective than do managers in the United States. Sales growth and achieving a greater market share are more important variables in the performance evaluation of Japanese managers.[5] This, combined with the fact that Japanese firms often do business in competitive export markets, explains the lower profitability ratios for Japanese companies. As previously mentioned, in Korea the government has played a major role in the economy in the post-World War II era. The government controls prices and profit margins in its effort to make Korean exports more competitive. Increased interest costs and depreciation charges due to the higher asset base often mandated by the government also put a downward pressure on corporate profits. The domineering role of the Korean government in corporate lending, investment, and pricing policies means that corporate profitability is not the sole measure of managerial performance in Korean companies, in contrast to U.S. firms that face relatively little direct intervention from the government in business decisions.

The above discussion clearly points to the need for several levels of "adjustments" that must be undertaken by those engaging in international comparisons of firms within the same industry. One adjustment relates to ensuring that the financial statements of the companies being analyzed are prepared according to the same set of generally accepted accounting principles. Companies that are listed on foreign stock exchanges will frequently provide secondary financial statements prepared in the GAAP of the foreign country where they are listed. The task of converting financial statements from another country's GAAP to their domestic standards may be a little daunting for most individual investors. The second adjustment, which is more subtle, is placing the financial statements and the ratios within the national context of the company's home country. Failure to do so can result in mistaken conclusions and erroneous decisions.

The authors of a research article[6] comparing companies from several countries concluded that:

> ". . . accounting measurements reflected in corporate financial reports represent, in one sense, merely numbers that have limited meaning and significance in and of themselves. Meaning and significance come from and depend upon an understanding of the environmental context from which the numbers are drawn as well as the relationship between the numbers and the underlying economic phenomena that are the real items of interest."

---

[5]See Bailes and Assada [1991].
[6]Choi et al [1983].

ADDITIONAL ISSUES IN INTERNATIONAL FINANCIAL STATEMENT ANALYSIS

Availability of Data

Anybody who has tried to do professional or academic research on a global sample of companies will attest that it is often difficult to access financial statements and data related to non-domestic companies. Naturally, the level of difficulty is related to the national origin and the level of multinationality of the company. It is generally easier to obtain annual reports from companies based in equity-oriented countries where companies are used to receiving requests from investors for their annual reports and other financial documents (such as regulatory filings) which are in the public domain. Companies in debt-oriented economies tend to be less willing to respond to requests for financial reports. In fairness to them, they simply may not be used to receiving such requests from their domestic constituents and do not consider it appropriate to expend resources to set up an investor relations infrastructure within their organization to respond to such requests. The exceptions to this situation are companies that have ventured abroad in search of business and capital. Such multinational companies recognize the need for investor relations in the markets where they have a presence and are, therefore, more willing to respond to requests for financial information. With the proliferation of corporate web sites, many companies now provide annual reports and other financial data about themselves through this medium. The internet offers several advantages to both the company and the public: it is less costly than traditional means of production and dissemination, it is more timely, and it is also environmentally friendly in that it uses less natural resources.

The difficulty of accessing information on foreign firms has also given rise to a database industry that gathers, organizes, and sells financial information on global samples of foreign companies. These databases vary in their coverage, their reliability, and their price. They often use templates to standardize the format of the information on the companies they cover. This can result in an inappropriate appearance of uniformity in the data provided. It can also minimize national differences and provide a veneer of comparability that is artificial and can be misleading to some users. It is likely that, as users become more sophisticated, they will be more discriminating of such databases. Other sources of financial data on foreign firms are the web sites and electronic databases of regulatory agencies as well as the web sites of various stock exchanges including the Amsterdam Stock Exchange, the Paris Bourse, and the New York Stock Exchange, among others.

Reliability of Data

Another important consideration in international financial statement analysis is the reliability of the financial information provided by preparers. The overall quality of the financial statements, particularly as relates to individual companies (i.e., at the micro-level), can be a function of a number of variables including the integrity of corporate management, the financial position of the company, and the attest value of its auditors. At the macro-level, the reliability of financial statements from various countries is likely to be affected by the level of transparency that prevails in the company's domicile, the scope and extent of audit required, and the degree of enforcement of financial reporting and securities regulations.

Users of non-domestic financial statements need to pay attention to these issues as they conduct international financial statement analyses. Clearly, institutional investors have more resources to research the variables cited above, particularly as they relate to specific firms. However, even individual investors need to be aware of at least some national characteristics as they use financial statements prepared in other countries. The two areas that are particularly relevant and fairly easy to research are the extent and scope of audit and the general level of enforcement of capital market regulations that exist in other countries. Investors could be in for a shock if they make economic decisions taking foreign financial statements at face value on the assumption that the audit and enforcement of capital market regulations in other countries mirror their own. This is not intended to be an ethnocentric comment but, rather, a caution of the potential pitfalls faced by investors who are uninformed about conditions in other countries.

Timeliness of Data

Related to the availability and reliability of financial information is the timeliness with which financial data are provided. In countries such as the United States, there are strict regulations on the timing and manner of dissemination of financial information. Great importance is placed on ensuring that information on corporate earnings and other significant developments likely to affect stock prices are disclosed concurrently to all investors. Securities laws are in place to deter trading based on insider information. However, in many countries, similar laws do not exist or are seldom enforced, with the result that certain individuals or groups are able to benefit from trading on information that they have obtained in advance of disclosures to other market participants. While a detailed discussion of this issue is not within the scope of this book, it is an important environmental variable of which investors need to be aware.

Also related to timeliness is the lag between the company's year end and the publication of its audited financial statements and annual report. In certain countries such as Brazil, Canada, Mexico, Korea, and the United States, annual reports are published between 30–60 days after year end. However, 61–90 days after year end appears to be the more typical time frame in which audited financial statements are published. Countries in this category include Argentina, Australia, the Netherlands, New Zealand, Singapore, Sweden, and the United Kingdom, among others. There are yet other countries where companies publish their audited financial statements beyond the first quarter of the following year (91–120 days). These countries include Austria, France, Germany, India, Italy, and Nigeria. One hopes that, with advances in information processing technology, companies will be able and willing to provide audited financial statements in a more timely manner.[7]

Language, Terminology, and Format

As indicated earlier, some companies still choose the do-nothing response in dealing with foreign users of their financial statements. These companies do not feel the need to accommodate foreign users of their financial statements and simply send the same annual report to foreign users that they do to domestic users. In such situations, if the languages differ for the preparer and the user, then the latter must find ways of overcoming the language barriers in order to make sense of the company's financial statements. However, there are also the differences that exist in the use of the same language in different countries (such as English in the United Kingdom and the

---

[7]This discussion is based on data presented in "International Accounting and Auditing Trends," edited by V. B. Bavishi [CIFAR 1995].

United States). Such differences can also give rise to differences in accounting terminology. Thus, what is *inventory* in the United States is *stock* in the United Kingdom, what is *sales* in the United States is *turnover* in the United Kingdom, *receivables* in the United States are *debtors* in the United Kingdom, *payables* in the United States are *creditors* in the United Kingdom, and *retained earnings* in the United States are *reserves* in the United Kingdom. Most terminology differences are not major barriers to international financial statement analysis and can be overcome with a modicum of effort on the part of users. However, there are situations when differences in definitions of terms can adversely affect the comparability of financial statements across countries. For example, the fairly innocuous accounting item, "cash and cash equivalents" can have different definitions in the accounting principles of various countries, as indicated in Exhibit 5-8. Similarly, "extraordinary items" can have different definitions across countries.

EXHIBIT 5-8 Global Variation in the Accounting Definition of "Cash"

DIFFERENCES IN THE DEFINITIONS OF CASH AND CASH EQUIVALENTS

	Canada	New Zealand	US	South Africa	UK	IASC
Treatment of cash and cash equivalents						
(a) net of short-term borrowings	x	x				
(b) net of short-term bank borrowings					x	
(c) gross			x*	x*		x
Treatment of equity securities as cash equivalents						
(a) specifically excluded		x				x+
(b) not specifically included	x		x	x	x	
Specific guidelines on maturity periods for cash equivalents						
(a) yes	x		x			x
(b) no		x		x	x	
Cash flow statement should disclose components of						
(a) cash and cash equivalents	x					x
(b) cash equivalents			x		x	
(c) no disclosure is required		x		x		

*netting is not mentioned
+unless they are in substance cash equivalents
Source: Wallace and Collier (1991)

Finally, the format of financial statements differs across countries. For example, in the United States, the balance sheet is organized in order of declining liquidity, with current assets and liabilities listed before long-lived assets and long-term liabilities. However, in Germany and the United Kingdom, the balance sheet items are listed in increasing order of liquidity, with the most liquid items appearing at the bottom of the balance sheet. Another example of a format difference in the balance sheet is that German companies tend to list the shareholders' equity section before the liabilities on the equity side of the balance sheet. Most of the format differences are purely cosmetic in nature and should not pose undue difficulties in international financial statement analysis.

SUMMARY

1. Companies respond to foreign users of their financial statements in a variety of ways. Corporate responses range from doing nothing additional for foreign users to preparing a set of secondary financial statements in the foreign user's language, currency, and accounting principles. Other responses include translating the financial statements into the user's language, in the user's currency, and partly in the user's accounting principles.

2. Users respond to foreign financial statements based on their resources and their level of interest in the foreign company. Their responses range from refusing to invest in foreign companies directly (in the case of some individual investors) to devoting considerable resources to monitor foreign companies' performance (in the case of institutional investors). Other responses include delegating the monitoring function to professional fund managers, relying on credit ratings, periodically meeting with company management, and, in the case of regulators, demanding a second audit where the original auditor's qualifications or procedures were not acceptable.

3. A number of adjustments are necessary in order to conduct international financial statement analysis. The financial statements must be translated into a common GAAP, typically the user's. The financial statements and the ratio analysis must also be placed in the context of the business environment in the company's home country.

4. Other factors that must be considered are the availability, timeliness, and reliability of the data, and the potentially misleading effects of differences in the language, terminology, and format used in the financial statements of foreign companies.

QUESTIONS

1. Describe the various ways in which corporations respond to foreign users of financial statements.

2. Why is there a wide range in corporate responses to foreign users of financial statements? What factors are likely to determine how much companies are willing to do in this arena?

3. Discuss how a) institutional investors, b) underwriters, and c) market regulators indicated that they coped with international accounting diversity as reported in the survey by Choi and Levich [1991].

4. What are some of the factors that investors must consider when comparing financial statements from companies based in different countries? Discuss the adjustments that are generally required in conducting cross-country comparisons of information contained in financial statements.

5. Discuss the major pitfalls in conducting cross-country ratio analysis. Are secondary statements prepared in the user's GAAP readily comparable to domestic financial statements? Explain.

6. Obtain an annual report from a foreign company that interests you and review the note containing its significant accounting policies. Discuss the main financial reporting issues you would be concerned about in comparing this company to a domestic company in the same industry.

7. Are there considerable differences in the timeliness and reliability of financial statement data across countries? How are these likely to affect financial statement analysis of companies across countries?

8. Investors cope with accounting principles differences in several different ways. Discuss at least two of these coping mechanisms and explain which approach(es) you favor, and why.

9. Non-U.S. companies listed on U.S. stock exchanges are not required to base their financial statements on U.S. GAAP. However, these companies are generally required to provide reconciliation disclosures that quantify any material differences between their reported net income and what their net income would be under U.S. GAAP. What are the most frequently disclosed types of material differences? Is U.S. GAAP net income usually larger or smaller than net income as reported under home-country GAAP? Why?

10. There are certain rules of thumb that are considered appropriate for financial ratios in a country. For example, current ratios of 2:1 and quick ratios of 1:1 are generally regarded as being desirable. Why might it be inappropriate to apply these rules of thumb when evaluating the liquidity of firms from other countries?

EXERCISES

1. Cost considerations and the need to tap capital providers in several countries sometimes result in companies preparing universal rather than country-specific secondary statements. If you were analyzing a universal secondary statement of a foreign company, what might be some of your concerns before making an investment decision? How would you get the answers you need?

2. Slightly more than half the institutional investors in the Choi and Levich study indicated that international accounting diversity affected their investment decisions due to the difficulty of measuring their decision variables. Obtain four company annual reports from different countries within the same industry. Using a few basic liquidity and profitability financial ratios (i.e., current, ROE, ROA) and what you already know about the countries and their business structure, which company would you invest in and why? List any concerns and difficulties you had in coming up with your answer.

3. Institutional investors often have difficulty analyzing measurement and disclosure items in an international context due to their non-comparability. Examples of problematic areas include discretionary reserves, goodwill, deferred taxes, inventory valuation, segmental information, asset valuation policies, and hidden reserves. Obtain two annual reports from different countries within the same industry and compare at least three problematic areas similar to ones listed above. In your opinion, are the differences significant enough to influence an investment decision? Explain.

4. There is a concern that relaxing domestic requirements for foreign issuers has a negative effect in that it reduces investor confidence in the market. Do the benefits outweigh the costs? Go to the web site of a regulatory body of your choice and list some of the practices and rulings it has passed in favor of, or against, foreign issuers in its jurisdiction.

5. Choose a company that issues both a domestic financial statement using its own GAAP and one in which it uses a foreign GAAP or IAS. Are there significant differences in the bottom line, policies and practices, format, etc.? Do the two sets of financial statements lead you to different conclusions about the operating performance of the company? Support your answers.

6. In the United States, foreign companies choosing to file financial statements with the SEC, prepared in their home-country GAAP, must provide a reconciliation to U.S. GAAP. Obtain the annual report of a non-U.S. company that contains a reconciliation to U.S. GAAP. Discuss the three items with the largest differences between the company's home-country GAAP and U.S. GAAP.

7. Go to Nokia's home page at *www.nokia.com* and bring up the company's most recent financial statements. Compare the Consolidated Profit and Loss statement prepared under international accounting standards to the Parent-only Profit and Loss statement prepared under Finnish Accounting Standards (FIN). Which statement makes Nokia appear more financially healthy? In your opinion, which GAAP best reflects economic reality, and why?

8. On the following page are the Consolidated Statements of Income and Parent Company Profit and Loss Statement of Rauma Corporation (Finland) from the company's 1997 annual report.

Rauma Corporation
Consolidated Statements of Income
December 31, 1997

	1997 FIM million
Net sales	10,866
Cost of goods sold	(7,918)
Gross profit	2,948
Selling, marketing, and administrative expenses	(2,288)
Other income and expenses, net	132
Operating profit	792
Share in results of associated companies	3
Interest and other financial expenses, net	(64)
Profit before extraordinary items and income taxes	731
Extraordinary items	-
Profit before income taxes	731
Income taxes	(212)
Profit before minority interests	519
Minority interests	-
Net profit	519
Earnings per share, FIM	9.72

Rauma Corporation
Parent Company Profit and Loss Statement
December 31, 1997

	1997 FIM million
Net sales	17
Cost of goods sold	(29)
Gross margin	**(12)**
Administrative expenses	(70)
Other income and expenses, net	158
Operating profit	76
Interest and other financial expenses, net	(191)
Loss before contributions,	
untaxed reserves and income taxes	**(115)**
Group contributions	380
Decrease in untaxed reserves	-
Increase in accelerated depreciation	(1)
Profit before income taxes	264
Income taxes	(75)
Net profit	189

Compare the net income and other important items in the two financial statements. Does this influence your opinion about the operating performance of the company? In your opinion, which statement is more informative from 1) a user perspective, 2) a management perspective?

9.   Company financial statements prepared under various GAAP have become an invaluable source of information to users doing cross-country comparisons among companies. Refer to Exhibit 5-9, which is Electrolux's (Switzerland) Parent Company income statement and balance sheet, consolidated income statement and balance sheet, and the Reconciliation from Swedish GAAP to U.S. GAAP from its 1998 annual report. Formulate a table and calculate the following ratios under the three GAAP:

EXHIBIT 5-9 Electrolux's Parent-only, Consolidated, and Limited Restatement

Parent company income statement

(SEKm)		1998	1997
Net sales		5,918	5,791
Cost of goods sold		–4,726	–4,559
Gross operating income		1,192	1,232
Selling expense		–727	–746
Administrative expense		–699	–736
Other operating income	(Note 3)	126	45
Other operating expense	(Note 4)	–43	–19
Operating income	(Note 23)	–151	–224
Group contributions		1,049	1,713
Interest income	(Note 7)	2,683	2,388
Interest expense	(Note 7)	–1,561	–2,257
Income after financial items		2,020	1,620
Allocations	(Note 17)	26	102
Income before taxes		2,046	1,722
Taxes	(Note 8)	–57	–70
Net income		1,989	1,652

Parent company balance sheet

ASSETS (SEKm)		Dec. 31, 1998		Dec. 31, 1997	
Fixed assets					
Intangible assets	(Note 10)		11		73
Tangible assets	(Note 11)		775		784
Financial assets	(Note 12)		30,739		28,595
Total fixed assets			31,525		29,452
Current assets					
Inventories, etc.	(Note 13)		593		482
Current receivables					
Receivable from subsidiaries		1,924		406	
Accounts receivable		431		458	
Tax refund claim		33		42	
Other receivables		40		36	
Prepaid expense and accrued income		162	2,590	119	1,061
Short-term placements		1,403		2,525	
Cash and bank balances		633	2,036	634	3,159
Total current assets			5,219		4,702
TOTAL ASSETS			36,744		34,154
Assets pledged	(Note 14)		30		10

EQUITY AND LIABILITIES (SEKm)		Dec. 31, 1998		Dec. 31, 1997	
Equity	(Note 15)				
Share capital	(Note 16)	1,831		1,831	
Statutory reserve		2,731		2,731	
Retained earnings		4,843		4,106	
Net income		1,989	11,394	1,652	10,320
Untaxed reserves	(Note 17)		548		574
Provisions					
Provisions for pensions and similar commitments	(Note 18)	192		848	
Other provisions	(Note 19)	149	341	156	1,004
Financial liabilities					
Payable to subsidiaries		5,395		4,404	
Bond loans		8,741		10,034	
Mortgages, promissory notes, etc.		5,538		4,189	
Short-term loans		3,060	22,734	2,103	20,730
Operating liabilities					
Payable to subsidiaries		345		292	
Accounts payable		516		460	
Other liabilities		55		43	
Accrued expense and prepaid income	(Note 21)	811	1,727	731	1,526
Total Equity and Liabilities			36,744		34,154
Contingent liabilities	(Note 22)		3,867		6,042

EXHIBIT 5-9 Electrolux's Parent-only, Consolidated, and Limited Restatement *(continued)*

Consolidated income statement

(SEKm)		1998	1997
Net sales	(Note 2)	117,524	113,000
Cost of goods sold		−86,899	−83,144
Gross operating income		30,625	29,856
Selling expense		−18,058	−18,850
Administrative expense		−6,336	−6,201
Other operating income	(Note 3)	141	149
Other operating expense	(Note 4)	−308	−404
Items affecting comparability	(Note 5)	964	−1,896
Operating income	(Notes 2, 6, 23)	7,028	2,654
Interest income	(Note 7)	1,349	1,285
Interest expense	(Note 7)	−2,527	−2,707
Income after financial items		5,850	1,232
Minority interests in income before taxes		76	51
Income before taxes		5,926	1,283
Taxes	(Note 8)	−1,951	−931
Net income		3,975	352
Net income per share, SEK	(Note 9)	10.85	0.95

Consolidated balance sheet

ASSETS (SEKm)			Dec. 31, 1998		Dec. 31, 1997
Fixed assets					
Intangible assets	(Note 10)		3,327		3,517
Tangible assets	(Note 11)		21,959		22,519
Financial assets	(Note 12)		2,599		1,744
Total fixed assets			27,885		27,780
Current assets					
Inventories, etc.	(Note 13)		16,957		16,110
Current receivables					
Accounts receivable		21,859		21,184	
Other receivables		3,123		2,014	
Prepaid expense and accrued income		2,078	27,060	2,718	25,916
Short-term placements		6,302		6,063	
Cash and bank balances		5,085	11,387	3,771	9,834
Total current assets			55,404		51,860
TOTAL ASSETS			83,289		79,640
Assets pledged	(Note 14)		2,635		2,973

EQUITY AND LIABILITIES (SEKm)			Dec. 31, 1998		Dec. 31, 1997
Equity	(Note 15)				
	(Note 16)				
Share capital		1,831		1,831	
Restricted reserves		11,427		9,716	
Retained earnings		7,247		8,666	
Net income		3,975	24,480	352	20,565
Minority interests			953		913
Provisions					
Provisions for pensions and similar commitments	(Note 18)	4,298		6,247	
Other provisions	(Note 19)	4,026	8,324	4,656	10,903
Financial liabilities					
Long-term bond loans	(Note 20)	6,777		7,827	
Mortgages, promissory notes, etc.	(Note 20)	11,018		10,864	
Short-term loans		11,275	29,070	9,788	28,479
Operating liabilities					
Accounts payable		10,476		9,879	
Tax liability		180		26	
Other liabilities		2,642		2,309	
Accrued expense and prepaid income	(Note 21)	7,164	20,462	6,566	18,780
TOTAL EQUITY AND LIABILITIES			83,289		79,640
Contingent liabilities	(Note 22)		1,658		2,083

EXHIBIT 5-9 Electrolux's Parent-only, Consolidated, and Limited Restatement *(continued)*

Notes to the financial statements

Note 25, (continued)		

APPLICATION OF US GAAP WOULD HAVE THE FOLLOWING APPROXIMATE EFFECTS ON CONSOLIDATED NET INCOME, EQUITY, AND THE BALANCE SHEET

A. Consolidated net income (SEKm)	1998	1997
Net income as reported in the consolidated income statement	3,975	352
Adjustments before taxes:		
Acquisitions	27	6
Timing differences	−306	669
Other	−49	19
Taxes on above adjustments	89	−191
Other taxes	12	−39
Approximate net income according to US GAAP, excluding divested operation	3,748	816
Divested operation	–	61
Approximate net income according to US GAAP	3,748	877
Approximate net income per share in SEK according to US GAAP, excluding divested operation	10.25	2.25
Approximate net income per share in SEK according to US GAAP (No. of shares in 1998 after a 5:1 stock split: 366,169,580)	10.25	2.40

B. Comprehensive income (SEKm)	1998	1997
Approximate net income according to US GAAP	3,748	877
Translation differences	910	473
Securities, unrealized changes in value	−56	−32
Provisions for pensions (minimum liability)	−1	−51
Approximate comprehensive income according to US GAAP	4,601	1,267

C. Equity (SEKm)	1998	1997
Equity as reported in the consolidated balance sheet	24,480	20,565
Adjustments:		
Acquisitions	−1,046	−1,090
Pensions	−163	−127
Securities	30	123
Timing differences	655	971
Other	−26	−45
Taxes on the above adjustments	−129	−247
Other taxes	217	182
Approximate equity according to US GAAP	24,018	20,332

D. Balance sheet (SEKm)

The table below summarizes the consolidated balance sheets prepared in accordance with Swedish accounting principles and US GAAP.

	According to Swedish principles		According to US GAAP	
	1998	1997	1998	1997
Intangible assets	3,327	3,517	2,366	2,546
Tangible assets	21,959	22,519	21,913	22,442
Financial assets	2,599	1,744	2,779	1,876
Current assets	55,404	51,860	58,642	55,710
Total assets	83,289	79,640	85,700	82,574
Equity	24,480	20,565	24,018	20,332
Minority interests	953	913	953	913
Provisions for pensions and similar commitments	4,298	6,247	4,518	6,461
Other provisions	4,026	4,656	3,371	3,685
Financial liabilities	29,070	28,479	32,378	32,403
Operating liabilities	20,462	18,780	20,462	18,780
Total liabilities and equity	83,289	79,640	85,700	82,574

a. Debt ratio $= \dfrac{\text{Total debt}}{\text{Total assets}}$ 　　c. Return on equity (ROE) $= \dfrac{\text{Net income}}{\text{Common equity}}$

b. Profit margin $= \dfrac{\text{Net income}}{\text{Sales}}$ 　　d. Return on total assets (ROA) $= \dfrac{\text{Net income}}{\text{Total assets}}$

Note: For U.S. GAAP ratios, use sales from the consolidated income statement.
Comment on the differences between ratios under Parent-only (Swedish GAAP), Consolidated (Swedish GAAP), and Consolidated (U.S. GAAP) prepared financial statements. Which GAAP produces the most favorable ratios for Electrolux? Do the results concern you? Explain.

CASES

Case

Brain Freeze

It was one o'clock in the morning, and Janet Greenley sat at her desk sipping her fourth cup of coffee. Janet's assignment was to analyze three company annual reports from different countries with the task of determining the most successful one. Assuming it was going to be easy, Janet waited until the night before it was due to begin the assignment. But there she sat, staring blankly at the annual reports.

Janet's problem was a lack of consistency in the annual reports. The three companies' reporting practices and policies differed, and even some of the same terms had different meanings. After spending an hour flipping through the annual reports and accomplishing little, Janet decided that her best bet was to restate the foreign financial statements to her domestic GAAP and then do a financial analysis. She figured that bringing the companies to a common accounting base would provide for her comparison across companies.

1) Do you agree with Janet's method of comparing foreign companies with one another?
2) What are some factors that must be considered when conducting cross-country comparisons among companies?
3) If you had Janet's assignment, what might you do to identify the most attractive company?

Case

Show Me the Money

Luke Skywalker, CEO of Vader Corporation based in Germany, was at a business luncheon with one of the company's long-time board members, Han Solo. The two were discussing ways the company could raise more U.S. investor interest for Vader Corporation's stock which was newly issued in the United States last year. For some reason, the stock price seemed undervalued and the volume of trading on the NYSE was rather low.

"Han, I believe that the only way Vader Corporation will attract more U.S. investors is if we provide them with U.S. GAAP secondary statements. I mean, it makes complete sense. The convenience translations we've been providing them just aren't enough for investors. They probably view Vader's stock as being too risky. We can definitely enhance the attractiveness of our shares, but only if we provide more user-friendly financial statements."

"Maybe you're right, Luke, but producing a separate secondary statement specifically for U.S. investors is going to cost us a fortune. Who knows if that's even our problem in the first place? I'd rather we spend the money developing a universal secondary statement that we can use across numerous countries for our financing needs. Not only will we save money, we'll be able to attract investor interest from countries all over the world. Forget the U.S. market—Hong Kong, Australia, France, here we come!"

1) Discuss some of the advantages and disadvantages of preparing a country-specific secondary statement compared to a universal secondary statement from both a corporate issuer and a user perspective.

2) Critique Han Solo's response to Luke Skywalker's suggestion. Do you agree or disagree? Explain.

3) If you had the deciding vote, whose position would you support and why?

REFERENCES

Bailes, J. C., and Assada, T. 1991. Empirical differences between Japanese and American budget and performance evaluation systems. *International Journal of Accounting*, 26 (2): 131–142.

Benes, N. 1999. Let the market reduce cross-shareholdings. *Asian Wall Street Journal*, Weekly Edition (February 8–14): 17.

Bhushan, R., and Lessard, D. R. 1992. Coping with international accounting diversity: Fund managers' views on disclosure, reconciliation and harmonization. *Journal of International Financial Management and Accounting*, 4 (2): 149–164.

Bindon, K., and Smith, T. 1997. Corporate financial data for international investment decisions. In F. D. S. Choi, ed., *International Accounting and Finance Handbook*, 2d ed. New York: John Wiley & Sons, 9.1–9.34.

Brown, R. R., Soybel, V. E., and Stickney, C. P. 1997. Achieving comparability of U.S. and Japanese price earnings ratios. In F. D. S. Choi, ed., *International Accounting and Finance Handbook*, 2d ed. New York: John Wiley & Sons, 7.1–7.18.

Business Week. 1998. Corporate Earnings: Who can you trust? *Business Week*, (October 5): 133–156.

Business Week, 1999. Fall of a Keiretsu: How giant Mistsubishi Group lost its way. *Business Week*, (March 15): 86–92.

Choi, F. D. S., Min, S. K., Nam, S. O., Hino, H., Ujiie, J., and Stonehill, A. I. 1983. Analyzing Foreign Financial Statements: The use and misuse of international ratio analysis. *Journal of International Business Studies*, (Spring–Summer): 113–131.

Choi, F. D. S., and Levich, R. M. 1991. Behavioral effects of international accounting diversity. *Accounting Horizons*, (June): 1–13.

Das, S., and Saudagaran, S. M. 1998. Accuracy, bias, and dispersion in analysts' earnings forecasts: The case of cross-listed firms. *Journal of International Financial Management and Accounting*, 9 (1): 16–33.

Das, S., and Saudagaran, S. M. 2002. Accuracy of analysts' earnings forecasts: A comparison of non-U.S. cross-listed firms and U.S. multinationals. *Journal of International Accounting Research*, Vol. 1: 61–74.

Samuels, J. M., Brayshaw, R. E., and Craner, J. M. 1995. *Financial Statement Analysis in Europe*. London: Chapman & Hall.

Sapsford, J. 1999. Japanese stocks tumble as longtime alliances fade. Cross-holdings unravel; Pressure on the market is expected to continue. *The Wall Street Journal*, (March 3): A13.

Schieneman, G. S. 1988. The effect of accounting differences on cross-border comparisons. *International Accounting and Investment Review*, (29 April): 1–14.

Sherman, R., and Todd, R., 1997. International financial statement analysis. In F. D. S. Choi, ed., *International Accounting and Finance Handbook*, 2d ed. New York: John Wiley & Sons, 8.1–8.61.

Stickney, C. R., and Brown, R. R. 1998. *Financial Reporting and Statement Analysis: A Strategic Perspective*, 4th ed. Fort Worth, TX: Harcourt Brace & Company.

U.S. Securities and Exchange Commission, Division of Corporation Finance. 1993. *Survey of Financial Statement Reconciliations by Foreign Registrants*, (May 1).

Wallace, R. S. O., and Collier, P. 1991. The "cash" in cash flow statements: A multi-country comparison. *Accounting Horizons*, (December): 44–52.

CHAPTER 6

FINANCIAL REPORTING IN EMERGING CAPITAL MARKETS

LEARNING OBJECTIVES

- Obtain an overview of the importance of emerging capital markets to developing countries.

- Recognize qualitative criteria for evaluating financial reporting in emerging capital markets.

- Consider important policy issues related to enhancing financial reporting capability in emerging capital markets.

For a group of countries whose political and economic importance has grown dramatically over the past two decades, relatively little has been written about financial reporting in emerging capital markets.[1] The Asian financial crisis that began in Thailand in July 1997, and quickly spread to a number of neighboring countries including Indonesia, Malaysia, the Philippines, and South Korea, has focused attention on the quality of financial reporting and auditing in emerging economies. It has also given rise to demands for more transparency in the financial reporting and governance structure of companies based in these countries. There has been a growing appreciation of the fact that financial reporting is a vital infrastructure requirement for the growth of emerging markets. As such, increasing attention must be devoted to improving the quality of financial reporting in these countries.

From the perspective of institutional investors, the globalization of financial markets has been synonymous with obtaining rapid access to portfolio investment opportunities anywhere in the world, including those in places once regarded as exotic or remote.[2] The 1990s can be regarded as the decade when these exotic financial markets, more popularly known as emerging capital markets (ECMs), captured the interest of investors worldwide with their promise of offering substantially higher returns than those attainable in more developed financial markets. World Bank statistics show that the aggregate net resource flows into emerging markets grew from US$98 billion in 1990 to over US$300 billion in 1997. These included debt, equity, and foreign direct investment from the private sector as well as from multilateral lending agencies such as the World Bank.[3]

The statistics below summarize the phenomenal growth of emerging capital markets over a relatively short period of time.[4] Consider the following:

- The market capitalization of ECMs increased almost nine-fold from US$319 billion in 1987 to US$2.9 trillion in 1999;
- Their share of world stock market capitalization increased during the same period from just over 4 percent to 8.5 percent;
- Trading in ECM securities increased from US$165 billion to US$3.1 trillion in that period;
- The number of domestic companies listed on the stock exchanges of ECMs more than tripled from 8,920 in 1990 to 26,314 in 1999 (during the same period, domestic listings in developed markets rose from 16,504 to 23,326);
- Several ECMs registered impressive returns on investment, in some cases exceeding over 100 percent of the U.S. dollar equivalent index value in just one year.

But these opportunities come at a cost. Despite their potential for significantly higher gains, investments in ECMs are also prone to greater volatility. As evidenced

---

[1]The term *emerging capital markets* is generally used to refer to capital markets in countries with less developed and transitional economies. Some of the other features of these markets are that they impose capital controls and foreign currency controls, and have high levels of government involvement in listed companies.

[2]The descriptions *exotic* and *remote* do not only imply geographical distance. These descriptions comprise a bundle of characteristics associated with emerging markets such as small market capitalization, low liquidity, high volatility of returns, limited number of premium-grade and investment-grade securities, and the lack of a well-developed domestic institutional investor base. See Price [1994] and Harvey [1995] for a discussion of these characteristics.

[3]From World Bank, Global Development Finance [1998].

[4]Compiled from IFC [1998] and Standard and Poor's [2000].

by the recent financial crises in Southeast Asia, Russia, Brazil and Argentina, the investment risk is generally much higher in these markets. The risks of investing in ECMs are associated not only with structural, political, and economic problems, although admittedly these factors are important.[5] Equally important, however, are informational problems stemming from the difficulty of obtaining adequate and reliable information useful for evaluating investment opportunities in these markets. Financial reporting is a crucial element of the information necessary for sustaining investor confidence in both developed and emerging capital markets. The quality of corporate financial reporting in ECMs varies considerably, however, and it has been increasingly difficult to ignore the impact of poor financial reporting on the performance of these markets.[6]

This chapter covers issues that are particularly relevant to financial reporting in ECMs. It provides an overview of ECMs and why these markets are important to developing countries in general. It discusses financial reporting issues relevant to the development of ECMs and their relationship with features of financial reporting, drawing attention to the choices facing emerging markets in regard to improving their financial reporting systems. The chapter provides criteria related to financial reporting by which ECMs can be analyzed and compared. By focusing on issues pertinent to developing economies, it provides financial statement users a better understanding of the financial reporting environment in these countries.

THE NATURE AND IMPORTANCE OF EMERGING CAPITAL MARKETS

The crucial role of financial reporting in ECMs can be positioned more broadly within the policy context of capital market development in less developed countries. An emerging capital market is a stock market located in a developing country.[7] Exhibit 6-1 lists the 79 countries whose capital markets are considered ECMs by the Standard & Poor's Emerging Stock Markets Data Base (2001).

The capital markets classified as emerging are quite diverse in terms of their size and history. Some ECMs, such as those in Taiwan, Brazil, South Africa, China, Mexico, and India, are quite large in terms of market capitalization and rank among the 20 largest capital markets globally. The market capitalization of shares traded on the stock exchanges of these emerging capital markets exceeds that of a number of developed countries. Moreover, some emerging capital markets, such as those in India, Malaysia, South Africa, and Zimbabwe, have existed since these countries' colonial eras, whereas others, such as those in Botswana and Ecuador, were established in the 1990s.

For most developing countries, relying on local stock markets as a means of raising large-scale capital is a relatively novel approach to enterprise financing, prompting references to it as a "non-traditional" source of capital to distinguish it from more "traditional" sources of informal and bank financing. A study by Saudagaran and Diga

---

[5]Structural problems of ECMs include the small size of their market capitalization, low liquidity, and limited investment choices. Political and economic problems are associated with political risk and uncertainty, macroeconomic stability (e.g., Argentina's recent economic crisis), and the possibility of unfavorable government regulations affecting capital market investments.

[6]The spate of accounting problems in the United States in 2001–2002, clearly demonstrate that investors in developed economies are not immune to problems arising from poor quality financial reporting.

[7]The World Bank [1994] defined a "developing country" as one whose average income per capita does not exceed a certain level established by the bank. In 1999, the cut-off was set at US$9,266.

EXHIBIT 6-1 Emerging Capital Markets by Geographical Location

Africa	Botswana, Cote d'Ivoire, Egypt, Ghana, Kenya, Malawi, Mauritius, Morocco, Namibia, Nigeria, South Africa, Swaziland, Tanzania, Tunisia, Zambia, Zimbabwe.
Asia	Bangladesh, China, Fiji, India, Indonesia, Kazakhstan, Korea, Malaysia, Mongolia, Nepal, Pakistan, Philippines, Sri Lanka, Taiwan, Thailand, Uzbekistan.
Europe	Bulgaria, Croatia, Czech Republic, Estonia, Greece, Hungary, Latvia, Lithuania, Macedonia, Malta, Moldova, Poland, Romania, Russia, Slovakia, Slovenia, Turkey, Ukraine, Yugoslavia.
Latin America	Argentina, Barbados, Bolivia, Brazil, Chile, Colombia, Costa Rica, Dominican Republic, Ecuador, El Salvador, Guatemala, Honduras, Jamaica, Mexico, Panama, Paraguay, Peru, Trinidad & Tobago, Uruguay, Venezuela.
Middle East	Bahrain, Iran, Israel, Jordan, Lebanon, Oman, Saudi Arabia, West Bank & Gaza.

Source: Standard & Poor's Emerging Stock Markets Factbook (2001).

EXHIBIT 6-2 Relative Importance of Commercial Banking and Securities Markets in ASEAN*

	Indonesia		Malaysia		Philippines		Singapore		Thailand	
	1980	1994	1980	1994	1980	1994	1980	1994	1980	1994
Total assets of commercial banks (US $ billions)	16	90	15	70	18	34	78	115	15	153
Stock market capitalization (US $ billion)	.07	47	12.4	199	3.5	56	24.4	135	1.2	132
Bond market capitalization (US $ billion)	nil	9	7	40	0.2	25	4	45	0.2	14
Ratio of bank assets to securities market capitalization	229	1.6	0.8	0.3	4.9	0.4	2.7	0.6	10.7	1.1

Note: *All figures are as of end of year.
Source: SEACEN (1991); World Bank (1994); IFC (1994) and (1990); FEER (1995).

(1997a) on countries belonging to the Association of Southeast Asian Nations (ASEAN) shows the dramatic rise in the importance of stock markets as a source of capital in these countries over the past two decades. As indicated in Exhibit 6-2, in all five ASEAN countries, the stock market capitalization grew exponentially between 1980 and 1994 and equity capital rose from insignificant levels to being at least as important a source of capital as bank loans in most of these countries. The development of active markets for corporate securities is generally seen as a step upward on the ladder of financial development. Multinational lending institutions such as the World Bank as well as development economists have generally agreed that a well functioning stock market provides the impetus necessary for the economic growth of these countries.[8] The benefits of ECMs to developing countries are varied and help to explain the role of financial reporting within these markets.

---

[8] See, for example, Asian Development Bank [1986], Frankel [1993], IMF [1994], Van Agtmael [1984], World Bank [1990].

First, many developing countries suffer from an investme[nt]
means that funds available fall far short of the amount need[ed]
development. In this regard, ECMs expand the investmen[t]
country, which attracts portfolio investments from overseas.
facilitated by the availability of investment options. Credit
oping countries has often been made on bases other than econo[mic]
sequently, available funds could be misallocated into such things as inefficient state
monopolies that sap the financial resources available for productive investments elsewhere. ECMs also allow enterprise funds to be raised in a more cost-effective manner. For example, according to the World Bank, the amount of new equity capital
raised by developing countries rose from virtually zero in 1987 to over US$32 billion
in 1997, representing about 10 percent of the total capital raised by developing countries in 1997.

ECMs can also positively influence the economic culture existing in less developed
countries (LDCs). Well functioning markets allow individuals to have a stake in enterprises in their respective countries and help to change cultural attitudes with respect
to participating in economic development activities and monitoring the socio-
economic contributions of enterprises. In turn, domestic enterprises are encouraged
to become more responsive and accountable to a greater number of stakeholders in
society. These changes are particularly important in transitional economies, i.e., countries attempting to change the basis of their economic system from reliance on state
central planning to reliance on the free operation of markets.

Finally, ECMs assist in developing information flows, a prerequisite for enhancing
the allocative efficiency of the economy. By providing market-based signals,
ECMs assist in channeling funds to the most efficient and productive uses. Also, active
stock markets serve as a barometer for a country's economic health by signaling expectations regarding macroeconomic variables such as economic growth and inflation. In
this role, ECMs provide important information for government macroeconomic
planning.

THE ROLE OF FINANCIAL REPORTING IN EMERGING CAPITAL MARKETS

Before ECMs can function effectively, it is essential to have in place a set of corporate
reporting policies and procedures geared towards supplying the information necessary
for making investment decisions. This view is well recognized by multilateral lending
institutions that support the strengthening of the accounting infrastructure in ECMs.
In its report on capital market developments in the Asia-Pacific region, the Asian
Development Bank [1995] stressed that "accounting information is an essential element of infrastructure for a financial system" [p. 229]. The World Bank [1989], in
turn, observed that "in developing countries, accounting and auditing practices are
sometimes weak, and financial laws and regulations do not demand accurate and
timely reports. Developing an effective accounting and auditing profession is essential
for building efficient financial markets" [p. 90]. Moreover, a *Euromoney* survey[9] of
investment institutions dealing on a regular basis with ECMs showed that the
accounting and legal infrastructure underlying an ECM was a major factor for evaluating the investment potential of the market.

---

[9]See "Taiwan Emerges on Top," *Euromoney*, [December 1993, pp. 68–70].

Financial reporting is central to regulations pertinent to establishing an active market for corporate securities. In particular, it is a fairly common practice in ECMs to require companies to submit a detailed prospectus of the offer and to satisfy the listing requirements of the domestic stock exchange if the company wants its securities to be traded in the exchange. Listing criteria generally consider characteristics such as the company's size (i.e., measured in terms of reported assets, revenues, or shareholders' equity), historical performance (i.e., profitability and financial stability), and future prospects. One of the main policy aims in ECMs is to ensure that only companies that satisfy minimum quality requirements are allowed to issue publicly traded securities. At the same time, governments also want to promote so-called entrepreneurial or start-up ventures that, by their nature, are riskier than more established companies. It is not unusual, therefore, that a tiered system exists in many ECMs with speculative securities being traded on a secondary or over-the-counter market, while "blue chip" or premium securities are traded in the main stock exchange. Financial reports provide an important basis for formulating an appropriate investment portfolio that could include a combination of these blue chip and second-tier companies.

Available evidence tends to bolster further claims that the financial reporting system is a crucial component of the infrastructure for developing domestic capital markets. A significant body of research shows that accounting reports are relevant to investors' buy and sell decisions. The importance of accounting reports for stock market investors has been demonstrated through capital market studies conducted in different countries and cross-country surveys of users.[10] The prevalence of accounting regulations worldwide can be attributed to the need to maintain the informational efficiency of capital markets. The worldwide pre-eminence of U.S. and U.K. capital markets has been associated, in part, with the stringent nature of financial reporting in these countries, which, in turn, resulted in the increased availability of information for decision-making purposes. The relationship between accounting information and the growth of domestic securities markets is a crucial policy issue for developing countries that aim to boost capital inflows to their economies.

CHARACTERISTICS OF FINANCIAL REPORTING IN EMERGING CAPITAL MARKETS

Recognizing the importance of adequate financial reporting and actually possessing a satisfactory financial reporting regime are two different matters. The pragmatic reality often falls far short of the desired goal in ECMs. In this section, three qualitative criteria for evaluating financial reporting in ECMs are discussed. These criteria are 1) information availability, 2) reliability, and 3) comparability. Focusing on these criteria assists in highlighting areas for improvement and policy formulation. While these criteria are qualitative in nature, they provide the focal point for developing benchmarks for comparing and improving the performance of financial reporting systems in these markets.

Availability

Availability means that financial and other information on publicly listed companies is adequate, timely, and conveniently accessible. The adequacy of corporate information is linked inextricably to issues of disclosure. There is a perception that disclosure

---

[10]See, for example, Choi and Levich [1990], Bhushan and Lessard [1992].

adequacy in ECMs lags behind that in developed capital markets. One method for measuring disclosure adequacy is to rank countries in terms of a specific disclosure index. A study that compared financial disclosures of industrial enterprises from 41 developed and emerging stock markets showed that enterprises in ECMs generally provided fewer disclosures compared to those in developed markets.[11] Exhibit 6-3 presents the disclosure ranking and scores of selected industrial companies from 20 ECMs relative to companies from 21 developed capital markets.

EXHIBIT 6-3 Disclosure Levels of Industrial Companies in Selected ECMs and Developed Capital Markets

Rank	Country	Average Score	Rank	Country	Average Score
1	United Kingdom	85	11	Spain Zimbabwe*	72
2	Finland Sweden	83	12	Japan Mexico*	71
3	Ireland	81	13	Nigeria*	70
4	Australia New Zealand Switzerland	80	14	Argentina* Belgium South Korea*	68
5	Malaysia* Singapore South Africa*	79	15	Germany	67
6	Chile* France	78	16	Italy Thailand*	66
7	USA	76	17	Philippines*	64
8	Canada Denmark Norway	75	18	Austria	62
9	Israel Netherlands Sri Lanka*	74	19	Greece* India*	61
10	Hong Kong Pakistan*	73	20	Colombia* Taiwan* Turkey*	58

*ECM
Source: CIFAR (1995).

Among the 21 countries ranked in the top half in terms of disclosures, only 6 (about 29 percent) were from ECMs (i.e., Malaysia, Singapore, South Africa, Chile, Sri Lanka, and Pakistan). In comparison, of the 20 countries in the lower half in terms of disclosure levels, 14 (about 70 percent) were from ECMs. Only 5 developed market countries were in the bottom half in terms of disclosure levels: Austria (18th), Italy (16th), Belgium (14th), Japan (12th), and Spain (11th). The results indicate that a

---

[11]See "International Accounting and Auditing Trends," published by the Center for International Financial Analysis & Research [CIFAR 1995].

higher proportion of companies in ECMs disclose less financial and other information compared to companies in developed capital markets. A significant degree of variability also exists among ECMs in terms of fundamental accounting disclosures. This variability is illustrated by the diversity in disclosure requirements in 12 selected ECMs (Exhibit 6-4).

EXHIBIT 6-4 Disclosure Requirements in Selected ECMs (*)

Panel A

Disclosures	Argentina	Brazil	Greece	Indonesia	Korea	Malaysia
1. Quarterly financial statements	•					
2. Notes showing accounting policies	•	•	•	•	•	•
3. Consolidated financial statements		•				•
4. Cash flow statements					•	
5. Earnings per share data		•		•	•	•
6. Segment information				•	•	•
7. Inflation-adjusted accounts	•	•				
8. Related party information		•		•	•	•
9. Extraordinary or unusual items	•	•		•	•	•
10. Discontinued operations				•		•
11. Post-balance sheet events	•	•		•		•
12. Forecast profits		•		•		•

Panel B

Disclosures	Mexico	Nigeria	Philippines	Poland	South Africa	Taiwan
1. Quarterly financial statements	•		•		•	•
2. Notes showing accounting policies	•	•	•	•	•	•
3. Consolidated financial statements	•	•	•	•	•	
4. Cash flow statements	•		•	•	•	•
5. Earnings per share data	•	•	•		•	
6. Segment information					•	•
7. Inflation-adjusted accounts	•					
8. Related party information	•	•	•	•		
9. Extraordinary or unusual items			•		•	•
10. Discontinued operations	•		•	•	•	
11. Post-balance sheet events	•	•		•	•	
12. Forecast profits	•	•			•	

(*) Disclosure requirements are based on stock exchange requirements and accounting standards in each country as of 1991. Information assembled from various sources including IFC (1994) and Coopers and Lybrand (1991).
Sources: Saudagaran and Diga (1997b)

As shown in Exhibit 6-4, differences in mandatory disclosures are apparent with respect to quarterly financial statements, consolidated and cash flow statements, segment information and inflation-adjusted accounts, related-party information, extraordinary items, discontinued operations, post-balance sheet events, and forecast profits. The only item that was mandatory in all 12 countries was the note on "significant accounting policies." Moreover, no country required disclosure of all information suggested in Exhibit 6-4. These variations in disclosure regulation suggest that disclosure practices, to the extent that they comply with extant requirements, also differ across ECMs.

In terms of timeliness of financial reporting, ECMs generally impose requirements for listed companies to furnish audited financial statements on an annual basis. Most ECMs require either quarterly or semi-annual financial statements to be released. The general trend has been towards quarterly financial reporting. In practice, however, the actual release of the financial statements varies from between two and six months after the end of the financial year.

In developed capital markets, research indicates that financial information is released continuously such that little, if any, new information exists when the financial reports are eventually published. Evidence concerning the effects of information release on share market activities in ECMs is quite limited. A major reason for the paucity of capital market-based research in ECMs is the difficulty of obtaining data regarding the public release of information in these markets and share price/volume changes over a sufficiently long period of time. Available evidence on Asia Pacific ECMs indicates that the notion of semi-strong efficiency (i.e., that publicly available information is immediately reflected in share prices and trading) retains qualified support in these ECMs.[12] In general, however, these ECMs showed less semi-strong efficiency than their developed market counterparts in that it took longer for the publicly available information to be impounded in the stock prices. The results suggest that the underlying infrastructure of ECMs is sufficiently different from those in developed markets to affect the efficiency by which information is processed.

Convenient access to financial information is also a key feature of information availability. In the larger and relatively more developed ECMs such as Taiwan and South Africa, real-time information is made available through online systems connected to organized securities exchanges. Ready access to such information is viewed as contributing to increased market efficiency and liquidity. In other ECMs, the public dissemination of information is limited by several factors. One is the absence of an efficient securities exchange agency that coordinates the retrieval and dissemination of corporate information. Financial reports may be collated and stored by a central government repository (e.g., Companies Registrar), allowing some form of limited public access to the stored information. Another major inhibiting factor is weakness in the research capability of local brokers and financial institutions. Shortages of qualified personnel, absence of effective competition among brokers, and a weak financial press often combine to retard the flow of financial and other information to investors.

Reliability

The second criterion for evaluating financial reporting is reliability. Reliability encompasses two requirements. First, financial reports need to be prepared on the basis of sound accounting requirements. Second, adequate steps should be taken to ensure compliance with these accounting requirements. In many ECMs, the absence of a strong capability to develop domestic accounting standards means that standards are borrowed from overseas. Some ECMs have attempted to emulate financial requirements in more developed capital markets by adopting International Accounting

---

[12]See, for example, Ariff and Johnson [1990], Ghon Rhee et al. [1990].

Standards (IAS). The IAS, in turn, are known to have incorporated accounting methods generally accepted in countries such as the United Kingdom and United States, widely considered the leading financial markets in the world. Exhibit 6-5 indicates the extent to which selected ECMs have adopted IAS as a basis for domestic financial reporting.

Exhibit 6-5 shows that a majority of ECMs have either wholly adopted IAS or used IAS to formulate domestic accounting standards. This adoption rate suggests that IAS generally enjoy considerable support in ECMs, perhaps more so than in developed capital markets with resources available to develop their own domestic standards. Paradoxically, the board membership of the IASB is dominated largely by representatives from developed capital markets. Adoption of IAS, however, does not necessarily

EXHIBIT 6-5 Adoption of IAS in Emerging Capital Markets

Wholly or Largely Adopted IAS as Domestic Standards	Used IAS to Formulate Some Domestic Standards	Did not Adopt IAS
Bangladesh	Brazil	Argentina
Barbados	China	Armenia
Cayman Islands	Colombia	Bolivia
Croatia	Greece	Botswana
Cyprus	Hong Kong(*)	Bulgaria
Czech Republic	India	Chile
Egypt	Kenya	Costa Rica
Estonia	Nigeria	Dominican Republic
Indonesia	Portugal	Ecuador
Jordan	Romania	El Salvador
Kuwait	Russia	Fiji
Latvia	Swaziland	Ghana
Lithuania	Taiwan	Guatemala
Macedonia	Turkey	Honduras
Malaysia	Uruguay	Iran
Mexico	Venezuela	Israel
Nepal	Zambia	Jamaica
Oman		Korea
Pakistan		Lebanon
Panama		Mauritius
Peru		Namibia
Philippines		Paraguay
Poland		Saudi Arabia
Singapore(*)		Slovakia
Slovenia		Tunisia
South Africa		Ukraine
Sri Lanka		Uzbekistan
Tanzania		
Thailand		
Trinidad & Tobago		
Zimbabwe		

(*) Hong Kong and Singapore are not generally considered ECMs but are included here because they exemplify developed capital markets that have only recently emerged as important global financial centers. *Source:* Saudagaran and Diga (I 997b) *updated 2002*

translate to perceived quality in accounting standards. Exhibit 6-6 summarizes an International Finance Corporation's (IFC) classification of ECMs on the basis of the perceived quality of their accounting standards.

EXHIBIT 6-6   Perceived Quality of Domestic Accounting Standards

Good	Adequate	Poor
Brazil	Argentina	China (**)
Chile	Colombia (**)	Indonesia (*)
Mexico (*)	Greece	
India (**)	Hungary	
Korea	Jordan	
Malaysia (*)	Nigeria (**)	
Philippines (*)	Pakistan (*)	
South Africa	Peru (*)	
Sri Lanka (*)	Poland (*)	
	Portugal	
	Taiwan (**)	
	Thailand (**)	
	Turkey	
	Venezuela	
	Zimbabwe (*)	

(*) Wholly adopted IAS
(**) Used IAS as basis for some domestic standards
Source: International Finance Corporation (1995)

A principal source of weakness in domestic accounting standards adopted in ECMs is that existing standards do not address specific areas of accounting that have significant impact on the financial statements. These include areas such as accounting for business combinations, investments, property and equipment, leases, foreign currency transactions and translations, long-term contracts, and financial instruments. The absence of standards in these areas creates significant uncertainty with respect to how particular transactions are to be accounted for in the financial statements. Companies often follow a variety of accounting treatments, some of which are dubious and result in potentially misleading financial statements. For example, the lack of standards on lease accounting and financial instruments affords companies significant scope for engaging in off-balance sheet financing that distorts the actual degree of financial leverage enjoyed by these companies.

Even where adequate financial accounting standards exist, enforcement is a potential problem in many ECMs. The most rigorous requirements mean little if enforcement is inadequate. In ECMs, particular political, economic, and socio-cultural factors significantly affect the strength of enforcement. Often, deficiencies in actual enforcement are traceable to a lax attitude towards financial reporting, weaknesses in the administrative mechanisms for enforcing standards, or both. The accounting and auditing profession in some countries may be relatively weak, owing to lack of government support or an inadequate degree of organization. The government agencies charged with monitoring compliance are understaffed or overburdened with other responsibilities. The absence of an effective government (or quasi-government) agency that monitors compliance with pertinent regulations would encourage widespread violations of extant regulations.

With respect to the audit function, substantial differences have been observed in regard to the level of assurance provided by an independent audit in various national settings. These differences are traceable to a variety of factors including the training and qualifications of local auditors, differences in audit standards and requirements, and differences in the nature of the audits conducted and in the availability of auditors. Reports issued by the United Nations and the World Bank in 1998 related to the Asian financial crisis were particularly critical of the Big Five international accounting firms for using less stringent auditing standards in developing countries than those used in developed countries.[13]

Enforcement capability is enhanced by the presence of adequate numbers of qualified auditors and accountants. A principal difficulty in many ECMs, however, is the shortage of qualified auditors capable of attesting to the reliability of financial statements. Exhibit 6-7 shows the relative proportion of auditors to the general population in selected emerging and developed capital markets.

EXHIBIT 6-7   Accountants and Auditors in Emerging and Developed Markets

Emerging Markets	No. of Auditors Per 100,000 Population	Developed Markets	No. of Auditors Per 100,000 Population
Chile	87	New Zealand	550
Argentina	71	Australia	539
Malaysia	48	UK	352
South Africa	35	Canada	350
Philippines	31	Singapore	273
Taiwan	17	Ireland	262
Mexico	15	USA	168
Poland	14	Hong Kong	110
Greece	12	Italy	110
Zimbabwe	11	Denmark	106
India	9	Switzerland	53
Sri Lanka	9	Netherlands	52
Nigeria	8	France	45
South Korea	7	Sweden	41
Thailand	5	Belgium	38
Colombia	2	Germany	26
Indonesia	2	Spain	18
Pakistan	2	Finland	10
Brazil	1	Japan	10

Source: Saudagaran and Diga [1997b]

As a group, ECMs have substantially fewer professional accountants and auditors than do developed capital markets. In particular, the proportions of auditors to total population in important global and regional financial centers such as the United Kingdom, the United States, Singapore, and Hong Kong are relatively high. The exception is Japan, which has the lowest proportion of auditors to total population

---

[13]See "Big Five criticised over global auditing standards: World Bank action may speed up international code," by Jim Kelly, *Financial Times* [October 19, 1998, p. 1] and "Auditors criticised on Asian standards," by Jim Kelly, *Financial Times* [October 26, 1998, p. 6].

among the important global financial centers. Analysis of the Japanese financial system shows, however, that bank finance continues to dominate the country's financial market, a condition similar to that existing in countries such as Germany and Switzerland. Moreover, compared to other important financial centers, the Tokyo Stock Exchange is relatively more restricted vis-a-vis foreign portfolio investments.

The shortage of qualified auditors in ECMs constrains the ability of these markets to enhance their enforcement capabilities, at least in the short term. The demand for audit services in these countries will likely increase significantly, however, as ECMs gear up to attract overseas investment inflows. In the long term, countries can seek to address the supply problems by expanding the opportunities for the education and training of auditors. Another potentially important development involves global and regional attempts to liberalize the trade in services under the recent World Trade Organization (WTO). The WTO is seeking to reduce barriers to the free movement of services, including accounting and auditing services, across countries. To the extent that this is accomplished, supply restrictions in some ECMs could be addressed by transferring accounting expertise from countries with a greater proportion of qualified auditors.

Exhibit 6-8 reports the results of the evaluation, by the Center for International Financial Analysis and Research [1995], of the comprehensiveness of audit reports

EXHIBIT 6-8   Comprehensiveness of Audit Reports in Emerging Markets

	Above Average	**Average**	**Below Average**
Emerging Markets	Greece Korea Mexico Philippines Thailand Venezuela	Argentina Brazil Chile Colombia India Indonesia Pakistan South Africa Sri Lanka Taiwan Turkey Zimbabwe	Malaysia Nigeria Portugal
Developed Markets	Australia Canada France Hong Kong Israel Italy Japan Netherlands Spain Switzerland United Kingdom United States	Austria Belgium Denmark Finland Germany Ireland Luxembourg New Zealand Norway	Sweden

Source: CIFAR (1995)

issued in the 20 ECM countries. Comprehensiveness was defined in terms of the scope of the audit and the amount of information disclosed in the audit reports. The results show only a few ECMs had audit reports comparable in scope to those in more developed markets such as Japan, the United Kingdom, and the United States. Overall, ECMs had audit reports that were at least as comprehensive as those found in most developed Continental European markets including Belgium, Germany, and Luxembourg. These differences in the scope and comprehensiveness of the audit affect the assessment of the reliability of accounts prepared by listed enterprises.

Comparability

The third criterion relates to the comparability of financial information, which can be broken into two dimensions. The first dimension of comparability is in terms of the specific accounting policies used to prepare financial reports. International organizations concerned with financial reporting, such as the IASB, OECD, and UN, have asserted that uniform rules for measurement and disclosure are necessary to achieve comparability.[14] Given the practical difficulties of achieving uniformity in an international setting, these organizations have generally settled for "accounting harmony," which, while not implying total uniformity, means that some degree of consistency and compatibility exists between the rules of countries.

Comparisons between enterprises located in different countries need to account for differences in the bases used for account preparation. These differences in accounting policies do not appear to be a major problem if adequate disclosures allow appropriate restatements to be made. Usually, however, reconciliations between results prepared using domestic standards and those of an alternative basis of accounting, e.g., IAS, are rarely provided in local financial statements. Research evidence indicates that while international accounting differences are viewed as important by international investors, they are not perceived to be an insurmountable barrier to international diversification. As discussed in Chapter 5, users are able to cope with accounting diversity by gaining insight into the nature and impact of accounting practices in different national settings. Knowledge of accounting differences is still a prerequisite for attaining practical comparability between enterprises.

To what extent does accounting measurement and valuation diversity exist in ECMs? The resources devoted to the effort for global accounting harmonization suggests that accounting practices differ significantly worldwide. A high degree of accounting diversity exists among ECMs. At various times, countries such as Argentina, Brazil, Greece, and Mexico, for example, have allowed or even required financial statements to be prepared using a basis other than historical cost. In the past, Argentina and Brazil, in particular, have endorsed the use of constant, rather than nominal, currency values in financial statements to adjust for the persistent inflation experienced in these countries.[15] The ECMs above also allow the upward revaluation of property and equipment, a practice not sanctioned in the United States. Discretionary and hidden reserves are also tolerated in Greece, Nigeria, and Poland,

---

[14]See, for example, IASC [1982], OECD [1986], United Nations [1988].

[15]Argentina and Brazil have recently reverted to historical-cost accounting as part of economic reform programs that have included switching to a new currency (i.e., new real) in Brazil and pegging its currency to the U.S. dollar in the case of Argentina.

thus increasing the potential that reported results are biased towards greater conservatism.[16]

The second dimension of comparability, often overlooked in the rush to promote accounting harmonization, is the need to understand the contextual significance of financial information. Even if accounting reports are prepared using the same policies, comparability does not exist if the underlying environmental factors, which provide significance to the information, differ between countries. As discussed in Chapter 5, it is important to recognize the danger of interpreting accounting numbers without taking into account the context in which they were derived. Reported profit growth measured in nominal currency, for example, needs to be interpreted cautiously, particularly in ECMs that have experienced significant levels of inflation or currency instability in recent years. Interpreting the degree of financial leverage also needs to take into account the institutional structure of finance in a country (e.g., in some countries, bank finance is organized through conglomerates of related enterprises), and the rate of industrial and economic growth (e.g., the telecommunications sector in many emerging markets is a rapidly growing sector requiring extensive capital investments of firms that wish to tap into the market). In the author's view, a thorough understanding of contextual variables is at least equally important as achieving international harmony of accounting rules.

FINANCIAL REPORTING POLICY ISSUES IN EMERGING CAPITAL MARKETS

Government policy towards financial reporting represents the cornerstone of improving the quality of accounting in ECMs. This section considers three important policy issues facing regulators in ECMs in regard to enhancing their financial reporting capability: 1) the choice between mandated and voluntary approaches to regulation, 2) approaches to strengthening enforcement capability, and 3) whether, and to what extent, accounting harmonization should be pursued. The aim here is to identify the policy options available to regulators and circumstances in which each option is likely to be desirable. These choices have a direct impact on users of financial statements.

Studies have recognized that financial reporting policy varies among ECMs because of differences in their political, economic, and socio-cultural backgrounds.[17] Moreover, factors in each country's national and international environments constrain policy options available to the government. Previous colonial links, for example, appear to strongly influence the choice of an accounting regulatory system. ECMs often share similar financial reporting legislation and practices with the countries by which they were formerly colonized. Conversely, some countries embark on a deliberate approach to reforming their financial reporting systems in response to changes in their environments. Recent examples of countries that are undergoing the adoption of new accounting systems include China, Russia, and Vietnam, countries that are increasingly adopting market-oriented measures in their economies. The search for an appropriate set of financial reporting policies depends on recognizing these differences in the underlying environments of countries.

---

[16]This is not to imply that these practices are unique to ECMs. Developed economies such as the United Kingdom's allow upward revaluation of property in financial statements, while discretionary reserves have long been a hallmark of European accounting in both developed and developing economies.

[17]See, for example, Cooke and Wallace [1990], Doupnik and Salter [1995].

In view of the diversity of conditions in ECMs, no single set of recommendations would be appropriate or desirable for all of these markets. Nonetheless, by focusing on the fundamental issues of information availability, reliability, and comparability, regulators will be in a better position to assess the relative merits of alternative policy options available. The rest of this section discusses the trade-offs associated with these policy options.

Information Availability

Facilitating the availability of financial and other information has not been an easy task in many ECMs. As mentioned earlier, cultural and economic factors often constrain the supply of information in these markets. In general, two policy options have been suggested in regard to increasing the availability of information. On the one hand, proponents of a free market approach suggest that disclosure adequacy is best advanced by allowing enterprises to decide on the appropriate level of disclosure according to their particular circumstances. Competitive market pressures would ensure that the optimal level of disclosure is achieved as firms compete to reduce the costs of obtaining funds from the market. The free market view is supported by studies showing that the level of voluntary disclosures of companies increases as they enter competitive financial markets.[18]

In comparison, advocates of the regulatory approach argue that an adequate framework of disclosure regulation is necessary because of the potential for market failure in the supply of financial information. This view might be gaining ascendancy following the recent financial reporting failures in the United States. Where financial information possesses characteristics of a public good, a strong probability exists that such information will be underproduced in the absence of regulatory mandates. Without adequate information, potential investors will be reluctant to participate in markets that are perceived to be "rigged" in favor of certain vested interests. The perception of unfair securities markets could be aggravated in ECMs where the level of information asymmetry appears to be greater than in more developed markets.[19]

An important reason for inadequate levels of disclosure in ECMs relates to cultural attitudes consistent with secrecy and lack of transparency over corporate affairs. These cultural attitudes are reinforced by the nature of large domestic enterprises in these countries, most of which are owned or controlled by family/clan-based groups. The phenomena of cross-ownerships and interlocking directorates are generally more prevalent in less-developed countries where economic wealth tends to be concentrated among a few, well-positioned groups.

If securities regulators perceive that some degree of mandatory disclosures are necessary in ECMs, care should be taken to ensure that such regulation enhances, rather than stifles, the growth of domestic securities markets. In an environment where firms have incentives not to disclose information voluntarily, accounting regulators must consider these incentives in evaluating the consequences of alternative mandatory reporting procedures.[20] First, imposing a greater number of mandatory requirements does not necessarily increase the amount of information available to investors if these requirements are offset by a reduction in voluntary disclosures. Second, the choices

---

[18]See, for example, Choi [1973], Meek and Gray [1989].

[19]See, for example, Bromwich [1985], Hilton [1994].

[20]See Dye [1985].

made by firms with respect to accounting policies are themselves sources of valuable information. As suggested by Gonedes and Dopuch [1974], accounting policy choices represent signals of private information.[21] As such, imposition of mandatory requirements could remove this potentially important source of information for investors. Third, in an environment characterized by increasingly globalized financial markets, accounting regulators should moderate the imposition of costly disclosure requirements if their market is to remain competitive as a site for raising capital.

Achieving an optimal balance of regulation is one of the most important issues facing securities regulators today, particularly in emerging capital markets. Overall, on the basis of current conditions in ECMs, the author's view is that a voluntary or laissez-faire approach is not appropriate in ECMs because of environmental factors that inhibit full disclosure and weaknesses in institutional capability to demand adequate information. Governments should consider taking a more active role in specifying minimum disclosure requirements, which do not have to be as onerous or extensive as those required in more developed capital markets, but are sufficient to provide a basis for making sound investment decisions.

Strengthening Enforcement Capability

Several factors account for differences in enforcement capability with respect to financial reporting regulations in ECMs. First, government attitude towards capital market development in general, and financial reporting in particular, varies across countries. In some countries, the development of active capital markets is afforded high priority in government policy-making. In other countries, a more dirigiste approach to financing is emphasized with the government playing a direct role in harnessing and allocating credit in domestic industries. Second, enforcement appears to be stronger if a designated government agency is responsible for regulating the securities market. These government agencies usually perform functions similar to the U.S. SEC, including formulating rules for public issuance of securities, approving specific offers of securities and listings, and defining the overall direction of capital market development. Finally, the size and quality of the accounting personnel significantly impact the enforcement capability in a country. Countries that have well-established accounting professions with a sizable membership body generally have stronger policy-making and enforcement capabilities with respect to financial reporting.

Another pressing policy dilemma facing regulators in ECMs is the extent to which the private sector should participate in setting and enforcing financial reporting rules. In some ECMs, greater reliance is placed on government edicts with respect to financial reporting. Reliance upon mandatory disclosures specified in law is apparent in countries such as China, Indonesia, Poland, and Peru. In comparison, a policy of private sector self-regulation is encouraged in other ECMs. The accounting profession in these countries often plays an important role in specifying the financial reporting standards applicable to private companies, including those listed in their stock exchanges. Examples of such countries include South Africa, Malaysia, and Mexico.

The choice of an overall regulatory approach potentially affects the capability to enforce accounting rules in these countries. Arguably, government-defined uniformity of accounting requirements facilitates the review of enterprise compliance with

---

[21]Cooper and Keim [1983] assert, however, that the signal associated with accounting choices must be unambiguous and credible if it is to be effective.

these rules. Uniformity also imposes fewer demands on skilled and professional accountants, who are generally in short supply in many ECMs. Conversely, uniformity based on strict government control could also inhibit the development of a more responsive financial reporting system. It has been observed, for example, that financial reporting is generally more "sophisticated" in countries that assign a greater role to the private sector, particularly the accounting profession, in shaping regulations.[22] Changes, apart from being implemented more rapidly, also are more likely to incorporate recent innovations in financial markets, such as the introduction of trading in financial derivatives, compared to countries that adopt a government-led regulatory approach.

On the basis of the above discussion, it seems appropriate that ECMs in their early stages of development should emphasize government-defined uniform accounting requirements. This option helps to maximize the use of scarce professional accounting personnel, facilitates compliance with extant requirements, and "educates" enterprises regarding the need to provide adequate disclosure. Effective enforcement of these reporting rules requires that a regulatory agency with sufficient administrative resources be established. For most ECMs, the model often emulated is that of the U.S. SEC.[23] Conversely, as ECMs reach a particular size and maturity and attain a greater number of well-trained accounting professionals (e.g., Argentina, Singapore, and South Africa), regulators can allow the private sector, i.e., stock exchanges and professional accounting bodies, to play a more active role in setting and enforcing financial reporting policies. The statutory regulatory agency could then play a supportive and supervisory role by monitoring the performance of these private sector organizations and by imposing credible, yet judicious, penalties for violations of extant rules.

Harmonization of Accounting Standards

Finally, the third policy issue facing regulators in ECMs is whether to pursue an active program of accounting harmonization. The issue is particularly important for countries adopting market-oriented economic policies after years of state central planning. Policy-makers will have to grapple with issues regarding the most appropriate financial reporting system for their country. The alternatives range from adopting aspects of regulation in economically advanced countries to formulating a system uniquely tailored to an ECM's particular circumstances. If accounting harmonization emerges as a preferred policy, a choice has to be made on whether accounting harmonization will be pursued following a regional or global model. The actual choice, however, will depend on the concurrent, yet diametrical, effects of regionalization and globalization on individual countries.

The regional model of accounting harmonization represents one policy option for countries. The regional model, representing the cluster approach to accounting harmonization, possesses specific advantages in terms of recognizing the shared interests of the member countries. Countries that are geographically proximate often share similar characteristics in terms of their historical, political, economic, and cultural backgrounds. Regional accounting harmonization might be pursued to further enhance the level of economic linkages among countries in the region.

---

[22]See Wallace and Briston [1993].

[23]Recent examples of ECMs that have adopted this model include Indonesia, Malaysia, Poland, and Thailand.

The other significant trend is the increasing level of integration of global financial markets. Globalization of finance is an increasingly significant policy issue for developing and transitional economies seeking to augment their domestic resources with foreign capital. Pressures to revise and transform financial reporting systems come from a variety of international sources. Foreign institutional investors can express their preferences for particular types of accounting regimes such as IAS or U.S. GAAP. Multilateral financial institutions such as the World Bank also support particular types of financial reporting. In such an environment, the global model of accounting harmonization represents a rational policy alternative for ECMs. Adoption of international accounting standards is consistent with moving towards the global concept of harmonization. International accounting standards offer a credible alternative for countries that do not have the resources to develop their own standards or that desire the benefits associated with possessing globally acceptable accounting standards. Some international accounting standards, however, could be inappropriate for the needs of ECMs. In the long term, the extent to which developed markets subsequently support international accounting standards is crucial to the ECM's decision.

The principal risk of pursuing accounting harmonization relates to the possibility that the accounting standards adopted are inappropriate for the particular ECM. The greater risk, however, is for an ECM to become uncompetitive because it does not have a sound basis of accounting that can be understood by investors elsewhere. In an increasingly interdependent and globalized economy, some form of accounting harmonization seems warranted. This assertion is particularly salient for ECMs because these markets depend substantially on the inflow of foreign portfolio investments for their continued growth. Rather than having such harmonization occurring by default, accounting regulators in ECMs should make a deliberate choice of accounting models with which they wish to harmonize their domestic accounting standards. The specific choices will depend on existing and planned economic linkages as well as political and socio-cultural similarities between the model country and adopting country.

Caveats Based on Recent Developments

The discussion in the chapter thus far has focused on the role and characteristics of financial reporting in ECMs. In doing so, we reported some descriptions and comparisons from surveys on the quality of accounting and comprehensiveness of auditing in emerging markets and developed markets. Until recently the conventional wisdom was that accounting in developed countries, particularly the United States, was uniformly superior to that in emerging markets. However, the year 2002 saw a spate of accounting scandals at well-known corporations in a number of developed capital markets such as the United States (Enron, WorldCom, Xerox, and Global Crossing), the United Kingdom (Centrica, Shell), France (Vivendi), and the Netherlands (Shell). Reports in the mainstream business press have questioned the superiority of U.S. accounting.[24] One article[25] concluded that U.S. companies are overvalued relative to Asian companies because the U.S. companies' more aggressive accounting practices make their quality of earnings more vulnerable. The article reported the

---

[24]See, for example, "Opening the case of the bogus bookkeepers" by M. Peel, *Financial Times* (May 3, 2001, p 11), and "Call to scrap U.S. rules on accounting in wake of Enron" by F. Guerrera and P. Norman, *Financial Times* (February 21, 2002, p.1).

[25]See "Asian Firms Avoid U.S.-Style Accounting Woes" by C. Karmin, *The Wall Street Journal* (May 29, 2002, p. C14).

results of a study by CLSA Emerging Markets that compared Asian and U.S. companies in three areas: pro forma accounting methods; the treatment of stock options in financial statements; and assumptions related to pension plan assets. It found that in 2001, S&P 500 firms in the United States used pro forma statements to report earnings that were inflated by 57 percent relative to U.S. GAAP. The difference was even more dramatic for NASDAQ 100 firms where a combined US$19 billion loss under GAAP became a US$82 billion profit under pro forma statements. Talk about creative accounting! In contrast, the difference between pro forma and GAAP earnings for Asian companies studied was only 4 percent. In comparing U.S. and Asian companies from similar industries and of comparable size, the study found that the average reduction in reported earnings if employee stock options were expensed was 13.7 percent for U.S. firms versus 6.8 percent for Asian firms. The third factor that made U.S. corporate earnings more vulnerable was the high rates of return assumed on their pension plan assets. While the average Asian company assumed a 6 percent return on its pension fund, U.S. companies assumed a 9.4 percent return. In view of the stock market slump since March 2000, U.S. firms are likely to be required to reduce their rate of return assumptions, which will result in their incurring tens of billions of dollars in additional expenses.[26] Thus, on each of the three items examined in the study, U.S. firms were shown to use accounting methods that tended to materially inflate their earnings and financial position. This evidence suggests that the quality of accounting is not just a concern in emerging capital markets.

Accounting in Selected Emerging Capital Markets

In the concluding section of this chapter, we briefly discuss accounting in two emerging capital markets, Mexico and China. Mexico is interesting because it requires companies to disclose the impact of inflation in their financial statements. China, the largest economy that is moving from a centrally planned to an open market economy, faces specific challenges in accounting during its transition. We examine samples of financial statements from each country to highlight some of their distinctive accounting practices.

Mexico

Accounting standards in Mexico are established by the Accounting Principles Commission of the Insituto Mexicano de Contadores Publicos (IMCP), which is an independent, nongovernmental association representing the accounting profession. The IMCP is the umbrella organization of state and local associations of registered public accountants. Through its various committees, it also promulgates auditing standards and rules of ethics for the accounting profession in Mexico. As is the case with most other countries, Mexican accounting principles are less detailed than those of the United States. However, the onset of NAFTA combined with the significant presence of U.S. multinationals and the major international accounting firms (i.e., Big Eight/ Seven/ Six/ Five/ Four . . . .) in Mexico have resulted in U.S. GAAP having considerable influence on Mexican accounting practices. However, there remain a number of areas of differences between Mexican GAAP and U.S. GAAP. These include: prior period items and changes in accounting policies, related-party disclosures, minority

---

[26]See "S&P Sheds Light on Accounting for Pension Costs" by C. Bryan-Low, *The Wall Street Journal* (October 24, 2002, pp. C1, C3); "FASB turns spotlight on pension rules" *Financial Times* (November 29, 2002, p. 16).

interest, research and development, deferred income taxes, accrued employee bene-fits, foreign currency fluctuations, extraordinary items, investments, and capitalization of interest. There are also special accounting practices and disclosures required for regulated industries. The most distinctive feature of Mexican accounting, however, is its continued use of inflation accounting. Long after countries such as the United States and United Kingdom abandoned inflation-adjusted accounting models in the mid-1980s, Mexico continues to require companies to adjust their financial statements to show the effect of inflation. This is a product of Mexico's experience with high rates of inflation over the past two decades.[27]

Accounting for inflation became mandatory under Mexican GAAP in 1984. The Mexican standard has elements of the general price level adjusted model, which was discussed in Chapter 4. It incorporates the effect of inflation on the net monetary assets (i.e., assets minus liabilities), the gains and losses from holding non-monetary assets, and the preservation of financial capital. As illustrated in the financial state-ments of FEMSA (a Mexican company) in Exhibit 6-9, income statements of Mexi-can companies include an item "Integral Result of Financing" not seen in historical cost-based financial statements. This item contains the nominal interest expense and interest income, the exchange gain or loss for the company's monetary items denom-inated in foreign currencies, and the gain or loss resulting from price level changes on the company's net monetary position. Inflation accounting rules in Mexico also require firms to restate all financial information in monetary units as of the end of the current period. To provide meaningful comparisons, all comparative data from prior years must also be restated to constant pesos at the end of the current period. For pur-poses of converting nominal monetary units to price-level adjusted units, firms are required to use the consumer price index statistics published by the central bank. Since 1990, all Mexican companies are required to use the calendar year as their fis-cal year.

The following is an extract from the Management's Discussion and Analysis (MD&A) section of FEMSA's annual report. It explains the adjustments made in the financial statements to reflect the change in the purchasing power of the Mexican peso:

> All of the figures in this report have been restated in constant Mexican Pesos ("Pesos" or "Ps.") with purchasing power as of December 31, 2001 and were prepared in accordance with Mexican Generally Accepted Accounting Principles ("Mexican GAAP"). As a result, all percentage changes are expressed in real terms. The restatement was determined as follows:
>
> • For the results of the Mexican operations, using factors derived from the Mexican National Consumer Price Index ("NCPI"). To restate December 2000 Pesos to December 2001 Pesos, the Company applied an inflation factor of 1.0440 and to restate September 2001 Pesos to December 2001 Pesos, the Company applied a 1.0097 infla-tion factor.
>
> • For the results of the Buenos Aires operations, using factors derived from the Argen-tine National Consumer Price Index of 0.9856 to restate December 2000 Argentine Pesos to December 2001 Pesos and of 0.9920 to restate September 2001 Argentine Pesos to December 2001 Pesos; and converting constant Argentine Pesos into Pesos, based on the December 31, 2001 exchange rate of Ps. 5.4 and Ps. 8.89 per Argentine Peso for Balance Sheet and Income Statement, respectively.

---

[27]Davis-Friday and Rivera (2000) describe the impact of differential financial reporting under Mexican and U.S. GAAP on the stock prices of Mexican firms listed on U.S. stock exchanges.

EXHIBIT 6-9 FEMSA's 2001 Mexican GAAP Income Statement

For the years ended December 31, 2001, 2000 and 1999. Amounts expressed in millions of US dollars ($) and in millions of constant Mexican pesos (Ps.) as of December 31, 2001.	2001		2000	1999
Net sales	$ 5,412	Ps. 49,681	Ps. 46,887	Ps. 42,739
Other operating revenues	21	196	78	70
Total revenues	5,433	49,877	46,965	42,809
Cost of sales	2,665	24,465	23,411	21,901
Gross profit	2,768	25,412	23,554	20,908
Operating expenses:				
Administrative	486	4,461	4,297	3,635
Sales	1,392	12,777	11,921	10,628
	1,878	17,238	16,218	14,263
Income from operations	890	8,174	7,336	6,645
Participation in affiliated companies	3	31	35	55
	893	8,205	7,371	6,700
Integral result of financing:				
Interest expense	97	893	1,078	1,137
Interest income	(50)	(458)	(424)	(453)
Foreign exchange loss (gain)	(32)	(293)	1,061	(124)
Gain on monetary position	4	39	(255)	(464)
	19	181	1,460	96
Other expenses (income), net	33	306	(187)	124
Income for the year before income tax, tax on assets and employee profit sharing	841	7,718	6,098	6,480
Income tax, tax on assets and employee profit sharing	307	2,820	2,407	2,084
Net income before extraordinary items	534	4,898	3,691	4,396
Effect of changes in accounting principles	3	27	—	—
Consolidated net income for the year	$ 531	Ps. 4,871	Ps. 3,691	Ps. 4,396
Net majority income	359	3,292	2,636	3,308
Net minority income	172	1,579	1,055	1,088
Consolidated net income for the year	$ 531	Ps. 4,871	Ps. 3,691	Ps. 4,396
Net majority income per share (US dollars and constant Mexican pesos):				
Per series "B" share				
Before changes in accounting principles	$ 0.061	Ps. 0.559	Ps. 0.440	Ps. 0.552
After changes in accounting principles	0.060	0.554	0.440	0.552
Per series "D" share				
Before changes in accounting principles	0.076	0.699	0.550	0.690
After changes in accounting principles	0.075	0.693	0.550	0.690

The accompanying notes are an integral part of this consolidated income statement.

An excerpt from the notes to FEMSA's consolidated financial statements provides additional insights into how Mexican firms recognize the effects of inflation:

> The recognition of the effects of inflation in the financial information consists of:
> - Restating non-monetary assets such as inventories and fixed assets, including related costs and expenses when such assets are consumed or depreciated.
> - Restating capital stock, additional paid-in capital and retained earnings by the amount necessary to maintain the purchasing power equivalent in Mexican pesos on the dates such capital was contributed or income generated, through the use of factors derived from the National Consumer Price Index (NCPI).
> - Including in stockholders' equity the cumulative effect of holding non-monetary assets, which is the net difference between changes in the replacement cost of non-monetary assets and adjustments based upon NCPI factors.
> - Including in the cost of financing the purchasing power gain or loss from holding monetary items.

Since FEMSA is listed on the New York Stock Exchange, it reconciles its financial statements to U.S. GAAP. Another note details the principal differences between Mexican GAAP and U.S. GAAP that FEMSA adjusts for in preparing its reconciliation to U.S. GAAP. Some of these differences are as follows. Under Mexican GAAP, the promotional costs related to the launching of new products are recorded as pre-paid expenses while they are expensed under U.S. GAAP. Similarly, under Mexican GAAP, start-up costs are capitalized and amortized after the start of operations using the straight-line method as opposed to being expensed as incurred under U.S. GAAP. Under Mexican GAAP, the maximum amortization period for goodwill is 20 years while it was 40 years under U.S. GAAP. Under SFAS No. 142, goodwill generated after June 30, 2001 is no longer subject to amortization. Another difference in accounting treatments is that under Mexican GAAP imported machinery and equipment are restated by applying the inflation rate of the country of origin and then translated at the year-end exchange rate of the Mexican peso, while under U.S. GAAP both domestic and imported machinery and equipment are restated using NCPI factors. As mentioned in Chapter 5, there also exist some important differences in accounting for deferred taxes. Under Mexican GAAP, deferred taxes are classified as non-current, while under U.S. GAAP the classification is based on the classification of the related asset or liability. Under Mexican GAAP, the effects of inflation on the deferred tax balance generated by monetary items are recognized in the result on monetary position, while under U.S. GAAP the deferred tax balance is classified as a non-monetary item. Finally, under Mexican GAAP, a change in statutory tax rate approved prior to the issuance of the financial statements is considered in the calculation of deferred taxes at the balance sheet date while under U.S. GAAP a change in statutory tax rate may not be considered until the enactment date.

People's Republic of China (PRC)

The authority to set accounting and auditing standards in China resides with the Ministry of Finance (MOF). The Accounting Law, which represents the highest accounting authority in China, was revised in 2000 and has as its objectives fraud prevention, investor protection, and management controls. In addition to Chinese Accounting Standards (CAS), all Chinese companies must comply with the Financial Accounting and Reporting Rules (FARR) enacted in 2001. The China Securities Regulatory Commission (CSRC), the country's capital market regulator, has the authority to require additional disclosures beyond that required by the MOF.

A distinct feature of the Chinese capital market is that Chinese companies issue several classes of shares. Companies listed on the domestic stock exchanges issue A and B class shares. Companies listed abroad issue various other classes of shares depending on their foreign listing location. Thus, firms listed in Hong Kong issue H shares, those in London issue L shares, and those in New York issue N shares. Originally, the A class shares were for domestic investors while the B class shares were for foreign investors. However, this partitioning has weakened over time. Since April 2001, Chinese investors have been allowed to purchase Class B shares. In November 2002, the CSRC and the People's Bank of China (the central bank) decided to also relax the constraints in the reverse direction. They announced that starting in December 2002, foreigners would be permitted to buy Class A shares. China's Class A share market has about 1,200 companies with about one-third being tradable and the remainder being non-tradable shares of state-owned companies. The recent relaxation by the Chinese authorities allows foreign institutional investors to purchase both the tradable and the non-tradable Class A shares. The tradable Class A shares had a total market capitalization of about US $160 billion in November 2002. The Chinese authorities set several conditions for the "Qualified Foreign Institutional Investor" (QFII) permitted to purchase Class A shares. All QFIIs are required to have paid-in capital of at least US$1 billion, investment portfolios of at least US$10 billion, a healthy corporate structure, and they must not have faced regulatory action by their domestic regulators in the past three years. These relaxations indicate an admission by the Chinese authorities that the partitioning of investors by nationality (Chinese versus foreign) and type of shares (tradable and non-tradable) were not sustainable.

So far, the different classes of shares have had accounting implications in that they have required Chinese companies to prepare their financial statements using different GAAPs. Financial reporting for companies issuing Class A shares was required in Chinese GAAP, for companies issuing Class B shares in International Accounting Standards (IAS), for H shares in Hong Kong GAAP, for L shares in IAS, and for N shares in U.S. GAAP. In addition, there were also different reporting standards for non-listed joint stock limited enterprises, for state-owned enterprises, and for other non-listed enterprises. The non-listed joint stock enterprises were subject to almost all Chinese GAAP. The MOF issued special industry standards for state-owned enterprises and required adherence to selected portions of Chinese GAAP for other non-listed enterprises.

The above discussion highlights the potpourri of accounting standards used by Chinese firms and the resulting challenges posed to financial statement users. The absence of a single set of standards makes it rather difficult to gain insights into the financial health of companies. It also makes it hard to compare business entities. This arrangement may have made sense as long as the Chinese government believed that state-owned enterprises and companies with only Class A shares did not need to raise capital from foreigners. It may also have been motivated by a desire to maintain opacity in the operations and financing of state-owned enterprises. The change in policy may reflect a desire to attract foreign investment in these entities along with an acceptance that foreign investors need greater transparency into the Chinese entities' operations and finances.

The differing standards do have a positive side from an international accounting perspective. China provides a unique setting in which to study de jure versus de facto harmonization. Since listed Chinese companies with Class A and Class B shares are required to provide two sets of financial statements—Chinese GAAP financial statements to Class A shareholders and IAS financial statements to Class B shareholders—

EXHIBIT 6-10 China Eastern Airlines Chinese GAAP Income Statement

Income Statement

(Prepared in accordance with PRC Accounting Regulations)
For the Period of January – December 2001

Unit: RMB Yuan

Items	Note	Current year (consolidated)	Current year (parent corp.)	Previous year (consolidated)	Previous year (parent corp.)
I. Revenue from Main Operations:	30	**12,839,339,288.79**	**10,836,053,949.83**	11,821,758,147.00	10,098,738,853.18
Less: Revenue for Civil Air Infrastructure Construction Fund		427,784,224.78	364,584,964.00	368,184,348.16	317,479,480.14
Revenue from Main Operations, net		12,411,555,064.01	10,471,468,985.83	11,453,573,798.84	9,781,259,373.04
Less: Main Operating Cost	31	9,895,680,220.39	8,309,081,958.21	9,119,344,878.75	7,894,754,222.36
Business Taxes and additional		296,836,879.42	255,111,509.28	271,339,202.01	235,781,341.74
II. Profit from Main Operations		**2,219,037,964.20**	**1,907,275,518.34**	2,062,889,718.08	1,650,723,808.94
Add: Other Operating Revenue	32	541,079,876.56	526,189,646.92	357,018,221.61	376,232,914.82
Less: Operating Expenses		1,297,765,706.82	1,205,229,653.27	1,349,875,214.28	1,280,465,097.67
General & Administrative Expenses		642,712,900.35	530.656,265.97	533,842,545.83	450,555,736.89
Financial Expenses	33	699,722,003.92	641,818,197.11	748,378,024.62	707,465,092.96
III. Profit from Operations		**119,917,229.67**	**55,761,048.91**	(212,187,845.04)	(411,529,203.76)
Add: Investment Income	34	57,296,511.88	94,242,771.53	53,839,446.05	163,423,373.84
Gains or Losses from Futures	–	–	–	–	–
Subsidy Income		750,000.00	750,000.00	1,069,600.00	1,069,600.00
Non-operating Income	35	33,312,379.60	25,092,544.34	281,258,809.38	283,972,830.69
Less: Non-operating Income	36	48,259,815.66	41,597,244.21	20,748,110.65	14,474,708.02
IV. Total Profit		**163,016,305.49**	**134,249,120.57**	103,231,899.74	22,461,892.75
Less: Income Tax		4,917,182.92	70,662.50	20,775,063.28	1,289,476.17
Gains or losses of Minority Shareholders		25,179,679.26	–	62,374,925.33	–
V. Net Profit		**132,919,443.31**	**134,178,458.07**	20,081,911.13	21,172,416.58
Add: Undistributed Profit at the Beginning of the Year (Deficit Shown in Degative)		41,595,432.49	79,029,006.02	141,799,852.68	155,195,589.44
Less: Decrease of Undistributed Profit to Reduce Registered Capital	–	–	–	–	–
Add: Transfer from Surplus Reserve		–	–	–	–
VI. Distribute Profit		**174,514,875.80**	**213,207,464.09**	161,881,763.81	176,368,006.02
Less Provision for Statutory Surplus Reserve		1,680,597.37	–	11,041,832.70	–
Welfare Fund		1,680,597.37	–	11,041,832.70	–
Provision for Staff & Worker's Welfare Fund	–	–	–	–	–
VII. Profit Attributable to Shareholders		**171,153,681.06**	**213,207,464.09**	139,798,098.41	176,368,006.02

it is possible to compare the level of harmonization between the two sets. In a study addressing this issue (Chen et al, 2002), the researchers examined 75 Chinese companies that provided financial statements in both Chinese GAAP and IAS. By comparing the two sets of earnings reported, they sought to determine whether the harmonization in accounting regulations (de jure) between Chinese GAAP and IAS was reflected in the accounting practices (de facto). They found that, contrary to the high expectations in China and abroad, harmonized accounting regulations did not result in correspondingly harmonized financial statements for Chinese firms. Exhibits 6-10 and 6-11 contain the income statements for China Eastern Airlines prepared under Chinese GAAP and IAS, respectively. A closer look at these statements reveals some important differences between the two. The Chinese GAAP income statement is presented for both the parent and the consolidated group, while the IAS statements are only for the consolidated entity. Several of the profit measures are different between the two sets of statements. Thus, while the Chinese GAAP income statement

EXHIBIT 6·11 China Eastern Airlines IAS Income Statement

Consolidated Profit and Loss Account

(Prepared in accordance with International Accounting Standards)
Year ended 31 December 2001

	Note	2001 RMB'000	2000 RMB'000
Traffic revenues			
Passenger		9,586,941	8,644,260
Cargo and mail		2,091,669	2,124,228
Other operating revenues		474,198	451,575
Turnover	3	12,152,808	11,220,063
Operating expenses			
Wages, salaries and benefits	4	772,896	797,594
Take-off and landing charges		1,702,899	1,572,216
Aircraft fuel		2,613,187	2,327,388
Food and beverages		567,168	498,640
Aircraft depreciation and operating leases		2,403,752	2,167,539
Other depreciation, amortisation, and operating leases		358,120	320,792
Aircraft maintenance		966,750	820,405
Commissions		487,009	645,482
Office and administration		849,217	724,046
Other		557, 139	567,709
Total operating expenses		11,278,137	10,441,811
Operating profit		874,671	778,252
Interest expense, net	5	(814,375)	(814,486)
Other income, net	6	248,741	340,642
Share of profit of an associated company	17	4,546	–
Profit before taxation	7	313,583	304,408
Taxation	9(a)	261,454	(99,637)
Profit after taxation		575,037	204,771
Minority interests	32	(33,324)	(29,242)
Profit attributable to shareholders		541,713	175,529
Basic earnings per share	10	RMB0.111	RMB0.036

has *total profit*, *net profit*, and *distributable profit*, the IAS income statement has *profit before taxation* and *profit after taxation*. However, the two sets of statements do have two common profit measures—*operating profit* and *profit attributable to shareholders*. Yet the numbers reported are very different under the two sets of GAAP:

In RMB'000	PRC GAAP	IAS
Total Revenues	12,839,933	12,152,808
Operating Profit	119,917	874,671
Profit attributable to Shareholders	171,154	541,713

The absolute operating profit reported by China Eastern Airlines in IAS is 729 percent of that in Chinese GAAP. The profit attributable to shareholders in IAS is 316 percent of that in Chinese GAAP. Even after we scale by the total revenue amounts under the two sets of GAAP, the income numbers are very different. Operating profit as a percentage of revenues under Chinese GAAP is 0.93 percent, while under IAS it is 7.2 percent. Similarly, profit attributable to shareholders under Chinese GAAP is 1.33 percent, while under IAS it is 4.46 percent. These numbers obviously provide a very different picture of the company under the two sets of GAAP even though Chinese GAAP is theoretically purported to be in harmony with IAS.

Commentators have attributed the difficulties with the financial reporting environment in China to a number of factors.[28] These include a shortage of well-trained accounting professionals; the selective enforcement of accounting and regulatory requirements; an environment of extensive corruption; issues related to independence, professional competence, and ethics of accounting professionals; and an inadequate supporting infrastructure that is manifested in excessive earnings management and low quality auditing. China will have to continue working on upgrading its accounting and auditing practices (as opposed to just its regulations) if it intends to attract foreign investors to its securities markets.

SUMMARY

1. This chapter considered reasons why sound financial reporting is central to the development of ECMs. The extent to which ECMs can address pitfalls and difficulties associated with their financial reporting rules and practices contributes significantly to the ability of these markets to attract global capital inflows.

2. Three characteristics of financial reporting were identified as being particularly relevant to ECMs. They are the availability, reliability, and comparability of financial and other information. Information availability was viewed in terms of the extent and quality of disclosures necessary for making investment decisions. ECMs are generally lagging in terms of their levels of disclosures compared to developed capital markets. Information reliability is linked to the soundness of domestic accounting standards as well as the enforcement capability in the country. Moreover, ECMs possess different capabilities with respect to enforcing existing standards because of constraints found in each country's national environment. Finally, comparability encompasses two important aspects. On one hand, differences in domestic accounting standards, quite prevalent among ECMs, affect the comparability of financial reports. In addition, the underlying environments in each country provide the contextual basis for interpreting the accounting numbers. Accounting harmonization generally focuses on a single facet of comparability, that of dissimilar accounting standards. As such, harmonization provides only a partial solution to the problem of comparing enterprises across different national settings.

3. The implications of various financial reporting policies on the political, economic, and socio-cultural conditions in ECMs must be considered. In this regard, three urgent areas of further inquiry can be identified. With respect to information availability, it is relevant to examine the implications of a mandated versus a voluntary approach to disclosure. The costs and benefits of these alternative approaches need to be considered in the context of ECMs, given their enforcement capabilities and reliance on external sources of capital. While the overall tendency is towards mandated disclosures, achieving an optimal balance of regulation appears more difficult in practice. Indeed, inadequate disclosure could seriously reduce investor confidence in the market. Conversely, burdensome disclosures could discourage otherwise qualified companies from raising capital in stock markets because the perceived costs of compliance outweigh the benefits of listing.

---

[28]See, for example, Xiao et al. (2000) and Tang (2000).

4. Enforcement of accounting regulation in ECMs is another important consideration for users of financial statements. The best accounting standards are only as good as the effectiveness of the regulatory process. Systematic inquiry needs to be made regarding the strength of regulatory mechanisms in ECMs, the factors limiting their effectiveness, and possible remedies for limitations that are uncovered. The issue of strengthening enforcement in ECMs is related to preferences for a government-led or a private sector-oriented approach to regulation. Uniform accounting requirements appear to provide benefits in view of the limited enforcement capability in ECMs. Nonetheless, there remains the question of whether a private sector-led accounting regime, similar to those that exist in the United Kingdom and United States, is more appropriate for ECMs. Methods for increasing the number and quality of accounting personnel in ECMs are also an important adjunct to enforcement effectiveness, regardless of the regulatory approach adopted.

5. Finally, users need to consider the impact of accounting harmonization on ECMs. Despite calls for increased accounting harmonization, little is known about the real benefits and costs. For example, will the adoption of international accounting standards provide greater benefits to emerging markets (e.g., in terms of attracting more foreign investment) or will such adoption retard the development of their capital markets? Another dimension of the comparability issue, which requires further inquiry, is the importance of contextual factors underlying accounting numbers. Knowledge of these contextual factors will assist users to correctly interpret the significance of accounting information in ECMs, which, in turn, would lead to better investment decisions.

QUESTIONS

1. How does the World Bank define a developing country? When did investors from developed countries start seriously investing in emerging capital markets?
2. What have been the "traditional" sources of capital in developing countries? How might this have impacted the financial reporting environment in these countries?
3. What is meant by "non-traditional" sources of capital in developing countries? In your view, how is the shift from "traditional" to "non-traditional" sources of capital likely to affect financial reporting in developing countries?
4. Why is a sound financial reporting system a crucial component of the infrastructure for developing domestic capital markets in developing countries?
5. What qualitative criteria must foreign investors consider in evaluating financial reporting that originates in emerging capital markets? Are these criteria necessarily different from those to be used for developed countries? Explain.
6. Discuss how the criteria referred to in question 5 can provide the focal point for developing benchmarks for comparing and improving the performance of extant financial reporting systems in emerging capital markets.
7. In light of Enron et al., do you consider problems with availability of financial information likely to be more severe in developing countries than in developed countries? If so, what are the factors that might contribute to this?
8. What two elements are essential to promote reliability in the financial reports prepared in a country? In emerging capital markets, which of these elements is easier to attain?
9. What are the two dimensions of comparability of financial information? Discuss the significance of each.
10. The chapter discusses three policy issues related to financial reporting in emerging capital markets. Briefly discuss each policy issue.

11. What are the two possible approaches to increasing the availability of high-quality financial information in emerging capital markets? Discuss the pros and cons of each.
12. What factors affect the level of enforcement of financial reporting and securities regulations in any country? How might authorities in emerging capital markets realistically strengthen their enforcement capability?

EXERCISES

1. The risks of investing in ECMs are not only associated with structural, political, and economic problems, but also with informational problems stemming from the difficulty of obtaining adequate, reliable, and timely information useful for evaluating investment opportunities in these markets. Research three ECMs and determine the timeliness and availability of financial reporting for each. Do publicly listed companies release quarterly or semi-annual financial statements? Are annual reports made available in a timely manner after the fiscal year end? Is actual practice different from required practice? Briefly summarize your findings for each ECM.
2. The quality of corporate financial reporting in ECMs varies considerably. This makes it difficult to ignore the impact of poor financial reporting on the performance of some of these markets. Choose an emerging capital market and obtain two corporate annual reports from it. Critique the quality of information provided in the annual reports and explain how this level of information may be affecting the performance of these markets.
3. Exhibit 6-1 lists 79 countries whose capital markets are considered ECMs by Standard & Poor's Emerging Stock Markets Factbook [2001]. Choose a country and obtain three corporate annual reports all within the same industry. How do the annual reports differ from reports in your home country? As a user, are you satisfied with the information provided in the annual reports? Discuss three key annual report items you would like to see improved.
4. Exhibit 6-5 illustrates that 19 out of 30 ECMs (63 percent) have either wholly adopted international accounting standards or have used international accounting standards to develop domestic accounting standards. However, international accounting standards are greatly influenced by more developed capital markets and are known to incorporate accounting methods generally accepted in countries such as the United Kingdom and United States. This results in some ECMs adopting accounting standards that might not be suitable to their stage of economic development or particular circumstances. Select and discuss specific ECMs where you think this might be the case.
5. Choose an emerging country and research the strength of enforcement of financial accounting standards and reporting. Is there a lax attitude towards financial reporting, or weaknesses in the administrative mechanisms for enforcing standards? Is there government support or an inadequate level of organization for the accounting and auditing profession? Is there an effective government or quasi-government agency that monitors compliance of pertinent regulations to discourage widespread violations of extant regulations?
6. Select an ECM and research the differences in training and qualifications of local auditors, audit standards and requirements, nature of audits conducted, and the availability of auditors compared to those in your home country. Include in your analysis anything the country is doing to improve its current situation with respect to the audit function.
7. Due to the differing economic, legal, political, and cultural environments surrounding each ECM, in addition to the high degree of accounting diversity that exists currently, should any accounting harmonization be pursued at all among ECMs? Explain.
8. As companies increasingly obtain financing overseas by listing on foreign stock exchanges, differences in auditing practices, procedures, and liabilities across countries have brought the auditing profession under much scrutiny and criticism. Choose an ECM and obtain a few local annual reports. Refer to the auditor's report, and, if possible, describe the auditing standards used. How do auditor liability, procedures, and standards differ from those in your home country?

9. One factor that can affect investor confidence in financial reporting is the timeliness of the annual reports. Choose an ECM and obtain three local annual reports all with the same fiscal year end. Carefully examine the auditors' reports of the three companies. When was the audit report issued (i.e., how long after the year-end date)? Is this period shorter or longer compared to companies listed in your home country? Explain.

10. A criterion for evaluating the reliability of an ECM's financial reporting system is whether the financial reports are prepared on the basis of sound accounting requirements. Choose an ECM that you are familiar with. Using any resources available to you, what GAAP (e.g., local GAAP, IAS) does the ECM use for financial reporting purposes? In your opinion, is this GAAP likely to inspire confidence in investors? Support your answer.

11. Substantial differences have been observed regarding the level of assurance provided by independent audits in various countries. Choose three companies from an ECM and find out who their auditors are. Would your level of assurance be reduced if the auditor was not one of the Big 4 accounting firms? Explain.

12. Go to the web site of Shanghai Petrochemical (China) at *www.spc.com.cn/* and pull up the most recent annual report. Answer the following questions.
    a) What is the basis of preparation the company uses for financial reporting purposes (e.g., domestic GAAP, IAS)?
    b) Who are their auditors?
    c) When was the audit report dated?
    d) What is the company's fiscal year-end date?
    e) Compare the Consolidated Balance Sheet (IAS) and the Income Statement (IAS) with the Consolidated Balance Sheet (PRC) and Income Statement (PRC). Which statement makes the company appear most financially healthy?
    f) Compare the Consolidated Profit and Loss Account (IAS) to the Consolidated Income Statement (PRC). Comment on the differences.

    After answering questions a–f, discuss what you found most interesting about Shanghai Petrochemical's financial reporting.

13. Go to the web site of China Southern Airlines (China) at *www.chinasouthernair.com/* and write a brief synopsis about the company.

14. Go to the web site of Ashanti Goldfields Company (Ghana) at *www.ashanti.com.gh/*.
    a) What does the company use as the basis of preparation for financial reporting purposes? Why do you suppose so?
    b) Examine the company's environmental and social disclosures. Are these disclosures more or less informative than those in your home country? Explain.

CASES

Case

Split Beans

Ryan Scott is a member of the South African Institute of Chartered Accountants, a professional accounting organization aimed at developing and maintaining quality accounting standards and procedures for all publicly listed companies. For the last four months, the organization has been unable to reach an agreement with other professional accounting bodies regarding the formulation of a national government policy that would improve the quality of financial reporting among ECMs.

You are a member of an organization that advocates a "free market approach," which would allow enterprises to choose the appropriate level of disclosure according to their particular circumstances. Specifically, your organization believes that competitive market pressures will ensure that an optimal level of disclosure is achieved since firms will compete to reduce the cost of obtaining funds from the market. However, other professional bodies have strongly advocated the mandatory regulatory approach and argue that an adequate level of disclosure regulation is necessary due to a potential market failure in the supply of financial information. Since financial information is characteristic of a public good, information is likely to be underproduced if mandatory regulations are absent, consequently stifling the growth of these markets.

1. If you were the CFO of a large publicly held company with headquarters in South Africa, what position would you like Mr. Scott to favor and why?
2. Describe some of the benefits of allowing companies the freedom of choosing their own disclosure policies versus mandating reporting procedures. As an investor, which approach would you like to see implemented? Be specific.
3. Does mandating reporting procedures necessarily increase the amount of information available to investors? Briefly explain.

Case

Gold Rush

Reece Khan, Investment Executive at Peterson and Company International, was just approached by a first-year hire, Trish Ventura, regarding a new investment opportunity in Croatia, an emerging capital market.

"Mr. Khan, this is an incredible opportunity and the returns would be fantastic. I've analyzed the company annual report ten times already, ran the numbers through twice, and I've even spoken to some of the executives at the company who gladly gave me the answers I needed. We've got to make this investment. The sooner, the better, so that we can maximize the company's returns before the investing public realizes what a gold mine they've been passing up. I'll bet my job on it!"

"Croatia? . . . But Croatia is an ECM. The country probably hasn't even developed sufficient corporate reporting policies and procedures to supply the information necessary for making investment decisions, let alone rely on them. What did your analysis reveal about the country's accounting and auditing profession, in addition to its accounting and legal infrastructure?"

"Good, okay, fair, and weak . . . so when do we invest?"

1. Pretend you are Mr. Khan. How would you respond to Trish Ventura and why?
2. What specifically did Trish forget to take into account or consider during her analysis of an ECM?
3. If you were Investment Executive for Peterson and Company International, would you recommend investing in any emerging capital markets?
4. Briefly summarize some of the reasons why investing in emerging capital markets is considered risky. Include the costs and benefits in your discussion.

REFERENCES

Ariff, M., and Johnson, L. W. 1990. *Securities Markets & Stock Pricing: Evidence from a Developing Capital Market in Asia.* Singapore: Longman.

Asian Development Bank (ADB). 1986. *Capital Market Development in Selected Developing Member Countries of the Asian Development Bank.* Manila: ADB.

Bhushan, R., and Lessard, D. R. 1992. Coping with international accounting diversity: Fund managers' views on disclosure, reconciliation, and harmonization. *Journal of International Financial Management and Accounting,* 4 (2): 149–164.

Biddle, G. C., and Saudagaran, S. M. 1991. Foreign stock listings: Benefits, costs, and the accounting policy dilemma. *Accounting Horizons,* 5 (September): 69–80.

Bromwich, M. 1985. *The Economics of Accounting Standard Setting.* London: Prentice-Hall and the Institute of Chartered Accountants of England and Wales.

Center for International Financial Analysis & Research (CIFAR). 1995. *International Accounting and Auditing Trends,* 4th ed., edited by V. B. Bavishi. Princeton, New Jersey: CIFAR.

Chen, S., Sun, Z., and Wang, Y. 2002. Evidence from China on whether harmonized accounting standards harmonize accounting practices. *Accounting Horizons*, 16 (3): 183–197.

Choi, F. D. S. 1973. Financial disclosure and entry to the European capital market. *Journal of Accounting Research*, 11 (Autumn): 159–175.

Choi, F. D. S., and Levich, R. M. 1990. *The Capital Market Effects of International Accounting Diversity.* Chicago, Illinois: Dow Jones-Irwin.

Cooke, T. E., and Wallace, R. S. O. 1990. Financial disclosure regulation and its environment: A review and further analysis. *Journal of Accounting and Public Policy*, 9 (2): 79–110.

Cooper, K., and Keim, G. 1983. The economic rationale for the nature and extent of corporate financial disclosure regulation: A critical assessment. *Journal of Accounting and Public Policy*, 2 (Fall): 189–205.

Davis-Friday, P. Y., and Rivera, J. M. 2000. Inflation accounting and 20-F disclosures: Evidence from Mexico. *Accounting Horizons*, 14 (2): 113–135.

Doupnik, T. S., and Salter, S. B. 1995. External environment, culture, and accounting practice: A preliminary test of a general model of international accounting development. *International Journal of Accounting*, 30 (2): 189–207.

Dye, R. A. 1985. Strategic accounting choice and the effects of alternative financial reporting requirements. *Journal of Accounting Research*, 23 (2): 544–573.

Frankel, J. A. 1993. *Recent changes in the financial systems of Asian and Pacific countries.* Center for International and Development Economics Research Working Paper No. c93–031, University of California at Berkeley.

Ghon Rhee, S., Chang, R. P., and Ageloff, R. 1990. *An overview of equity markets in Pacific-Basin countries.* Pacific-Basin Capital Markets Research, edited by S. Ghon Rhee and R. P. Chang. Amsterdam: North Holland.

Gonedes, N., and Dopuch, N. 1974. Capital market equilibrium, information production, and selecting accounting techniques: Theoretical framework and review of empirical work, in studies on financial accounting objectives. *Journal of Accounting Research*, (Supplement): 48–129.

Harvey, C. R. 1995. The risk exposure of emerging equity markets. *The World Bank Economic Review*, 9 (1): 19–50.

Hilton, A. 1994. Emerging Markets. *Professional Investor*, (March): 31.

Hofstede, G. 1980. *Culture's Consequences: International Differences in Work-Related Values.* Sage.

International Accounting Standards Committee (IASC). 1982. *Objectives and Procedures.* London: IASC.

International Finance Corporation (IFC) 1995. *Emerging Stock Markets Factbook 1995.* Washington, D.C.: IFC.

International Finance Corporation (IFC). 1998. *Emerging Stock Markets Factbook 2000.* Washington, D.C.: IFC.

International Monetary Fund. 1994. *International Capital Markets: Developments, Prospects, and Policy Issues.* Washington, D.C.: IMF.

Meek, G. K., and Gray, S. J. 1989. Globalization of stock markets and foreign listing requirements: Voluntary disclosures by continental European companies listed on the London Stock Exchange. *Journal of International Business Studies* 20 (2): 296–314.

Organization of Economic Cooperation and Development. 1986. *Harmonization of Accounting Standards: Achievements and Prospects.* Paris: OECD.

Price, M. M. 1994. *Emerging Stock Markets: A Complete Investment Guide to New Markets Around the World.* New York: McGraw-Hill.

Rivera, J. M., and Salva, A.S. 1995. On the regional approach to accounting principles harmonization: A time for Latin American integration? *Journal of International Accounting Auditing & Taxation*, 4 (1): 87–100.

Saudagaran, S. M. 1991. The SEC and the globalization of financial markets. *Research in Accounting Regulation*, 5: 31–53.

Saudagaran, S. M., and Biddle, G. C. 1992. Financial disclosure levels and foreign stock exchange listing decisions. *Journal of International Financial Management and Accounting*, 4 (2): 106–147.

Saudagaran, S. M., and Biddle, G. C. 1995. Foreign listing location: A study of MNCs and stock exchanges in eight countries. *Journal of International Business Studies*, 26 (2): 318–341.

Saudagaran, S. M., and Diga, J. G. 1997a. The impact of capital market developments on accounting regulatory policy in emerging markets: A study of ASEAN. *Research in Accounting Regulation*, (Supplement): 3–48.

Saudagaran, S. M., and Diga, J. G. 1997b. Financial reporting in emerging capital markets: Characteristics and policy issues. *Accounting Horizons*, 11 (2): 41–64.

Saudagaran, S. M., and Diga, J. G. 1998. Accounting harmonization in ASEAN: Benefits, Models, and Policy Issues. *Journal of International Accounting Auditing & Taxation*, 7 (1): 21–45.

Standard and Poor's. 2000. *Emerging Stock Markets Factbook 2000*. New York: S&P.

Standard and Poor's. 2001. *Emerging Stock Markets Factbook 2001*. New York: S&P.

Tang, Y. 2000. Bumpy road leading to internationalization: A review of accounting development in China. *Accounting Horizons* 14 (1): 93–102.

United Nations. 1988. *Conclusions on Accounting and Reporting by Transnational Corporations*. New York: UN.

Van Agtmael, A. W. 1984. Emerging Securities Markets. London: *Euromoney*.

Wallace, R. S. O., and Briston, R. J. 1993. Improving the accounting infrastructure in developing countries. *Research in Third World Accounting* 2: 201–224.

Walter, I. 1993. Emerging equity markets: Tapping into global investment flows. ASEAN *Economic Bulletin* 10 (1): 1–19.

World Bank. 1989. *World Development Report 1989*. New York: Oxford University Press.

World Bank. 1990. *Financial Systems and Development*. Washington, D.C.: International Bank for Reconstruction and Development.

World Bank. 1994. *World Development Report 1994*. New York: Oxford University Press.

Xiao, J. Z., Zhang, Y., and Xie, Z. 2000. The making of independent auditing standards in China. *Accounting Horizons*, 14 (1): 69–89.

CHAPTER 7

MANAGERIAL ISSUES IN INTERNATIONAL ACCOUNTING

LEARNING OBJECTIVES

- Examine budgeting and performance evaluation issues for international firms.

- Discuss global risk management tools and strategies including multinational capital budgeting and foreign exchange risk management.

- Identify the main constituents of cross-border transfer pricing policies, define the transfer pricing methods, and consider the issues in devising a transfer pricing strategy.

- Recognize the critical role of information technology systems in the effective recording, processing, and dissemination of financial and managerial accounting information.

In the first six chapters of this book, the focus was primarily on financial reporting issues in the global arena. In this chapter, we turn our attention to a number of managerial accounting issues that are relevant to executives and other stakeholders in companies that do business globally. The areas we focus on are budgeting and performance evaluation, global risk management, transfer pricing, and information technology.

BUDGETING AND PERFORMANCE EVALUATION

Most companies use budgeting and performance evaluation as tools in their strategic planning and control systems. As more companies get involved in global business, it is important for their managers to monitor and refine their budgeting and performance evaluation techniques to ensure that they are just as relevant for their operations abroad as they are in the company's home-country environment. Multinational companies (MNCs) need to set up a balanced set of financial and non-financial performance measures to get an accurate picture of the performance of their managers and subsidiaries in different parts of the world.

Budgeting and performance evaluation are critically linked in that the budget sets the performance criteria on which the operating units within the company will be evaluated ex post (i.e., at the end of the budget period). If the budget is to motivate the employees and to help create goal congruence between the employees and the organization, then it must set appropriate criteria and provide reasonable targets for the employees to attain. Along with all the budgeting and performance evaluation issues that organizations must contend with in the purely domestic context, there are additional considerations that must be factored into designing budget and performance evaluation systems for subsidiaries and affiliated entities located in other countries. This section highlights the main issues in this area.

Using Appropriate Performance Measures

It is critical that corporate management select appropriate bases of measuring performance at the start of the budget process. There are several criteria that can be used to measure performance. Seldom is one single basis likely to be appropriate for all units within a MNC.[1] Thus, while unit material and labor cost, quality of product, and production levels or plant capacity utilization rates are appropriate for a manufacturing division in Indonesia, sales revenue, market share, and customer satisfaction might be the meaningful measures for the regional sales division located in Singapore. Similarly, different performance evaluation criteria might be required for a unit organized as a service center versus another organized as a profit center. Selecting appropriate performance measures also requires corporate management to periodically review the criteria for each unit as its strategic role in the company changes or its local business environment evolves. For example, in the late 1980s when Hungary was first emerging from the communist system, the Hungarian subsidiary of sports equipment maker Adidas might have had a very different strategic role for the company than it does today. Given the limited purchasing power of Hungarians at the time and the restrictions on repatriating profits out of Hungary, Adidas was hardly concerned about its

---

[1]Gupta and Govindrajan [1991] argue that subsidiaries fall into four categories (global innovators, integrated players, implementers, and local innovators) and that companies should use different performance evaluation measures for each type of subsidiary.

Hungarian subsidiary contributing to the firm's profit. Its main objective then was to create brand visibility and name recognition for its products among Hungarian consumers.[2] However, a decade later, with the integration of Hungary in the EU, it is possible that Adidas has different expectations of its Hungarian subsidiary. As indicated by this example, not only are the same performance measurement criteria not appropriate for different units; they may not even be appropriate for the same unit at different points in time.

Another related issue is whether a company should limit itself to financial measures, albeit different ones for different units (i.e., sales, net income, return on assets, etc.). In certain situations where financial criteria are either inappropriate or insufficient, companies may need to include non-financial criteria in addition to, or in lieu of, financial criteria based on what they perceive as the primary role of the foreign subsidiary in the firm's overall strategy. For example, the main financial criterion for a service unit might be actual costs relative to budgeted costs. However, the more important criterion might be non-financial, such as user satisfaction. Some of the important non-financial measures are customer satisfaction, employee morale, delivery performance, name recognition, and relationship with host governments. Additional non-financial measures might relate to environmental performance (i.e., reducing emissions of pollutants in the air, water, or ground) and community relations. An important benefit of non-financial measures is that they can be reported on a timely basis and problems identified can be addressed promptly before they negatively affect the company's financial performance.

Using Appropriate Currencies

Another budgeting and performance evaluation issue specific to companies engaged in global business relates to the choice of appropriate currency for measuring the performance of foreign subsidiaries. Should a MNC based in the United Kingdom evaluate its subsidiary in India in British pound sterling or in Indian rupees? Depending on the direction and magnitude of the change in the rupee relative to the pound during any reporting period, results could be very different under the two currencies. It is possible for the Indian subsidiary to be very profitable when measured in rupees but considerably less profitable in pounds if the rupee has weakened relative to the pound during the year.

There are two factors that companies must consider when selecting the currency to be used. First is the role of the specific subsidiary in the company's overall strategy. This is related to the earlier discussion about appropriate performance measures. If the subsidiary's current role is to contribute to the overall profits of the MNC, then it is appropriate to use the parent's currency to measure performance. However, if the subsidiary's current role is something different (i.e., research and development), then it might be appropriate to use the local currency. The second factor relates to where the prime responsibility for foreign currency risk management resides. If the company has a centralized treasury operation at corporate headquarters with exclusive

---

[2]While visiting Budapest in 1990, the author saw long, orderly queues (lines) outside the Adidas store and was told that people actually took time off from work to stand in line for hours to buy Adidas products. It was apparent that, at the time, Adidas was not making a profit from its Budapest store or else it would have opened additional stores. Yet the Budapest store served a useful purpose in Adidas' long-term strategy in Hungary by whetting the appetite of Hungarian consumers for its products.

authority to manage foreign currency risk, then the local currency is the one that ought to be used for measuring the foreign subsidiary. However, if foreign currency risk management is decentralized with each subsidiary having autonomy in this regard, then it is reasonable to use the parent's currency for performance evaluation. The rationale is that local subsidiaries cannot be held accountable for the effect of exchange rate fluctuations on their profitability if they are not given the authority to manage their currency exposure. Since corporate headquarters has the sole authority in this regard, it should also be responsible for the gain or loss resulting from exchange rate fluctuations.

Transfer Pricing Policies

The need to link responsibility and authority is also relevant in the arena of transfer pricing policies used within an organization for its intrafirm activity. Transfer pricing is covered in detail later in this chapter. However, at this point, it is sufficient to note that it is the price at which goods or services are transferred between affiliated entities within an organization. Transfer prices can be market based (i.e., arm's length), cost based, or negotiated. The type of transfer pricing policies within an organization impacts the revenues (of selling divisions) and costs (of buying divisions) and, therefore, can have a nontrivial effect on the profitability of each subsidiary engaged in intrafirm trade.

Naturally, companies will select transfer pricing policies based on overall objectives of the entity such as tax minimization, moving funds internationally, etc. However, in designing performance evaluation systems, MNCs need to factor in the types of transfer pricing policies in place for each subsidiary. The performance of subsidiaries may not be comparable if they use different transfer pricing policies. More importantly, subsidiaries that are required to source products or components internally at other than market-based prices lack control, in a sense, of their own profitability. This is particularly so when the intrafirm transfer price forced on them by the parent compares unfavorably with prices in the open market. This will be discussed later in this section.

Other Considerations

There are a number of other factors that must be considered in setting up meaningful performance evaluation systems for subsidiaries located in other countries. The underlying objective ought to be to suitably motivate employees and to have appropriate measures of performance for the subsidiary. For a company that has subsidiaries in a number of countries, comparability might be another desired ingredient of the performance evaluation system. A number of macro-economic variables could adversely affect comparability. First, differing levels of inflation are likely to impact performance measurement in different countries. For example, it is difficult to compare the performance of subsidiaries in Chile and Peru if the two countries have materially different levels of inflation. Second, differing levels of political stability across countries can significantly impact the performance of different divisions. The economic climate in a country that is in political turmoil is likely to suffer, thereby adversely affecting a subsidiary in that country. Third, the labor situation in a country (to be distinguished from labor relations within the firm) can have a significant impact on the operations of the subsidiary in that country. Thus, when truck drivers in France blockade the country's freeways, this adversely impacts performance of the subsidiary located there.

Distinguishing Between Manager Performance and Subsidiary Performance

The differing economic, political, and business conditions between countries and even within countries at different points in time necessitate that companies be flexible and pay attention to company-specific variables in designing performance evaluation systems. However, if they are to suitably motivate and reward the managers of their foreign subsidiaries, it is critical that MNCs distinguish between manager performance and subsidiary performance. It should be clear from the discussion above that there are a variety of factors that affect subsidiary performance, but over which managers may not necessarily have control. In certain instances, the subsidiary manager lacks control because the parent has decided that it is in the greater interest of the organization to centralize a particular function or to mandate a certain policy. Examples of this are a centralized treasury function where foreign currency risk management is based at corporate headquarters and the imposition of other than market-based transfer pricing methods on subsidiaries. In each of these cases, the subsidiary manager lacks control of a function that can have a significant impact on the performance of the subsidiary. The argument that the policy chosen is for the benefit of the company as a whole is little solace to the subsidiary manager if he is evaluated on performance that is impacted by factors over which he has no control. Then there are the macro-economic variables cited above (i.e., inflation, labor strife, political instability) over which not even headquarters has any control, but which nevertheless can significantly impact performance of subsidiaries in various countries. If the company is to have a performance evaluation system that adequately motivates and rewards managers based on factors that are within their control, it needs to recognize the differential impact of these factors on subsidiaries and institute systems that recognize them. Failure to do so is likely to result in a disconnection between the actual performance of managers and that measured by the performance evaluation system. This will adversely impact the company's ability to attract and retain the better managers.

Some Comparative Evidence on Budgets and Performance Evaluation Systems

Researchers have examined how budgets and performance evaluation systems are used globally. Much of the research has compared practices in Western countries (e.g., Australia, United Kingdom, United States) to that in Japan. A review of the evidence from these studies is instructive. Studies[3] that have compared budgeting and performance evaluation practices in Japan and the United States have found that 1) the average length of time spent in preparing budgets was greater in the United States than in Japan, 2) U.S. firms tended to focus on profitability measures of performance in their budgets (such as return on investment), while Japanese firms tended to focus on sales volume and market share, 3) U.S. firms used budget variances primarily to evaluate division managers' forecasting ability and management ability, while Japanese firms used budget variances primarily for the timely recognition of problems and to improve the next period's budget, and 4) the compensation and promotion of American managers was more likely to be impacted by their budget performance than was those of Japanese managers. It was remarkable to see how differently U.S. and Japanese firms rated return on investment (ROI) as a performance evaluation measure in both these studies (68 percent for U.S. firms versus 3 percent for Japanese firms in the

---

[3]See Bailes and Assada [1991], and Shields et al. [1991].

Bailes and Assada study; 75 percent for U.S. firms versus 7 percent for Japanese firms in the Shields et al. study).

Another study that compared management control systems and performance evaluation between British and Japanese firms similarly found that British firms tend to focus on control systems to increase short-term profits at the expense of longer-term benefits in areas like R&D and management training, while Japanese firms focused more on strategic planning and emphasized growth in sales and market share.[4] A more recent study compared management accounting practices in Australia and Japan.[5] Its main finding was that, while management accounting practices of Australian companies emphasize cost control tools at the manufacturing stage, Japanese companies pay much greater attention to cost-planning and cost-reduction tools at the product design stage. The emphasis of Australian companies suggests that they pay greater attention to accounting tools that are mainly used for planning and controlling costs and financial reporting. In contrast, the focus of Japanese companies on target costing suggests their greater emphasis to cost management.

GLOBAL RISK MANAGEMENT

The recent economic turmoil in Southeast Asia and Argentina is a reminder, if one was needed, of the importance of global risk assessment and management on an ongoing basis. MNCs must continuously monitor their exposure and balance it with their appetite for risk. Proper risk management for international companies must include a broad range of risk-management tools and strategies.

Multinational Capital Budgeting

Multinational companies are constantly acquiring and disposing of assets globally in the normal course of business. Shareholder wealth is created when the MNC makes an investment that will return more (in present value terms) than what it costs. Among the most important decisions that MNC managers face is the choice of capital projects globally. These investments will determine the firm's competitive position in the marketplace, its overall profitability, and, ultimately, its long-run survival.

Multinational capital budgeting, like domestic capital budgeting, focuses on the cash flows of prospective long-term investment projects. It is used both in traditional foreign direct investment analysis, such as the construction of a chain of retail stores in another country, as well as cross-border mergers and acquisitions activity. Capital budgeting for a foreign project uses the same net present value (NPV) discounted cash flow model used in domestic capital budgeting. However, multinational capital budgeting is considerably more complex due to the consideration of a number of additional factors,[6] discussed below.

PARENT VERSUS PROJECT CASH FLOWS. Parent (i.e., home-country) cash flows must be distinguished from project (i.e., host-country) cash flows. While parent cash flows reflect all cash flow consequences for the consolidated entity, project cash

---

[4]See Demirag [1994].

[5]See Wijewardena and De Zoysa [1999].

[6]See Eiteman [1997].

flows look only at the single country where the project is located. For example, cash flows generated by an investment in Spain may be partly or wholly taken away from one in Italy, with the end result that the net present value of the investment is positive from the Spanish affiliate's point of view but contributes little to the firm's worldwide cash flows.

FINANCING VERSUS OPERATING CASH FLOWS. In multinational investment projects, the type of financing package is often critical in making otherwise unattractive projects attractive to the parent company. Thus, cash may flow back to the parent because the project is structured to generate such flows via royalties, licensing fees, dividends, etc. Unlike in domestic capital budgeting, operating cash flows cannot be kept separate from financing decisions.

FOREIGN CURRENCY FLUCTUATIONS. Another added complexity in multinational capital budgeting is the significant effect that fluctuating exchange rates can have on the prospective cash flows generated by the investment. From the parent's perspective, future cash flows abroad have value only in terms of the exchange rate at the date of repatriation. In conducting the analysis, it is necessary to forecast future exchange rates and to conduct sensitivity analysis of the project's viability under various exchange rate scenarios.

LONG-TERM INFLATION RATES. Differing rates of national inflation and their potential effect on competitiveness must be considered. Inflation will have the following effects on the value of the project: a) it will impact the local operating cash flows both in terms of the prices of inputs and outputs, and also in terms of the sales volume depending on the price elasticity of the product, b) it will impact the parent's cash flow by affecting the foreign exchange rates, and c) it will affect the real cost of financing choices between foreign and domestic sources of capital.

SUBSIDIZED FINANCING. In situations where a host government provides subsidized project financing at below-market rates, the value of that subsidy must be explicitly considered in the capital budgeting analysis. If a company uses the subsidized rate in the analysis, there is an implicit assumption that the subsidy will exist through the life of the project. Another approach might be to incorporate the subsidized interest rates into the analysis by including the present value of the subsidy rather than adjusting the cost of capital.

POLITICAL RISK. This is another factor that can significantly impact the viability and profitability of foreign projects. Whether it be through democratic elections or as a result of sudden developments such as revolutions or military coups, changes in a country's government can affect the attitude towards foreign investors and investments. This can affect the future cash flows of a project in that country in a variety of ways. Political developments may also affect the life and the terminal value of foreign investments.

TERMINAL VALUES. While terminal values of long-term projects are difficult to estimate even in the domestic context, they become far more difficult in the multinational context due to the added complexity from some of the factors discussed above. An added dimension is that potential acquirers may have widely divergent perspectives on their value of acquiring the terminal assets. This is particularly relevant if the assets are located in a country that is economically segmented due to a host of restrictions on cross-border flow of physical or financial assets.

In conducting multinational capital budgeting analyses from a parent's perspective, the additional risk arising from projects located abroad can be handled in at least two ways. One possibility is to add a foreign risk premium to the discount rate that would be used for a domestic project. This higher rate is intended to capture the additional uncertainties arising from exchange risk, political risk, inflation, and such factors. The second possibility is to adjust the cash flows for the foreign projects to reflect the additional risk. The discount rate stays the same as for domestic projects. Thus, the additional complexities resulting from doing business abroad must be incorporated in the analysis through adjustments to either the discount rate or the projected cash flows. Rather than make these adjustments arbitrarily, firms can use wide-ranging publicly available data, historical analysis, and professional advice to make reasonable decisions.

Managing Foreign Exchange Risk

Financial risk management is concerned with minimizing the company's exposure to changes in currency exchange rates, interest rates, and credit risks related to customer receivables; placement of liquid funds; and trading in derivative instruments. While these risks are an inherent part of international business, corporate managers have various instruments available to manage them. In this section, we focus primarily on managing foreign exchange risk since it has the most direct impact on international financial and managerial accounting within MNCs.

As previously discussed in Chapter 3, foreign exchange risk arises from the potential for random fluctuations of foreign currency exchange rates. These fluctuations can affect the company's profitability, the carrying value of its assets and liabilities, and its global competitiveness. It must be noted that fluctuations in exchange rates affect companies to varying degrees based on the level of exposure of their assets, liabilities, and income to exchange rate variations. Exposure describes the level of risk of the affected values to changes in exchange rates. Ultimately, it is the foreign exchange exposure that is relevant to each company and is likely to determine the level of resources each company devotes to foreign exchange risk management.

PROS AND CONS OF MANAGING FOREIGN EXCHANGE RISK. The level of risk economic entities take is generally a function of an implicit or explicit cost-benefit analysis combined with their capacity for risk. Managers who refrain from active management of foreign exchange risk may do so for a variety of reasons. First, they consider the use of risk management instruments such as forward contracts, options, and futures as speculative and argue that these activities lie outside the company's realm of expertise. Second, such managers claim that foreign currency exposures cannot be measured with precision. Third, they argue that since they do all their business in their domestic currency, they do not have any foreign currency exposure. However, as was also mentioned in Chapter 3, they could still have exposure if their competitors do business in foreign currencies. Fourth, they argue that all business is risky and the firm gets rewarded for bearing risks. Finally, they assert that the firm's balance sheet is hedged on an accounting basis particularly when their domestic currency is their functional currency.[7]

---

[7]See Dufey and Giddy [1997].

Management should only devote company resources to managing foreign exchange risk if the related cost can be justified on economic grounds. The benefits to the company's shareholders must exceed the cost of implementing a foreign exchange risk-management program, and hedging activities at the corporate level must be the least costly way to realize these benefits. Managers actively engaged in foreign exchange risk management cite the following benefits from an active foreign exchange risk-management program that reduces the volatility of the firm's reported earnings. First, since there is a direct relation between risk and the required rate of return, a less volatile earnings stream reduces the firm's cost of capital. Second, a less volatile earnings stream also has the potential for tax savings under a nonlinear tax regime. Corporate after-tax income and cash flows increase with less volatile pretax income in progressive tax regimes.[8] A reduction in earnings volatility can effectively lower the company's tax rate in the long run and create gains for shareholders. Finally, hedging activities can help securities analysts get a more precise value of the firm's assets, thereby providing them a comprehensive picture of the company's exposure.

Thus, risk management does matter to companies interested in maximizing shareholder wealth. A passive strategy towards risk management can be harmful in that it has the effect of deliberately assuming certain risks. An active risk management strategy attempts to minimize risk to acceptable levels in view of the costs of reducing exposure.

TYPES OF FOREIGN EXCHANGE EXPOSURE AND HEDGING METHODS. There are three main types of foreign exchange exposures: 1) translation exposure (alternatively referred to as accounting exposure), 2) transaction exposure, and 3) economic exposure (also known as operating exposure). These exposures were discussed in detail in Chapter 3 and will not be repeated here. The main hedging instruments available to companies are currency forward contracts, currency options, money market hedges, and currency futures. Their main features and relative merits are briefly discussed below.

A forward contract is a commitment to exchange currencies in the future at a rate that is set today. While the amount of the transaction, the maturity date, and the exchange rate are all determined in advance, no money changes hands until the settlement date. Forward contracts are one of the most popular tools in foreign exchange risk management. Their disadvantage is that they are accompanied by a risk that one of the parties to the contract will not perform on the maturity date. The default risk also results in certain companies not having access to forward contracts in sufficiently large amounts to cover all their foreign exchange exposure.

A foreign exchange option is the right, but not the obligation, to buy or sell a currency on or before a given date at an agreed price. The right to buy is a *call*, and the right to sell is a *put*. The option buyer pays an up-front fee (i.e., a premium) to the option seller. In a sense, what the buyer gets for this fee is the ability to not exercise the option if the currency exchange rate "improves" during the life of the option. MNCs use options in a variety of ways. Some use them in contingent activities such as bidding on contracts denominated in foreign currencies where they will need the protection only if they win the contract. Others use them as protection for future transactions. Yet others use them for existing receivables and payables. Because options have an explicit up-front fee, managers sometimes feel the pressure of having to justify using them.

---

[8]See Smith and Stulz [1985].

A money market hedge is essentially an interest-bearing bank debt or an interest-earning bank deposit (in another currency) intended to offset a receivable or payable (in that currency), respectively. It achieves the same result as a forward contract with the difference that the company has a cash inflow or outflow today rather than at the maturity date of the receivable or payable. By creating an offsetting liability in the case of a receivable or an offsetting asset in the case of a payable, the company protects itself against fluctuations in the exchange rate during the credit period.

Currency futures are a variation on forward contracts. They are similar to forward contracts in that they also are an agreement to exchange currencies at a set price at a future date. However, they differ from forwards in that they are standardized in terms of amounts and delivery dates, and are traded on organized exchanges. While forwards can be for any amount that two parties to the contract agree to, futures are for standard amounts that are smaller than the average forward contract. Similarly, while forward contracts can have any delivery date based on the mutual agreement of the transacting parties, currency futures have standard delivery dates typically in March, June, September, and December. While forwards can be entered into at any time and at any location, futures are traded on organized exchanges. The most important feature of currency futures is the timing of the cash flows. Unlike forward contracts where the cash flow happens only at maturity, with futures cash can change hands every day during the life of the contract when there is a change in the price of the contract. This daily compensation feature considerably reduces the default risk that is present in forward contracts. Most large companies prefer forwards because they can be customized. Futures are preferred when credit risk is a concern. Exhibit 7-1 on the following page provides a graphical overview of the management of foreign exchange risk in a corporation.

TRANSFER PRICING

The growth in the global flow of goods and services and the increase in cross-border mergers and acquisitions have dramatically increased the volume of intrafirm trade (i.e., transactions between related firms in one or more countries). Transfer pricing relates to the pricing of goods and services that change hands between entities engaged in intrafirm trade. Some estimates indicate that intrafirm trade makes up fully half of all global trade.[9] As one observer put it, a multinational company "can produce its products anywhere, using resources from anywhere, by a subsidiary located anywhere, to a quality found anywhere, to be sold anywhere."[10] Since intrafirm trade and transfer pricing are closely related, the growth in intrafirm trade has resulted in a greater focus on transfer pricing. This section examines transfer pricing as a managerial accounting issue of import in the global arena. Specifically, it covers 1) the major constituents affected by transfer pricing, 2) the different transfer pricing methods, 3) recent developments in transfer pricing policies globally, and 4) research evidence on variables affecting international transfer pricing method choices.

---

[9]See "Domestic Myths on Globalization" by M. V. Whitman [*The Wall Street Journal*, October 27, 1995, A14].

[10]See Naisbitt [1994, p. 50].

EXHIBIT 7-1 Management of Corporate Foreign Exchange Exposure

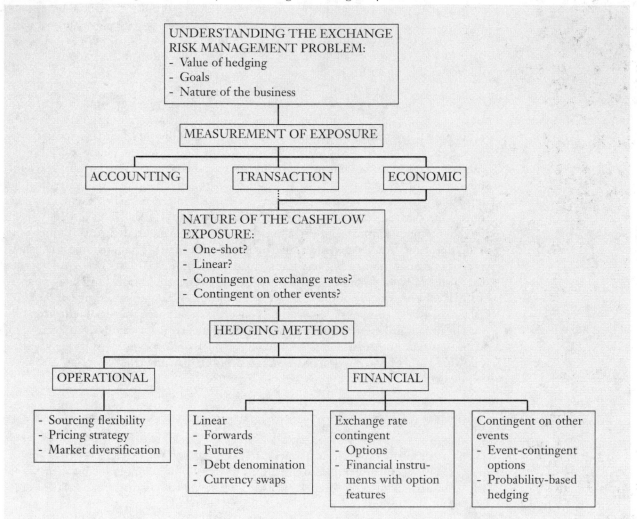

Source: Dufey and Giddy (1997). Reprinted by permission of John Wiley & Sons, Inc.

Major Constituents Affected by Transfer Pricing Choices

A multinational firm's transfer pricing policies typically have numerous objectives. These include avoiding foreign currency restrictions and quotas, minimizing taxes and tariffs, minimizing exchange risks, increasing share of profits from joint ventures, bypassing profit repatriation restrictions, and optimizing managerial performance evaluation and reward systems. This should make it clear that though transfer pricing has important ramifications on a firm's global tax liability, it is more than just a tax issue. The transfer pricing policy objectives listed above point to the fact that transfer pricing choices made by a firm affect a number of constituents both within and outside the firm. Consequently, there is much more to establishing a firm's transfer pricing policies in the global arena than just tax minimization. Exhibit 7-2 provides a list of conditions that would induce high and low transfer prices on intrafirm trade between parent and affiliated companies.

EXHIBIT 7-2 Conditions in Subsidiary's Country Influencing Intrafirm Transfer Pricing Level

Conditions Inducing Low Transfer Prices on Flows from Parent and High Transfer Prices on Flows to Parent	Conditions Inducing High Transfer Prices on Flows from Parent and Low Transfer Prices on Flows to Parent
High ad valorem tariffs	Local partners
Corporate income tax rate lower than in parent's country	Pressure from workers to obtain greater share of company profit
Significant competition	Political pressure to nationalize or expropriate high-profit foreign firms
Local loans based on financial appearance or subsidiary	Restrictions on profit or dividend remittances
Export subsidy or tax credit on value of exports	Political instability
Lower inflation rate than in parent's country	Substantial tie-in sales agreements
Restrictions (ceilings) in subsidiary's country on the value of products that can be imported	Price of final product controlled by government but based on production cost
	Desire to mask profitability of subsidiary operations to keep competitors out

Source: Arpan (1972).

Internal Constituents

Employees within the different divisions of a company can be affected by the transfer pricing method selected. Assuming that the employees are evaluated based on the profitability of their division, employees of the buying division would prefer a lower intrafirm transfer price while employees of a selling division would prefer a higher intrafirm transfer price. The corporate tax compliance division would prefer a transfer price that is a reasonable reflection of an arm's-length transaction in the event that the firm is audited by the tax authorities. Senior management at the corporate level would probably prefer the transfer pricing method that maximizes the firm's consolidated earnings since their salary and other compensation (e.g., stock options) are likely to be based on the firm's overall performance.

Stockholders of the company, like top management, are probably also concerned about the firm's overall after-tax earnings and would, therefore, prefer transfer pricing methods that help maximize consolidated earnings and minimize the firm's global tax liability. Stockholders would, however, be adversely impacted by overly aggressive transfer pricing policies if these were to result in the firm being subject to scrutiny by tax authorities which, in turn, could result in huge penalties and bad publicity for the firm if it were deemed to be cheating on its taxes.

External Constituents

Domestic government agencies include the national and local tax collecting agencies, the customs agency, the legislative body, and other regulatory and enforcement agencies. The domestic tax collecting agencies are interested in collecting their "fair share" of taxes. They would like to ascertain that the firm is not using transfer pricing as an income-shifting mechanism to inappropriately reduce its domestic tax liability. Similarly, the customs agency wants to ensure that the firm is paying the appropriate duties on the import and export of items to and from its affiliated entities in other countries. The legislative body is interested in monitoring the impact of the laws it has passed on the overall tax revenue of the government. It might also, however, have other concerns related to the effect of its laws on the competitiveness of domestic companies vis-a-vis their counterparts in other countries.

Foreign government agencies similarly want to ensure that they are collecting the taxes owed them by companies based in other countries. Historically, there has been an adversarial relationship between multinational companies and the tax collecting agencies of the countries in which they do business. Due to the presence of MNCs in multiple locations, there is a deep-seated suspicion that they use differences in marginal tax rates in the various jurisdictions to shift their profits globally and, thereby, lower their tax liability. Customs authorities have similar concerns.

Competitors of multinational firms can also be affected by the latter's transfer pricing practices. There is a concern that multinational firms are able to subsidize their affiliates in certain countries by charging them artificially low transfer prices that make them more competitive in that market. Critics argue that, in the extreme, such practices are predatory and anti-competitive since they are used to drive competitors out of business, after which the multinational firms can boost their prices and profitability in that country. In this regard, one frequently hears of charges of "dumping" by multinational companies. Simply put, dumping occurs when a firm sells products in another country at a price below its own cost. The regulations of the World Trade Organization (WTO) call for penalties against firms engaging in dumping and similar unfair trade practices.

Joint venture partners represent yet another external constituent that is impacted by the transfer pricing decisions. As indicated in Exhibit 7-2, in countries where it has a joint venture (as opposed to a fully owned subsidiary), a multinational might want to charge higher transfer prices for goods flowing into that country and lower transfer prices for goods flowing out of that country since it must share profits in that country with its joint venture partner. Naturally, the joint venture partner would prefer lower transfer prices for flows into the country and higher transfer prices for flows out of the country since that would result in increasing profits in the joint venture.

Suppliers in the home country and elsewhere are affected by transfer pricing policies to the extent that these policies affect the procurement practices within the organization. Certain suppliers will be helped and others hurt depending on the transfer pricing method used by the company.

Customers of the multinational company may also be impacted by its transfer pricing policies. The level of impact will depend upon the type of product and the type of market. The impact of transfer pricing policies on customers will be less when the product has multiple suppliers and the market is competitive. However, in monopolistic or oligopolistic conditions, the transfer price will have a greater impact on final customers since the retail price of the product in the importing country will likely reflect the transfer price.

As is evident from the above discussion, management must weigh the interests of the various constituents in setting transfer prices within the organization. The complex matrix of interests presents management the challenge of devising a strategy that maximizes corporate profitability without violating the rights of any constituent group or breaking the rules of any jurisdiction in which it operates.

Transfer Pricing Methods

Essentially, transfer pricing methods can be split into three categories. They are 1) market-based methods, 2) cost-based methods, and 3) negotiated transfer prices.

Market-based transfer pricing methods require the existence of comparable products on the market. Since this approach is most reflective of arm's-length pricing, it presents fewer challenges in administering since it is easy to defend to various constituents. It also forces the various divisions to operate under market conditions and make the best use of scarce resources, and permits a less subjective evaluation of the performance of the various divisions. However, in situations where there is no comparable market for intermediate products being transferred between divisions, it is difficult to discern a market-based transfer price. In such a situation, cost-based transfer prices might be the solution. However, they present a series of other problems that are related to cost accounting systems. Cost allocations can be arbitrary, they rely on historical costs, and they may be far removed from market realities. In companies with centrally mandated procurement, cost-based systems provide selling divisions little incentive to control costs since they can pass on the higher costs of inefficient manufacturing to the buying divisions. In certain cost-plus-type methods, there might be a perverse incentive to have higher costs since the selling division's margin is a fixed percentage of its costs, and a fixed percentage of a higher cost is a higher amount. Finally, negotiated transfer pricing methods may be an alternative to cost-based methods where comparable arm's-length market prices are not readily available. In a decentralized procurement environment, negotiated pricing may also be used between buying and selling divisions based on marginal revenue and cost analysis.

The degree of detail and level of enforcement of transfer pricing methods across countries is a function of a number of factors, including the resources available to the tax authorities in each country. While a detailed review of the transfer pricing rules in individual countries is beyond the scope of this book,[11] it is useful to briefly consider the main transfer pricing methods that are incorporated in tax regulations globally. The main transfer pricing methods for sales and transfer of tangible items are outlined below.

THE COMPARABLE UNCONTROLLED PRICE METHOD (CUP). This method is most useful when a commodity-type product is being transferred within the organization and when the selling or buying division has engaged in transactions for the product with outside parties. Under the CUP method, the arm's-length price is the price in comparable uncontrolled sales, adjusted for factors such as the quality of the product, contractual terms (i.e., credit terms, transport terms, etc.), level of the market (i.e., wholesale, retail, etc.), date of the transaction, and foreign currency risks. The regulations permit the use of data from indirect sources such as public exchanges or quotation media if

1. The data are widely and routinely used in the industry to negotiate prices for uncontrolled sales,
2. The data are used to set transfer prices in the controlled transaction in the same way as they are used by uncontrolled parties in the industry to set market prices, and
3. The amount charged in the controlled transaction is adjusted to reflect differences in product quality and quantity, terms, transportation costs, market conditions, and other factors.

---

[11]See O'Connor [1997], Tang [1997], and Felgran and Yamada [2001] for a detailed discussion of transfer pricing regulations and related tax laws in selected countries.

THE RESALE PRICE METHOD (RPM). Under this method, the arm's-length price is equal to the applicable resale price to an independent purchaser, less an appropriate gross profit margin. The gross profit is computed by multiplying the applicable resale price by the margin percentage normal in comparable uncontrolled transactions. This method is generally used in the transfer of tangible assets. It assumes that the buying division does not add value to the item and cannot be used when this condition is violated (i.e., when the buying division adds substantial value to the item before reselling it).

THE COST-PLUS METHOD (CPLM). Under this method, the transfer price is the cost of producing the item plus an appropriate gross profit markup. This method is typically used in cases involving the manufacture, assembly, or other production of goods that are transferred between affiliates or when one party is a subcontractor for the other. A typical cost-plus analysis might include adjustments for the complexity of manufacturing or assembly, differences in sales and purchase terms, and foreign currency risks. The cost-plus method is generally appropriate when the following conditions are met: 1) exact product market comparables are not available; 2) potential comparables are similar to the affiliated firm in terms of manufacturing functions performed, risks assumed, and level of intangibles; and 3) reliable accounting and other data are available for the comparables.

THE COMPARABLE PROFITS METHOD (CPM). This method is based on the premise that similarly situated taxpayers should earn similar returns over a reasonable time period. The CPM evaluates whether the transfer price in a controlled transaction is arm's length based on objective profit-level indicators obtained from uncontrolled taxpayers that engage in similar activities under similar circumstances. Profit-level indicators are ratios that measure relationships between profits and costs incurred. Acceptable profit-level indicators include rate of return on capital employed, ratio of operating profit to sales, and ratio of gross profit to operating expenses. In order to reasonably measure returns that accrue to uncontrolled comparables, the regulations require that profit-level indicators be obtained from a three-year period (i.e., the taxable year under review and the preceding two taxable years). In applying this method, adjustments must be made for differences in the sales conditions, risk assumed, functions performed, and foreign exchange risk.

THE PROFIT-SPLIT METHOD (PSM). This method is applied in complex situations where the other methods are not adequate to price the functions performed in either tax jurisdiction. The regulations provide for two profit-split methods. Under the comparable profit-split method, the combined profit of the controlled parties is allocated between the parties in similar fashion to those of uncontrolled parties with similar types of transactions and activities. Under the residual profit-split method, there is a two-step process. The first step is to allocate operating income to each party to the controlled transaction to provide a market return for its routine contribution to the business activity. The second step is to allocate residual profit among the controlled taxpayers based on the relative value of their contribution of intangible assets to the relevant business activity that was not accounted for as a routine contribution.

The main transfer pricing methods for intangible assets are the comparable uncontrolled transaction method (CUT), the comparable profit method (CPM), and the profit-split method (SPM). CPM and SPM have already been discussed above. The

CUT method sets a royalty rate by reference to uncontrolled transactions in which the same or similar intangibles are transferred under similar circumstances. As in the case of the CUP method for tangible assets, the CUT method relies on product market comparables. The controlled and uncontrolled transactions must be used in connection with similar products or processes within the same general industry or market, and have similar profit potential.

For the intrafirm transfer of both tangible and intangible assets, taxpayers may use an unspecified transfer pricing method that is reasonable under the facts and circumstances if none of the methods discussed above can reasonably be applied. Finally, despite the increasing volume of intrafirm trade in services, there are no established methods for transfer pricing of services.

Advanced Pricing Agreements

With the growing volume of intrafirm trade, multinational companies' transfer pricing practices have come under the microscope of tax authorities all over the world. Every country is determined to maximize and protect its tax revenues, and foreign multinationals are considered a legitimate target in this endeavor. However, since aggressive enforcement by a country is typically reciprocated by other countries, multinationals often find themselves in the crossfire. In the past decade, MNCs have sought less costly ways of settling, and even preempting, transfer pricing disputes with tax authorities. One such mechanism is an Advanced Pricing Agreement (APA).

An APA is an agreement between a company and a tax authority under which the tax authority will accept an agreed transfer pricing method used by a company for a fixed term. Such agreements are formal in nature, with set terms and limits. They are reached through a process of formal inquiry, and negotiations are based on law. Apple Computer was the first company to enter into such an agreement in early 1991 when it signed agreements with the tax authorities in Australia and the United States to determine in advance how its intrafirm transactions would be priced for tax purposes. A number of countries including Australia, Canada, Germany, Japan, the Netherlands, Mexico, Romania, the United Kingdom, and the United States have formal APA type procedures in place.

The APA process has its advantages and disadvantages. Once an agreement has been reached with the tax authority, it removes some of the uncertainty as to how the transfer pricing activities will be treated for tax purposes. Since the applicant and the tax authority work together to agree in advance on the transfer pricing method, it makes the relationship between the company and the tax authority less adversarial and more cooperative. It can also reduce the taxpayer's record-keeping burden. On the minus side, the taxpayer may have to divulge some proprietary information as part of the APA process. It does not protect the company from subsequent scrutiny of its transfer pricing activities. The monetary cost of obtaining an APA can be considerable, and taxpayers need to balance this against the cost of undergoing a transfer pricing tax audit in the jurisdiction. An international transfer pricing survey conducted by Ernst & Young[12] found that corporate views on APAs and the likelihood that they would be used in the future ranged widely between MNCs from different countries.

---

[12]See Ernst and Young [1994].

Research Evidence on Determinants of International Transfer Pricing Methods

Most of the research on choice of transfer pricing methods has used surveys due to the absence of independent sources of information on this subject. A study of U.S. MNCs found that large firms tended to choose market-based transfer pricing methods.[13] This may be related to the fact that these firms are more visible and are more likely to be monitored closely by government agencies in the countries in which they do business. Another study reported the results of surveys of Fortune 500 companies in 1977 and 1990.[14] Its findings are summarized in Exhibit 7-3. As evident therein, the overall profitability of the company ranked highest in both surveys. Other factors that ranked high in both surveys (although their ranks changed slightly) were differentials in income tax rates and income tax legislation among countries, restrictions imposed by foreign countries on repatriation of profits or dividends, and the competitive position of subsidiaries in foreign countries. There were also major changes in the ranks of some of the factors between 1977 and 1990. The ones that declined in importance were performance evaluation of foreign subsidiaries (from 5 to 10), rules and requirements of financial reporting for subsidiaries in foreign countries (from 10 to 16), and rates of inflation in foreign countries (from 13 to 18). Among the factors that rose in importance between 1977 and 1990 were maintaining good relationships with host governments (from 11 to joint 6), the need of subsidiaries in foreign countries to seek local funds (from 16 to 11), and antitrust legislation of foreign countries (from 20 to joint 13). These changes suggest that companies respond to developments in the economic and legal environment of the countries where they do business.

With the improvement in information technology and the growing cooperation between tax authorities in various countries, the level of monitoring of MNCs is likely to continue to increase. This will require corporate management to pay greater heed to their transfer pricing practices to avoid running afoul of tax authorities and other constituents in the countries in which they do business.

INFORMATION TECHNOLOGY

Information technology (IT) is increasingly perceived as a vital ingredient in the management of companies that do business globally. MNCs face pressure to do business faster, cheaper, and on a wider global scale, and they are turning to IT for help. Executives in MNCs need a great deal of timely information if they are to manage their worldwide operations in a globally coordinated manner.

Ironically, the problem for many companies is not one of too little data but of too much. The sort of complex, integrated resource planning systems now available generate large amounts of data on virtually every aspect of an organization's performance. The trouble is that, despite what their proponents may claim, many IT systems lack the reporting and analysis tools necessary to use the data generated. Turning data into information and information into intelligence can be equally difficult with technology as without. Many companies still see accounting packages as basic data manipulation and analysis tools, rather than aids to making business decisions. This section covers IT issues facing global companies.

---

[13]El-Eryani, M. F., Alam, P., and Akhter, S. H. "Transfer pricing determinants of U.S. multinationals," *Journal of International Business Studies*, [Third Quarter 1990, pp. 409–425].

[14]Tang, R. Y. W. "Transfer pricing in the 1990s," *Management Accounting* [February 1990, pp. 22–26].

EXHIBIT 7-3 Environmental Variables Impacting International Transfer Pricing

Ranking of Average Importance Score		Variables	Average Importance Score	
1990	**1977**		**1990**	**1977**
1	1	Overall profit to the company.	4.04	3.94
2	4	Differentials in income tax rates and income tax legislation among countries.	3.45	3.06
3	2	Restrictions imposed by foreign countries on repatriation of profits or dividends.	3.32	3.24
4	3	The competitive position of subsidiaries in foreign countries.	3.31	3.16
5	6	Rate of customs duties and customs legislation where the company has operations.	3.04	2.99
6,7,8	8	Restrictions imposed by foreign countries on the amount of royalty or management fees that can be charged against foreign subsidiaries.	2.90	2.85
6,7,8	11	Maintaining good relationships with host governments.	2.90	2.75
6,7,8	9	The need to maintain adequate cash flows in foreign subsidiaries.	2.90	2.83
9	7	Import restrictions imposed by foreign countries.	2.71	2.89
10	5	Performance evaluation of foreign subsidiaries.	2.69	3.01
11	16	The need of subsidiaries in foreign countries to seek local funds.	2.61	2.40
12	12	Devaluation and revaluation in countries where the company has operations.	2.44	2.71
13,14	15	Antidumping legislation of foreign countries.	2.38	2.45
13,14	20	Antitrust legislation of foreign countries.	2.38	2.14
15	17	The interests of local partners in foreign subsidiaries.	2.36	2.30
16	10	Rules and requirements of financial reporting for subsidiaries in foreign countries.	2.34	2.78
17	14	Volume of interdivisional transfers.	2.31	2.53
18	13	Rates of inflation in foreign countries.	2.24	2.57
19	19	Risk of expropriation in foreign countries where the company has operations.	2.01	2.23
20	18	U.S. government requirements on direct foreign investments	1.94	2.27

Source: Tang (1992)

Since information may be used for a variety of purposes within an organization, it is useful to distinguish between the types of business information. Transactions are structured business communications that record basic business activity such as the purchase of inventory or the payment for supplies. These systems require strict controls to ensure that all transactions are recorded and that no unauthorized transactions enter the system. Reports are periodic or ad hoc information groupings on various aspects of a business. Examples would be monthly or quarterly financial statements or a customer's recent activity statement. They are generated by running an application program which extracts and organizes the relevant information from a database. Messages are specific point-to-point transmissions of information sent on the company's information network.

Complexities Involving IT Systems for MNCs

Managers in MNCs must deal with more diverse information than those in single-country firms because information from foreign affiliates and from the parent must be combined (e.g., preparing consolidated financial statements). The differences between the various group entities place significant demands on the information systems of MNCs. The demands of the international environment are considerably greater than those faced in the purely domestic setting. The main areas of differences between MNCs and domestic firms in IT are 1) factors affecting system design, 2) factors affecting system operation, and 3) factors affecting regulation.

The main issues in system design for MNCs (relative to domestic firms) are the need to deal with different languages and currencies. Thus, while a domestic firm in Japan can design a system that is set up to deal with Japanese alphabet characters and with a single currency—the Japanese yen—a Japanese MNC will need a system that can deal with multiple languages and currencies. This places additional demands on systems that need to generate reports by aggregating data from transactions originally recorded in different languages and currencies.

A major issue affecting system operation is the likelihood that the system must be accessible around the clock due to the global presence of the company. While domestic companies can afford to have the system down for maintenance and other support activities during certain hours of the day, the IT systems of MNCs must be designed to permit them to undertake maintenance activities simultaneously with operational processing. Differences in language and equipment between locations can also increase support demands and create operation problems. Given the need to deal with different equipment, training is also more demanding and costly.

Finally, when it comes to regulation, domestic firms need to deal with one set of regulations in designing and operating their information systems. MNCs must deal with a multitude of regulations and restrictions related to the type of information that can be transferred and the form of transmission. Many countries are at the very early stage of establishing regulations, which creates even more uncertainty for MNCs as they develop their IT systems.

Global IT Challenges and Strategies

In the area of IT, MNCs face challenges in effectively resolving differences between the needs and capabilities of headquarters and foreign subsidiaries. Managers in different environments have not only different ways of analyzing and resolving issues, but also different information needs. The fact that the basis for decisions may be fundamentally different presents challenges in using a uniform information system globally. While headquarters prefers a common IT system to facilitate comparability and conformity in the data generated worldwide, subsidiaries want systems that are designed for their specific needs to enable them to better service their local clientele and respond to local threats and opportunities.

MNCs also face some very serious IT challenges when they engage in cross-border mergers and acquisitions. There is emerging anecdotal evidence that suggests that IT strategy is critical in the success of cross-border mergers and acquisitions. The experience of two cross-border mergers in the auto industry is instructive. The Daimler Chrysler merger proceeded relatively smoothly from an IT perspective because the two companies gave it sufficient attention during the merger process. Also, given the difference in the two companies' products and markets (Daimler being in the high-end market; Chrysler being a volume player), it was feasible for Daimler and Chrysler to run separate IT systems, which combine simply at the financial reporting level. BMW's merger with Rover, on the other hand, has had considerable problems from the IT perspective, partly because very little attention was paid to integrating the IT systems of the two entities during the merger process. Given the similarity in the two companies' products and markets, this has proved particularly expensive to the post-merger organization. For the past five years, BMW has had to duplicate back office functions for its Rover division, and it may eventually have to write off Rover's IT system and treat it as a costly price of the merger process.

The following four approaches can help provide a match between a firm's global business strategy and its global IT system: 1) independent global operations, 2) parent mandated, 3) cooperative, and 4) integrated.

INDEPENDENT GLOBAL OPERATIONS. Under this approach, subsidiaries are fairly autonomous. The equipment used in information systems reflects national communications standards and offerings and local availability of trained personnel. As a result, the IT system is not integrated globally. This is an advantage in that it permits greater local responsiveness. However, it is disadvantageous in that it makes it difficult for the MNC to implement global initiatives and strategies.

PARENT MANDATED. This approach is essentially the opposite of the previous one. The parent mandates a particular IT system on all the subsidiaries, regardless of local conditions. This approach facilitates global strategies and coordination but is not particularly responsive to local needs and customs. There is a greater chance of local rejection.

COOPERATIVE. Under this approach, the parent influences rather than mandates the IT choices of its subsidiaries. Joint application development efforts are undertaken between various entities within the group. Subsidiaries have latitude in modifying applications developed centrally to better fit into their environment. The advantage of this approach is that systems developed cooperatively are more likely to be used by subsidiaries since they were part of the development process. The main disadvantage is that the development period can be long and the end product is still not fully integrated.

INTEGRATED. Under this approach, systems reach across national boundaries to meet diverse objectives and are integrated using international standards and a common IT infrastructure. While data is shared worldwide, application modules are divided into global and local modules. In a sense, this is the ideal in that the system selectively allows for both commonality and diversity and is based on interaction between the parent and subsidiaries. An integrated IT system is probably the most difficult to attain.

The internet and e-commerce revolution means that the technology now exists for companies of any size and nationality to do business anywhere in the world. However, in order to be successful, companies need appropriate IT systems to allow common reporting, pricing, purchasing, and timely delivery. From a financial reporting perspective, the IT system needs strong multicurrency, multilingual reporting, and consolidation capabilities. While the opportunities offered by globalization are enormous, appropriate IT systems are critical to companies wishing to avail themselves of these opportunities.

SUMMARY

1. In order to remain competitive globally, MNCs need to institute budgeting and performance evaluation measures that are congruent with the company's mission, objectives, and strategies. Both financial and nonfinancial measures must be included, based on the primary role of each unit within the organization.

2. Global risk assessment and management are another important aspect of managerial planning and control. Multinational capital budgeting is important in making wise choices related to foreign investments. There are a number of additional factors (such as exchange rates, inflation rates, political risk, terminal value, subsidized financing, etc.) that must be considered which are not issues in domestic capital budgeting.

3. Foreign exchange risk management is critical for any company that faces significant levels of foreign currency exposure. There are a number of derivative financial instruments such as forward contracts, options, money market hedges, and futures that can serve as useful tools in managing foreign exchange risk.

4. Transfer pricing has many internal constituents (e.g., management, employees, stockholders) and external constituents (e.g., domestic and foreign government agencies, competitors, customers, suppliers). Consequently, in setting transfer pricing policies, companies have to consider the impact on all these groups.

5. There are a number of transfer pricing methods, each of which has its advantages and disadvantages and is best suited under a certain set of conditions.

6. In recent years, companies and tax authorities in certain countries have been entering into advance pricing agreements (APA) in an effort to reduce future conflicts on the amount of taxes the company owes in the tax authority's jurisdiction.

7. Companies engaged in global business need to pay attention to instituting appropriate IT systems within their organization if they are to be successful. IT systems are necessary for the timely recording, processing, and dissemination of financial and managerial accounting information.

8. There are a number of alternative approaches to setting up IT systems (i.e., independent global operations, parent mandated, cooperative, integrated). Companies must select the approach that best fits their operational structure.

QUESTIONS

1. What are the factors that make budgeting and performance evaluation more complex for MNCs than for purely domestic firms? What problems might an MNC encounter if it ignores the impact of certain international business issues in designing its budgeting and performance evaluation systems?

2. It is generally said that responsibility must be linked with authority in order to motivate managers and to hold them accountable for the performance of the unit they manage. Discuss situations where responsibility and authority sometimes get divorced in the global context. Explain why it is important to factor this into designing performance evaluations systems within an MNC.

3. Discuss how multinational capital budgeting differs from domestic capital budgeting. What adjustments need to be made to address the effects of these differences?

4. Why does the management of foreign exchange risk occupy a prominent place in the global risk management strategies of MNCs? Identify the financial instruments available to manage foreign exchange risks and discuss their pros and cons.

5. Why is international transfer pricing about more than tax minimization? Who are the various stakeholders affected by a company's cross-border transfer pricing policies?
6. Why is information technology increasingly perceived as a vital ingredient in the management of companies that do business globally? Discuss the challenges and strategies that MNCs must consider in designing their information technology systems.

EXERCISES

1. Arbitrary transfer prices can be a great concern to governments because of tax implications. The article, "The Corporate Shell Game" (pp. 48–49) from the April 15, 1991 issue of *Newsweek* serves as an example.

   A U.S. company that manufactures goods through its German subsidiary sells them to its Irish subsidiary, which, in turn, sells the goods back to the U.S. parent company. The German subsidiary manufactures the goods at a cost of $80, which is the same price the Irish subsidiary pays for the goods. Although Germany has a tax rate of 48%, no tax is paid by the German subsidiary since no profit is earned on the transaction. The Irish subsidiary sells the goods to the U.S. parent for $150, earning a $70 profit. But because the tax rate is only 4% in Ireland, the Irish subsidiary pays a mere $2.80 ($70 × .04) in taxes. The U.S. parent then sells the goods for $150, earning no profit and paying no taxes (34%) in the United States. Consequently, the only tax the U.S. parent ever pays is $2.80, and that is the tax paid in Ireland.

   With this example in mind, suggest a few things countries can do to prevent and control transfer pricing abuses by multinationals operating within their jurisdiction.
2. As companies continue to grow globally, the importance of global risk assessment and management has motivated MNCs to adopt a broad range of risk-management tools and strategies. Obtain two MNC annual reports and describe each company's foreign exchange risk management programs, policies, and hedging activities. Based on the information provided, do the programs in place appear adequate? Support your answer.
3. Blade Craze Corporation (United States) is a manufacturer of in-line skates for enthusiasts of all ages. During the last five years, the cost of raw materials and labor have continued to rise in the firm's U.S. manufacturing facility. As a result, the CEO of Blade Craze Corp. is considering establishing a new manufacturing subsidiary overseas to take advantage of lower production costs elsewhere. Investment advisors to the CEO have suggested Malaysia and Thailand as two possible locations.

   Below is the summary of the subsidiary's expected after-tax cash flows for the first five years in each location. Even though most operating cash flows will be in ringgits or baht, the company anticipates some U.S. dollar-denominated expenses.

Blades Malaysia

In millions	2000	2001	2002	2003	2004
MR cash inflows		3,500	4,000	5,500	4,800
MR cash outflows	15,000	2,000	900	700	1,000
US $ cash outflows		200	150	125	75

Blades Thailand

In millions	2000	2001	2002	2003	2004
TB cash inflows		25,000	22,500	23,000	24,800
TB cash outflows	35,000	2,000	2,200	1,900	3,000
US $ cash outflows		125	175	200	none

Additional information:
Exchange rates for 2000 are 3.8 Malaysian ringgit (MR) = US$1 and 39.5 Thai baht (TB) = US$1. It is expected that the Malaysian ringgit will depreciate 3 percent a year against

the dollar and the Thai baht will appreciate 4 percent a year against the dollar. Blade Craze Corporation's weighted average cost of capital for both projects is 12 percent.

a. Determine the net present value of both projects.

b. If you were Blade Craze Corporation's investment advisor, which location would you choose for the new subsidiary? Why?

4. Chateau Miel of Francland (a country) has exported premium wine to the United States for the past 20 years. However, due to the growing popularity of California wines among U.S. consumers, Chateau Miel is considering acquiring a vineyard in Napa, California. The original investment would be 25 million francs ($5,000,000 at the current spot rate of F 5.0 = US$1) in fixed assets, which are depreciated over 5 years using the straight-line method. An additional 5 million francs ($1,000,000) will be needed for working capital. The following U.S. dollar forecasts were used to evaluate the capital project:

End of Year	Sales Revenue in U.S.	Unit Sales Price	Exchange Rate (francs/$)	Fixed Cash Operating Expenses	Depreciation
0			5		
1	$2,500,000	$10	5	$250,000	$1,000,000
2	$2,000,000	$12	5.5	$275,000	$1,000,000
3	$2,750,000	$15	5.5	$300,000	$1,000,000

Additional information:

- For capital budgeting purposes, Chateau Miel assumes sales proceeds at the end of the third year (after income taxes in both countries) to be equal to the net book value of fixed assets only.
- The United States imposes no restrictions on the repatriation of funds. Hence, any free cash flow can be repatriated to Francland immediately.
- Variable manufacturing costs are 40 percent of sales.
- The combined U.S. federal and state corporate tax rate is 40 percent, and Francland's is 55 percent. Tax credit for taxes paid in another country are allowed by both countries.
- Chateau Miel's weighted average cost of capital is 15%.

Using the information above, calculate the net present value a) in U.S. dollars using a U.S. perspective b) in francs using a Francland perspective. Should Chateau Miel acquire a California vineyard? Explain.

CASES

Case

Tech Sonic Incorporated

Tech Sonic Inc. is a large multinational computer chip manufacturer with headquarters in Okayama, Japan. The company's production and manufacturing facilities are located in Europe, East Asia, Germany, and the United States. The company's products are distributed primarily through contracted retail establishments and company-owned outlets around the world. Because of Tech Sonic's vertically integrated global operations, the company has achieved a competitive advantage when it comes to adapting to new and changing market conditions. Approximately 40 percent of the company's products are transferred to facilities in the United States.

Transfer Pricing Policy
Prices of goods transferred between divisions are equal to the current market price less a 15 percent discount. However, due to a recent increase in the corporate tax rate in Japan, the CEO is considering whether alternative transfer prices in conjunction with differences in tax rates between countries might help improve the company's worldwide after tax earnings.

Among the memory chips that sell well in the United States is the Tech960 which is manufactured by Tech Sonic in both Taiwan and Malaysia. Due to differential cost structures in the Malaysian and Taiwanese subsidiaries, prices quoted for the Tech960 by these two subsidiaries can vary by as much as 20 percent. The Malaysian subsidiary is currently quoting a price of US$ 175 per unit while the Taiwanese subsidiary is quoting a price of US$ 205 per unit. The US subsidiary must pay an import duty of 10 percent on these chips. Tech Sonic USA is able to sell these chips at retail in the United States at US$350 per unit. Tech Sonic Japan (the parent) sets transfer prices among its various units based on what it considers to be best for the overall company.

Mr. Satoh, the chief financial officer of Tech Sonic, has been asked to look into the tax ramifications of the intra-company transactions. His research indicates that the relevant effective tax rates for the Tech Sonic subsidiaries in Malaysia, Taiwan, and the United States are 18 percent, 22 percent, and 38 percent, respectively. He expects these tax regimes to stay fairly stable in the foreseeable future (although things could change in the United States depending on who wins the forthcoming presidential and congressional elections). Mr. Satoh has also done some research on the likely impact of exchange rate changes. Tech Sonic's bankers have informed Mr. Satoh that the following is the range of exchange rates that are currently projected for the next few months:

	Spot	30 days	90 days	180 days
Japanese yen/US$	105	104	103	102
Japanese yen/Malaysian ringgit	27.6	27.4	27.2	26.9
Japanese yen/Taiwan dollar	3.31	3.52	3.70	3.94

1. What are the issues that Mr. Satoh must consider in setting intra-firm transfers and transfer pricing policies within Tech Sonic?
2. Discuss various transfer pricing scenarios that Tech Sonic might adopt and the likely impact of each on the Tech Sonic subsidiaries as well as the parent company.

REFERENCES

Arpan, J. S. 1972. *Intracorporate Pricing: Non-American Systems and Views*. New York: Praeger Publishers.

Bailes, J. C., and Assada, T. 1991. Empirical differences between Japanese and American budget and performance evaluation systems. *International Journal of Accounting*, 26 (2): 131–142.

Demirag, I. S. 1994. Management control systems and performance evaluations in Japanese companies: A British perspective. *Management Accounting* (UK), (July–August): 18–20, 45.

Dufey, G., and Giddy, I. H. 1997. Management of corporate foreign exchange risk, in *International Accounting and Finance Handbook*, edited by F. D. S. Choi. New York: John Wiley.

Eiteman, D. K. 1997. Foreign investment analysis. *International Accounting and Finance Handbook*, edited by F. D. S. Choi. New York: John Wiley.

Felgran, S. D. and Yamada, M. 2001. Transfer pricing: a truly global concern. *Financial Executive*, November 2001: 21–23.

Gupta, A. K., and Govindrajan, V. 1991. Knowledge flows and the structure of control within multinational corporations. *Academy of Management Review*, 32 (2): 768–792.

Kachelmeier, S. J., and Towry, K. L. 2002. Negotiated transfer pricing: Is fairness easier said than done? *Accounting Review*, 77 (3): 571–593.

Naisbitt, J. 1994. *Global Paradox*. New York: William Morrow & Co.

Neelankavil, J. P., Mathur, A., and Zhang, Y. 2000. Determinants of Managerial Performance: A cross-cultural comparison of the perceptions of middle-level managers in four countries. *Journal of International Business Studies*, 31 (4): 121–140.

O'Connor, W. 1997. International transfer pricing. *International Accounting and Finance Handbook*, edited by F. D. S. Choi. New York: John Wiley.

Shields, M. D., Chow, C. W., Kato, Y., and Nakagawa, Y. 1991. Management accounting practices in the U.S. and Japan: Comparative survey findings and research implications. *Journal of International Financial Management and Accounting*, 3 (1): 61–77.

Smith, M. J. 2002. Ex ante and ex post discretion over arm's length transfer prices. *Accounting Review*, 77 (1): 161–184.

Smith, W. S., and Stulz, R. M. 1985. The determinants of firms' hedging policies. *Journal of Financial and Quantitative Analysis*, 20 (4): 341–406.

Tang, R. Y. W. 1992. Transfer Pricing in the 1990s. *Management Accounting*, (February): 22–26. Copyright, Institute of Management Accountants, Montvale, NJ.

Tang, R. Y. W. 1997. *Intrafirm Trade and Global Transfer Pricing Regulations*. Westport, CT: Quorum Books.

Wijewardena, H., and De Zoysa, A. 1999. A comparative analysis of management accounting practices in Australia and Japan: An empirical investigation. *International Journal of Accounting*, 34 (1): 49–70.

DIRECTORY OF
RELEVANT WEB SITES

International Organizations

Confederation of Asian and Pacific Accountants	www.capa.com.my
European Federation of Accountants	www.euro.fee.de
Federation of European Stock Exchanges	www.fese.be
International Accounting Standards Board	www.iasb.org.uk
International Federation of Accountants	www.ifac.org
International Federation of Stock Exchanges	www.fibv.com
International Monetary Fund	www.imf.org
International Organization of Securities Commissions	www.iosco.org
Organization for Economic Cooperation and Development	www.oecd.org
United Nations Conference on Trade and Development	www.unctad.org
World Bank	www.worldbank.org
World Trade Organization	www.wto.org

National Professional Accounting Organizations

Belgium – Institut des Experts Comptables	www.accountancy.be
Canada – Canadian Institute of Chartered Accounts	www.cica.ca
China – Chinese Institute of Certified Public Accountants	www.cicpa.org.cn
Germany – Institute der Wirtschaftsprufer	www.wpk.de
Hong Kong – Hong Kong Society of Accountants	www.hksa.org.hk
India – Institute of Chartered Accounts of India	www.icai.org
Japan – Japanese Institute of Certified Public Accountants	www.jicpa.or.jp
Malaysia – Malaysian Institute of Accountants	www.mia.org.my
Netherlands – Koninklijk Nederlands Instituut van Registeraccounts	www.nivra.nl
New Zealand – Institute of Chartered Accountants of New Zealand	www.icanz.co.nz
Nigeria – Institute of Chartered Accountants of Nigeria	www.ican.org.ng
Philippines – Philippines Institute of Certified Public Accountants	www.picpa.com.ph
Singapore – Institute of Certified Public Accountants of Singapore	www.accountants.org.sg
South Africa – South African Institute of Chartered Accountants	www.saica.co.za
South Korea – Korean Institute of Certified Public Accountants	www.kicpa.or.kr
U.K. – Institute of Chartered Accountants in England and Wales	www.icaew.co.uk
U.S. – American Institute of Certified Public Accountants	www.aicpa.org

National Accounting Standard Setting Organizations

Australia	www.aasb.com.au
Denmark	www.fsr.dk
France	www.finances.gouv.fr
Germany	www.drsc.de
Israel	www.iasb.org.il
Japan	www.asb.or.jp
Malaysia	www.masb.org.my
Netherlands	www.rjnet.nl
South Korea	www.kasb.or.kr
Spain	www.icac.mineco.es
Sweden	www.redovisningsradet.se
Switzerland	www.fer.ch
United Kingdom	www.asb.org.uk
United States	www.fasb.org

Selected Stock Exchanges

Country	Stock Exchange	
Argentina	Buenos Aires	www.bcba.sba.com.ar
Australia	Australian	www.asx.com.au
Austria	Wiener	www.wbag.at
Bahrain	Bahrain	www.bahrain.stock.com
Belgium	Brussels	www.bxs.com
Brazil	Sao Paulo	www.bovespa.com.br
Canada	Toronto	www.tse.com
Chile	Santiago	www.bolsadesantiago.com
China	Shanghai	www.sse.com.cn
Czech Republic	Prague	www.pse.cz
Denmark	Copenhagen	www.xcse.dk
Egypt	Cairo & Alexandria	www.egyptse.com
Finland	Helsinki	www.hexgroup.com
France	Paris	www.bourse-de-paris.fr
Germany	Frankfurt	www.deutsche-borse.com
Ghana	Ghana	www.gse.com.gh
Greece	Athens	www.ase.gr
Hong Kong	Hong Kong	www.hkex.com.hk
Hungary	Budapest	www.bse.hu
India	Mumbai	www.bseindia.com
Indonesia	Jakarta	www.jsx.co.id
Iran	Tehran	www.tse.or.ir
Italy	Italian	www.borsaitalia.it
Japan	Tokyo	www.tse.or.jp
Kenya	Nairobi	www.nse.co.ke
Malaysia	Kuala Lumpur	www.klse.com.my
Mexico	Mexican	www.bmv.com.mx
Netherlands	Amsterdam	www.aex.nl
New Zealand	New Zealand	www.nzse.co.nz
Norway	Oslo	www.ose.no
Philippines	Philippines	www.pse.org.ph
Poland	Warsaw	www.wse.com.pl
Portugal	Lisbon	www.bvl.pt
Russia	Moscow	www.mse.ru
Singapore	Singapore	www.singaporeexchange.com
South Africa	Johannesburg	www.jse.co.za
South Korea	Seoul	www.kse.or.kr
Spain	Madrid	www.bolsa.madrid.es
Sweden	Om Stockholm	www.omgroup.com
Switzerland	SWX Swiss	www.swx.ch
Taiwan	Taiwan	www.tse.com.tw
Thailand	Thailand	www.set.or.th
Turkey	Istanbul	www.ise.org
United Kingdom	London	www.londonstockexchange.com
United States	American	www.amex.com
	NASDAQ	www.nasdaq.com
	New York	www.nyse.com

Other Web Sites of Interest

Accountancy Magazine	www.accountancymagazine.com
Asia-Pacific Economic Cooperation (APEC)	www1.apecse.org.sg
Asian Wall Street Journal	www.dowjones.com/awsjweekly
Association of Southeast Asian Nations (ASEAN)	www.asean.or.id/
Business Week	www.businessweek.com
Central and Eastern Europe Business Information Center	www.mac.doc.gov
Central Europe Online	www.centraleurope.com
China Ministry of Finance	www.mof.gov.cn
China News Digest International	www.cnd.org
China Securities Regulatory Commission	www.csrc.gov.cn
Deloitte Touche	www.deloitte.com
Ernst & Young	www.ey.com
European Union (EU)	www.europa.eu.int
Far Eastern Economic Review	www.feer.com
Federation of European Accountants	www.euro.fee.be
Financial Executives International	www.fei.org
Financial Times	www.ft.com
Hoover's Online	www.hoovers.com
Inside China Today	www.insidechina.com
Institute for Global Ethics	www.globalethics.org
International Institute for Management Development (IMD)	www.imd.ch/wcy
International Risk Management Institute	www.irmi.com
International Search Engine	www.vls.law.vill.edu
International Tax Treaties	www.danzigerfdi.com
KPMG	www.kpmg.com
Library of Congress Country Studies	www.lcweb2.loc.gov
Political and Economic Risk Consultancy	www.asiarisk.com
PricewaterhouseCoopers	www.pwcglobal.com
Russian Information Services	www.alice.ibpm.serpukhow.su
U.S. National Association of State Boards of Accountancy	www.nasba.org
U.S. Securities and Exchange Commission (SEC)	www.sec.gov
U.S. SEC Electronic Data Gathering, Analysis, & Retrieval (EDGAR)	www.sec.gov/edgarhp.htm
Wall Street Journal Interactive Edition	www.wsj.com

LIST OF

ABBREVIATIONS

ACCA	Association of Chartered Certified Accountants (UK)
AcSB	Accounting Standards Board (Canada)
ADB	Asian Development Bank
ADR	American Depositary Receipt
AFA	ASEAN Federation of Accountants
AIC	Asociacion Interamericana de Contabilidad
AIMR	Association for Investment and Management Research
APA	Advanced Pricing Agreement
APB	Accounting Principles Board (US)
ASEAN	Association of South East Asian Nations
CAPA	Confederation of Asian and Pacific Accountants
CCA	Current Cost Adjusted
CERCLA	Comprehensive Environmental Response, Compensation, and Liability Act
CPI	Consumer Price Index
CPLM	Cost Plus Method
CPM	Comparable Profits Method
CTA	Cumulative Translation Adjustment
CUP	Comparable Uncontrolled Price
EC	European Commission
ECM	Emerging Capital Market
ECU	European Currency Unit
EITF	Emerging Issues Task Force
EMU	(European) Economic and Monetary Union
EPA	Environmental Protection Agency
EU	European Union
FASB	Financial Accounting Standards Board (US)
FEE	Federation des Experts Comptables Europeens
FSR	(Danish) Foreningen af Statsautoriserede Revisorer
G4+1	Australia, Canada, New Zealand, United Kingdom, United States + IASC
GAAP	Generally Accepted Accounting Principles
GAAS	Generally Accepted Auditing Standards
GATT	General Agreement on Tariffs and Trade
GPLA	General Price Level Adjusted
IAS	International Accounting Standards
IASB	International Accounting Standards Board
IASC	International Accounting Standards Committee
ICC	International Chamber of Commerce
ICFTU	International Confederation of Free Trade Unions
IDS	Integrated Disclosure System
IFAC	International Federation of Accountants
IFC	International Finance Corporation
IFRS	International Financial Reporting Standard
IMF	International Monetary Fund
IOSCO	International Organization of Securities Commissions

IRE	(Belgian) Institut des Reviseurs d'Enterprises
ISA	International Standards on Auditing
ISAR	International Standards of Accounting and Reporting
IT	Information Technology
LDC	Less Developed Country
LIFO	Last-in, First-out
MDS	Multijurisdictional Disclosure System
MNC	Multinational Corporation
NAFTA	North American Free Trade Agreement/Area
NASDAQ	National Association of Securities Dealers Automated Quotation
NIVRA	Nederlands Institut van Register Accountants
NPV	Net Present Value
NYSE	New York Stock Exchange
OECD	Organisation for Economic Cooperation and Development
PP&E	Property, Plant and Equipment
PRPs	Potentially Responsible Parties
PSM	Profit Split Method
R&D	Research and Development
RIFS	Remedial Investigation and Feasibility Study
ROI	Return on Investment
RPM	Resale Price Method
SEC	Securities and Exchange Commission
SFAS	Statement of Financial Accounting Standards
SIC	Standard Interpretation Committee
UN	United Nations
USAID	United States Agency for International Development
WICE	World Industry Council for the Environment
WTO	World Trade Organization

INDEX